Management in South-East Asia

South-East Asia is widely agreed to be a region of growing importance economically in today's globalized world, containing contains a diverse range of dynamic economies, ranging from the 'highly developed' through to the 'newly emerging'.

Management in South-East Asia specifically focuses on current and future developments in areas such as business culture, enterprises and human resources, covering a range of topics, industries, size of firms and countries, (Malaysia, Singapore, Thailand, Vietnam, three of which are capitalist economies, with the latter a transitional communist one). These locations also comprehend a variety of business cultures, with a variety of religious values, ranging from Buddhist to Islamic, and ethnic identities.

This book was previously published as a special issue of the *Asian Pacific Business Review*.

Chris Rowley is Professor of HRM at Cass Business School, City University, London, and Director of the Centre for Research in Asian Management.

Malcolm Warner is Professor and Fellow Emeritus, Wolfson College, and Senior Research Associate, Judge Business School, University of Cambridge.

Management in South-East Asia

Business Culture, Enterprises and Human Resources

Edited by
Chris Rowley and Malcolm Warner

Routledge
Taylor & Francis Group

LONDON AND NEW YORK

First published 2007 by Routledge
2 Park Square, Milton Park, Abingdon, Oxon, OX14 4RN

Simultaneously published in the USA and Canada
by Routledge
711 Third Avenue, New York, NY 10017, USA

Routledge is an imprint of the Taylor & Francis Group, an informa business

© 2007 Chris Rowley & Malcolm Warner

Typeset in Times 11/12pt by the Alden Group, Oxfordshire

British Library Cataloguing in Publication Data
A catalogue record for this book is available from the British Library

Library of Congress Cataloging in Publication Data

ISBN 10: 0-415-38334-X (hbk)
ISBN 10: 0-415-49495-8 (pbk)

ISBN 13: 978-0-415-38334-9 (hbk)
ISBN 13: 978-0-415-49495-3 (pbk)

Dedication

For Jean and Clive Rowley for their continuing support

CONTENTS

1 Introduction: Business and Management in South East Asia
CHRIS ROWLEY & MALCOLM WARNER   1

2 Conflicting Cultural Imperatives in Modern Thailand:
Global Perspectives
PHILLIP NIFFENEGGER, SONGPOL KULVIWAT &   14
NAPATSAWAN ENGCHANIL

3 Accruals Accounting in Government – Developments in Malaysia
ZAKIAH SALEH & MAURICE W. PENDLEBURY   32

4 Telecommunication Industry in Malaysia: Demographics Effect on
Customer Expectations, Performance, Satisfaction and Retention
NORIZAN MOHD KASSIM   47

5 Implementing e-HRM: The Readiness of Small and Medium Sized
Manufacturing Companies in Malaysia
LAI WAN HOOI   74

6 Internationalization Strategies of Emerging Asian MNEs – Case Study
Evidence on Singaporean and Malaysian Firms
A. B. SIM   95

7 Human Resources, Labour Markets and Unemployment:
The Impact of the SARS Epidemic on the Service Sector in Singapore
GRACE O. M. LEE & MALCOLM WARNER   114

8 Multinational NGOs and Expatriation: A Case Study of a NGO
in Vietnam
YING ZHU & DAVID PURNELL   135

9 Trust and Uncertainty: A Study of Bank Lending to Private SMEs
in Vietnam
THANG V. NGUYEN, NGOC T. B. LE & NICK J. FREEMAN   153

10 Conclusion: Whither Business and Management in South East Asia?
MALCOLM WARNER & CHRIS ROWLEY   175

Index   183

Business and Management in South East Asia: Studies in Diversity and Dynamism

Introduction: Setting the Scene

CHRIS ROWLEY* & MALCOLM WARNER**

*Faculty of Management, Cass Business School, City University, London, UK, **Wolfson College and Judge Business School, University of Cambridge, UK

This scholarly collection of fieldwork and research from a range of leading international authors across the management field is both timely and topical. The South East Asian region remains a diverse and dynamic part of the 'greater Asia' area and an important economic bloc. It contains a range of economies and types of firms and operating environments. However, the region has often received less academic and research interest and focus than East and North East Asia, although there have been many recent dynamic developments. This collection, we hope, will greatly contribute to the growing literature on South East Asia (see, for example, Rowley and Bhopal, 2005; 2006a; 2006b).

Furthermore, countries in South East Asia do also appear in the mass media and the business-related press, albeit sometimes not in the ways one may wish. For example, Thailand often appears for its political links to business, Malaysia for similar reasons and also issues of ethnicity and Vietnam is covered not just for being a fast growing transition economy with great potential, but also currently as a location for 'bird flu' (Avian Influenza, H5N1 virus). Singapore appears for its highly educated population but often draconian laws. Nevertheless, some topical media stories on these South East Asian countries are important.

Reports on Thailand note a promised huge investment in infrastructure (for example, electricity generation, transport, housing, irrigation, health and education) of 1.7 trillion Baht (US$4 billion) or 26 per cent of gross domestic product (GDP) as there is fear that inferior infrastructure is accelerating the loss of manufacturing jobs to cheaper Asian rivals (China and Vietnam) and putting its status as a regional hub for car and electronic components industries under threat (*Economist, 2005b*). Therefore, one response is to turn the country into a centre for regional trade and business, hence the new infrastructure, but it may also require a shift from generic mass manufacturing into specialist markets with higher, defensible profits, such as fashion industries, long stay tourism and medical tourism, for example, one-third of Bumrungrad Hospital's (Bangkok's top private clinic) 1 million patients is now foreign, while some see Thailand as a good alternative to China, offering safe, profitable well-managed projects, as well as a more open political climate and better middle management (*Economist, 2005b*). Another issue concerns business-politics links. For instance, the prime minister has been dogged by allegations and criticisms about a conflict of interests and the use of political power to further family business interests. This led in early 2006 to this family selling their stake (49.6 per cent) in Shin Corp, its telecoms business empire they founded, for US$ 1.9 billion (capital gains tax free) to the Singapore government's investment arm, Temasek Holdings, representing Thailand's largest foreign takeover (Kazmin, 2006c).

Media coverage of Malaysia revolves around its multi-ethnic population and the long-term debate on positive discrimination of the post-New Economic Policy of 1970, which was billed as a 'temporary' measure, but when it expired in 1990 was renamed with hardly any changes (*Economist, 2005a*). Linked to this is the saga of Proton, the national car maker, at the forefront of plans to reform the state-owned industrial sector. Proton's losses have increased as its domestic market share shrank, from 70 per cent (2001) to 40 per cent (2005) with the dismantling of tariff barriers in 2008 a further massive threat (Burton & Milne, 2006). This corporate reform involved Volkswagen (VW) establishing a technical alliance in 2004 to produce VW cars at Proton's under-used plants, with the idea of the possibility of this being developed into a strategic alliance. However, this alliance has collapsed due to continued political interference and resistance with '... questions of national honour' (Burton, 2006: 19) as it is the last big survivor of the ambitious programme of the 1980s to industrialize the country, and job losses – Proton employs more than 90,000 people as subcontractors (Burton & Milne, 2006). This antagonism and collapse should not have been a great shock as it is commonplace. For example, Proton's previous partnership with Mitsubishi Motors in 2004 was marked by frequent disputes (Burton, 2006).

Much of the coverage of Vietnam concerns its rapid economic development. The economy is expected to maintain its rapid growth after the fastest growth in 2005 in nearly a decade (averaging 7 per cent between 2000–04) driven by surging exports and a 17 per cent rise in foreign visitors, although inflation is at 8–9 per cent and World Trade Organization membership freed China from quotas on the garments industry, which has damaged Vietnam's exports (Kazmin, 2006a).

An indication of developments was the doubling in value of Vietnam's stock market (established in 1999–2000), pushing it past US$1 billion, when Vinamilk, the country's top diary products company, was listed, making 24 companies now listed (Kazmin, 2006b).

In Singapore the government collects S$530 million (£181 million) in annual maid levies (employers pay S$200–295 monthly) but foreign domestic workers (accounting for 25 per cent of 600,000 migrant workers) are excluded from its main labour laws, but subject to laws such as being expelled if they get pregnant (Burton, 2005). Wider coverage would allow greater protection against abuses, violence and even death (147 maids died from accidents or suicide between 1999–2005) (Burton, 2005).

Comparative Background

To assist readers, we provide some comparative perspective on these selected economies in South East Asia.[1] This is in terms of key basic data, such as those related to population, labour markets and the economy. These can be seen in Table 1.

Coverage and Themes

The present authors cover a range of countries in South East Asia, and a plethora of organizations, issues and topics. We cover Thailand, Malaysia, Singapore and Vietnam. The spatial spread includes both newly industrialized countries (NIC) and late developing countries (LDC). The organizations include not only the more commonly covered ones, such as headquarters (HQ) and multinational enterprises (MNEs), but also less frequently covered ones, such as small and medium sized enterprises (SMEs) and non-governmental organizations (NGOs). The issues and concepts include the investment development path (IDP), foreign direct investment (FDI), human resources (HR), human resource management (HRM) and e-HRM, cultures, accounting, marketing and customer satisfaction, internationalization strategies, the impact of epidemics, strategy, structure and control and banking, risk and lending decisions. We organize the contents of coverage and themes of our collection in Table 2 by country, theme, basis and author. We then provide comprehensive overviews of the studies that make up this edited collection.

Contents

Our collection starts with a broad 'macro' piece from Niffenegger *et al.*, 'Conflicting Cultural Imperatives in Modern Thailand: Global Perspectives'. Prior to the 1990s, Thailand existed for centuries with little cultural change and was never colonized by another Asian or western power. Yet, the twentieth century brought the introduction of new western technology, values and capital flows. Devaluation of Thai Baht in July 1997 is held to have triggered the Asian Financial Crises, from which several nations in the global economy are still recovering. Thailand has made a moderate economic comeback but progress has been slow. From a − 10.8 per cent

Table 1. Key data (2005) in selected South East Asian economies in comparative perspective

	Thailand	Malaysia	Singapore	Vietnam
Size				
Geographical ('000 km^2)	513.00	333.00	1.00	332.00
Population**				
Total (millions)	64.2	26.1	3.5	83.5
Urban (%)	20	59	100	25
Age cohorts (years of age)				
0–14 (%)	24	32.6	20.0	27.9
15–64 (%)	68.5	63.1	72.8	66.4
65 and over (%)	7.5	4.3	8.2	5.8
Labour Market				
Labour force (millions)	36.3	10.9	2.2	44.03
Unemployment (%)	1.4	3.5	4.3*	2.4
By sector**				
Agriculture (%)	40.1	13.4*	0.3	63.0
Industry (%)	24.5	28.6*	25.8	} 37.0
Services (%)	35.5	49.9*	73.9	}
Economic:				
GDP (US$ billion)	143.0	61.0	91.3	39.2
GDP (% growth)	5.6	5–6	4.0	7.6
GDP per capita (US$)**	2,190	3,905	21,230	480
Value Added as % of GDP by sector				
Agriculture (%)	10.0	8.7	0.0	22.0
Industry (%)	44.0	45.3	35.0	40.0
Services (%)	46.0	53.5	65.0	38.0
FDI Flows (US$ millions)**	1,949	3,451*	11,409	1,450

*2004
**2003
Compiled from various sources: Economic Planning Unit (2005), Yearbooks, Departments of Statistics, World Bank, Asia Development Bank, and so on.

GDP growth rate in 1998, the economy has improved to an estimated growth rate of about 4–5 per cent in 2005. However, an obstacle to needed investment spending on new technology and industrial development is the ratio of non-performing loans (as a percentage of total loans), which has remained stubbornly high, conservatively estimated at about 11 per cent (2003).

The authors, Niffenegger *et al.*, examine some of the conflicting cultural imperatives between Thailand and western cultures (specifically the USA), as well as some potential avenues for future Thai economic growth and development. The authors compare the effects of national culture on business values/practices and restructuring approaches, arguing that despite possession of its own uniqueness, Thailand resembles most Asian countries (for example, collectivism and power distance) in terms of cultural roots (Hofstede, 1980). Thus, Thai management styles and practices are relatively similar to those of other Asian countries. On the

Table 2. Content by country, themes, basis and author

Country	Themes	Basis	Authors
Thailand	Culture Comparison Cultural imperatives	Macro	Niffenegger *et al.*
Malaysia, UK	Accruals accounting Development Comparison	Government accountants Questionnaire	Saleh & Pendlebury
Malaysia	Customer expectations Quality Performance, satisfaction and retention	Telecommunications Interviews Questionnaire	Kassim
Malaysia	HRM HR practices E-HRM readiness	SMEs Manufacturing industry Observation, Interviews, Questionnaire	Hooi
Malaysia, Singapore	MNEs Internationalization strategies Comparison	MNEs Case Studies Interviews	Sim
Singapore	HR Labour markets Employment	Service sector Hotels Interviews	Lee & Warner
Vietnam	Organizational strategy and structure Control of subsidiaries Expatriation	Non-profit organizations, NGOs Case Study Interviews	Zhu
Vietnam	Risk and uncertainty Trust Bank lending to SMEs	SMEs State and private owned banks Interviews	Nguyen *et al.*

other hand, the variations between Thailand and western countries are well-evidenced in the literature as cultural differences (for example, uncertainty avoidance and masculinity) (Hofstede, 1980). For Niffenegger *et al.* it can be said that Thailand possesses its own uniqueness which rests on the essence of Thai Buddhism as expressed in the 'Four Noble Truths'.

Assessing any culture using only such cultural dimensions seems insufficient in truly understanding national culture, especially a country like Thailand that is rooted in Buddhism. In fact, criticisms of Hofstede's approach exist, namely, that 'four or five dimensions are not enough' (Hofstede, 2002). Thus, Niffenegger *et al.*'s work integrates Hofstede's (1980) five cultural dimensions with the basic doctrine of Thai Buddhism. Niffenegger *et al.* argue and support the view that the practices of Thai Buddhism and capitalism differ in six ways, the first two being conflicting cultural imperatives. First, of a tradition of spiritualism based on

Buddhism (rooted mainly in the 'Four Sublime States of Consciousness' and the 'Four Noble Truths') which is different from the western culture's need for achievement and material rewards as a sign of success. Second, in the form of building business relationships through traditional, social business networks, forged over time, which is different from western culture's need for new regulatory procedures and enforcement agencies, with modern and public reporting of data.

Niffenegger *et al*'s work provides a challenge to other researchers to develop specific measures to confirm these ideas. The authors believe that successful Thai economic development will incorporate both confrontation and compromise in the attempt to integrate Buddhist and capitalist principles to create a more competitive and self-reliant Thailand. Further studies of the evolving 'Thai model' can provide insights into potentially successful international business strategies for foreign companies that operate in the other countries of South East Asia.

Staying with Malaysia, Saleh and Pendlebury's contribution, 'Accruals Accounting in Government – Developments in Malaysia', argues that there has been much debate over the use of accruals accounting by national governments. Accruals accounting, it is argued, improves performance measurement and accountability and control, encourages more efficient use of resources and provides a better basis for comparison with alternative service providers. However, there are also significant difficulties, not least identifying and valuing the wide range of assets that exist in the public sector. Nevertheless, accruals accounting has been successfully adopted in some countries, including New Zealand, Australia and the United Kingdom. Saleh and Pendlebury's study, examines the potential for the introduction of accruals accounting by the Malaysian government. The first stage of this examination traced the origins of the move to accruals accounting in the UK and compared this with Malaysian developments. The authors also drew on the results of a questionnaire survey of government accountants. The survey obtained views and opinions on current financial accounting and reporting practices as well as on likely developments and innovations in external financial reporting by the government.

It is argued by Saleh and Pendlebury that in the UK the principles of accruals accounting were introduced not for financial reporting and financial account-ability purposes, but for the managerial accounting reasons of decision making, control and performance measurement. Similar to this experience, Malaysia has also focused primarily on management accounting reasons for the development of governmental accounting and is now considering the use of accruals accounting in an attempt to improve further its financial management procedures, according to Saleh and Pendlebury.

The willingness in Malaysia to adopt private sector solutions, including many of the reforms of new public financial management, combined with the pressures facing any government of achieving 'best value' from the resources available, suggest to Saleh and Pendlebury that accrual accounting's ability to provide a measure of the full cost of resources consumed, rather than simply the cash payments, might be an attractive option. Saleh and Pendlebury's survey reveals that although the current accounting and reporting system was generally felt to have been able to meet its main objectives, there was also a clearly felt need for improvements, including a move to accruals accounting. If accruals accounting is introduced, then the experience from other countries points to the need for a comprehensive and well-planned training programme, argue Saleh and Pendlebury. This will obviously be required for the preparers of accounting information but will also be particularly important for the users of the information. Many of the benefits of accruals accounting will be lost if the information it provides is not used effectively.

In sum, Saleh and Pendlebury used an exploratory approach to understand accounting developments in the Malaysian government. The study could be extended by broadening the categories of respondents to include, for example, users of governmental financial information and professional accountants, whose views would be a useful contribution to the debate concerning changes to the governmental accounting system in Malaysia.

Continuing with Malaysia, we find in Kassim's study of 'The Telecommunication Industry in Malaysia: Demographics Effect on Customer Expectations, Performance, Satisfaction and Retention', a highly interesting examination of differences in customer expectations, perceptions of performance and satisfaction and retention of telecommunications service quality in this multi-ethnic environment. Kassim's study was accomplished in two stages. In stage one, a preliminary questionnaire was constructed from discussions with five executives from each of the five telecommunications operators in Malaysia, two Malaysian authorities, two management professors and 15 users who were experts on the issues. The scale used was a forced response, six-point Likert type as prior knowledge through exploratory study suggested a high likelihood of favourable responses to the attitude under study as the survey was conducted in a conservative market where respondents were more guarded in offering praise. Five types of satisfaction measurements were developed and tested: a) service coverage; b) billing integrity; c) quality of line; d) customer service; e) customer service outlet. These measurements were developed and empirically tested using confirmatory factor analysis (CFA). The 42 indicators used to measure the five dimensions in the questionnaire were then reduced to 28 appropriate indicators.

In stage two, the most appropriate survey method (in the Malaysian context) for Kassim was a personally administered survey. Of the 425 questionnaires distributed, 120 completed questionnaires were found to be unusable due to missing responses and unexplained outliers. Analysis of multivariate covariance was used to determine the effect of a number of demographic variables (gender, ethnicity, age, marital status, education and income). Overall, Kassim's findings suggest that some demographic variables have significant effects on some dimensions – service coverage, billing integrity, quality of line, customer service and customer service outlet – involved in expectations, perceptions of performance and satisfaction and retention, with income having the most effects, and gender, ethnicity and marital status, the least.

The findings of Kassim's study have important implications for business and management, such as in decision making in the area of customer satisfaction and retention. An understanding of how customer groups differ demographically provides insights for managers in designing and implementing effective customer acquisition and retention strategies. Service providers would also find the contribution's findings useful as it suggests that perceptions of performance level of service vary between gender, ethnic, age, marital status, education and income. Therefore, it is important for marketing managers to be sensitive to different demographic groups in terms of service when developing corresponding marketing and advertising strategies. Kassim's study also found for the first time a relationship between demographics and retention, especially for income. Kassim's work supports the non-demographic literature about building customer retention and loyalty efforts that are not necessarily targeted at all customers. Thus, this study makes a contribution to knowledge about demographics' effects on overall retention.

Remaining focused on Malaysia, we find Hooi's piece, namely, 'Implementing e-HRM: The Readiness of Small and Medium Sized Manufacturing Companies in Malaysia'. This study argues that in line with rising competition as a result of liberalization and globalization it is important that enterprises adapt to remain competitive. Enterprises are going digital to improve profitability, quality of working life and employee retention. To respond to global changes and to move forward there is a need for HR managers to adopt what Hooi calls an 'e-business vision'. However, Hooi argues that electronic services are still an unknown territory for many HR managers. Furthermore, not much research has been carried out on e-HRM at the Malaysian workplace.

The author, Hooi, examines in depth the extent of e-HRM practised in SMEs in the manufacturing sector in five main areas of HRM believed to have significant impacts on competitiveness: recruitment, compensation, development, communication and performance appraisal. Hooi's study also focuses on the fact that the readiness and feasibility of implementing e-HRM is dependent on the availability of resources (expertise, financial and technical) and employee attitudes. Hooi finds that a large number of companies still support the use of conventional HRM practices. Except for communication purposes, conventional methods are widely used in most of the other HR functions. The main constraints in the implementation of e-HRM are the lack of financial resources and expertise. Technical infrastructure for e-HRM seems to be in place and would not be a problem if companies decided to implement e-HRM, it is argued. On the positive side, most employees were ready and receptive towards e-HRM according to Hooi. Hooi's research concludes that it is feasible to implement e-HRM in the SMEs in Malaysia provided that measures are taken to overcome certain constraints.

Therefore, Hooi's research provides insights on the adoption of e-HRM by SMEs in manufacturing and their readiness to implement e-HRM to address various issues in HRM. Hooi's contribution gives an insight on the feasibility of introducing e-HRM. The results of the study will also help managers and HR and information technology (IT) professionals to understand the benefits of e-HRM and how technology can be applied in their organizations.

The next piece broadens our geographical and thematic focus – as while it is still partly on Malaysia – it also takes in the nearby city-state of Singapore. Sim's work is on 'Internationalization Strategies of Emerging Asian MNEs – Case Study Evidence on Singaporean and Malaysian Firms'. While research on Asian

MNEs is growing, knowledge of their nature, organization and operations is still in its infancy. Therefore, Sim's interest is in whether differences in characteristics and strategic traits of MNEs from different Asian countries are due to variations in the levels of development in these countries (such as NICs and LDCs), as predicted by the IDP thesis (Dunning, 1993). Sim argues that a considerable knowledge gap about these strategic advantages still exists and as comparative empirical research on Asian MNEs is limited, further comparative research is warranted. Thus, Sim's research examines the internationalization characteristics and strategies of emerging Asian MNEs from Malaysia (representing a rapidly developing country) and Singapore (an NIC). Empirical data from ten matched case studies are examined, particularly in relation to the IDP explanation from a micro or firm level perspective.

Sim's findings indicate that the emerging Singaporean and Malaysian MNEs, while exhibiting characteristics such as that described in extant theories, also suggest some differences. In terms of spread, the firms tended to concentrate their operations in the Asian area, while the more progressive firms, particularly Singaporean, had invested in the developed countries. Both the Malaysian and Singapore government played key and direct roles in the promotion of outward FDI. The spread and operations of the firms (all Chinese owned) was aided by the use of their extensive ethnic and social networks, according to Sim. For the author, western theories have overlooked the active role played by the state and neglected the contextual perspective in the internationalization of Asian firms. Thus, there is a need to examine MNEs within the context of their institutional and socio-cultural embeddedness.

Sims finds that the internationalization of the sample firms lay in their search for markets and low cost bases, which was similar to other Asian MNEs, but different from western MNEs. In terms of scale and scope, the Singaporean firms were ahead of the Malaysian firms in their move to developed countries for strategic asset seeking purposes. The internationalization strategies of the firms were largely founded on cost-based competencies and other location-based advantages, brought together by an extensive web of ethnic networks and aided by government encouragement and the institutional framework, according to Sim. Some differences between the Singaporean and Malaysian firms were found by the author. Increasingly, the more progressive firms (particularly Singaporean) were extending beyond their current competitive advantages to those that capitalize on differentiation benefits had moved to advanced countries to strategically position for new markets and technologies. For Sim this trend seems to indicate a move towards the ownership specific advantages specified by the IDP. The characteristics of the Malaysian firms were generally consistent with the IDP's first wave (Stage 2), while a majority of the Singaporean firms reflected the second wave (Stage 3) for Sim. Thus, Sim's findings provide some support for the IDP concept. Whether the future strategies of the sample firms (and that of other Asian MNEs) will result in them resembling western MNEs remains to be seen and warrants further research. These findings, and their managerial and research implications, are discussed further by Sim.

Next, we move our focus totally towards the city-state economy of Singapore, with Lee and Warner's investigation of 'Human Resources, Labour Markets and

Unemployment: The Impact of the SARS Epidemic on the Service Sector in Singapore'. This examines the links between epidemics and their economic and HR consequences in a contemporary setting, specifically in terms of their implications for HR, labour markets and jobs. To exemplify this, the authors specifically look at the 2003 SARS (Severe Acute Respiratory Syndrome) crisis vis-à-vis its impact on the Singapore economy, its HR, labour market and its levels of employment and unemployment.

With the advent of SARS, Singapore's rate of growth in the service sector turned sharply negative in the second quarter of 2003, falling to -4.2 per cent from positive growth of 1.7 per cent in the previous quarter of 2003. Since the service sector accounts for about two-thirds (65.7 per cent) of Singapore's GDP the SARS crisis had a noticeable damaging impact, it led to a 3.9 per cent fall in GDP in the second quarter of 2003. SARS initially affects the economy by mainly reducing demand. Consumer confidence did in fact dramatically decline in a number of economies, leading to a significant reduction in private consumption spending. Much of the impact stemmed from the great degree of uncertainty and fear generated by SARS. Service exports, particularly tourism-related, were to be most hard hit. The decline in tourist arrivals shocked Singapore – the figures were 61.6 per cent lower over the previous year in April 2003, contracting by 70.7 per cent in May. As visitor-arrivals dropped, hotel occupancy rates slumped significantly. The hotels and restaurants sector in the last of these shrank sharply in the second quarter by 33 per cent, after sliding 5.1 per cent in the first quarter of 2003. Visitor-arrivals plunged by 62 per cent in the second quarter, while hotel occupancy rates fell to an average of 20 to 30 per cent, compared to normal levels of 70 per cent or above. Revenues at some restaurants halved. Attendance at main attractions was at least 50 per cent down and retail sales dropped by 10 to 50 per cent.

Lee and Warner hypothesize that the greatest impact would be seen vis-à-vis HRM in the service sector and on particular sub-sectors, such as the hotel industry. The authors conclude that the *demand* and *supply* 'shocks' investigated affected both the demand for, and the supply of, labour in the sector, with observable HRM consequences for hotel employment. Hotels froze recruitment and overtime, dismissed casual workers and cut pay at every level. These implications for HRM and strategic management practice, theory development, as well as longer-term economic policy, are discussed further by Lee and Warner. The main implications for management relate to the degree managers can be proactive vis-à-vis external environmental threats, such as the SARS epidemic. It is clear that government agencies and enterprises with proactive policies were able to deal with the crisis more effectively. Enterprises can minimize exposure, make it clear what employees have to do, have a plan ready and last, enforce robust policies. In terms of strategic HRM theory, Lee and Warner argue that having effective scenarios to cope with external crises fits very well into their organizational vision that is, an environmental scanning strategy, a formulation strategy implementation and an evaluation and control model. In short, organizations must have a 'game-plan'. The strategies can be forward-looking responses to expected trends and events or retrospective responses to past trend and events, or a mixture of these two. But it is better, they conclude, to be *proactive* than reactive.

Our geographical focus changes again for the last two contributions – to a fast growing, but under-researched, country – Vietnam. Zhu and Purnell's 'Multinational NGOs and Expatriation: A Case Study of a NGO in Vietnam' covers an under-researched organizational form. There is extensive research into MNE organizational strategy and structure, HQ control of subsidiaries, and expatriation in profit driven organizations. However, limited research has been carried out using case studies of non-profit organizations. Therefore, Zhu and Purnell's pilot case study addresses these issues in non-profit organizations operating in a developing economy. Semi-structured interviews were used to examine organizational strategy, structure and control in an NGO. The role of expatriates and expatriate relationships with other organizational and contextual stakeholders were also investigated.

Zhu and Purnell's work has five sections. Section 2 reviews the theoretical and empirical literature pertaining to structure, strategy and organizational control as well as expatriation management. A framework for fieldwork design is presented in Section 3. Section 4 outlines the research findings. Section 5 concludes the work by identifying the theoretical and empirical implications for NGOs' expatriation management. Zhu develops three propositions based on the theoretical framework. First, organizational ideology, politics, strategy and structure have significant impacts on the NGO's subsidiary strategy formulation and implementation. Second, expatriates working for the NGO will have intrinsic ideological motivations that will lead to expatriate work satisfaction despite cross-cultural difficulties. Third, expatriates working for the NGO will have a distant relationship with HQ and cooperative relationships with local governments, employees and communities.

Zhu and Purnell's findings show that propositions one and two are fully supported and proposition three is partially supported. The case study reveals to Zhu and Purnell a unique approach to management of the global-local conflict that exists. The power of ideology in subsidiary strategy formulation is evident. The global-local conflict can be well managed by expatriates who realize the importance of the local context, but subscribe to the organization's ideology in strategy formulation. Organizational structure and politics provide a forum for which HQs can listen to reasons for subsidiary-specific changes to strategy and policy. HQ control of subsidiaries can be established through organizational culture. Eventually, expatriate failure can be reduced through intrinsic ideological motivation and autonomy. Therefore, the findings from Zhu and Purnell's work indicate that the HQ's ideology, politics, strategy and structure have substantial impacts on the strategy formulation and implementation at subsidiaries. In addition, expatriate ideology and intrinsic motivations contribute greatly to successful expatriation outcomes.

Next we remain with Vietnam – but return to an earlier organizational form, SMEs – with Nguyen *et al.*'s study entitled 'Trust and Uncertainty: A Study of Bank Lending to Private SMEs in Vietnam'. These authors argue that previous empirical studies concur that SMEs tend to be high-risk borrowers, particularly in developing and transitional economies. This clearly poses a challenge for banks in such countries when making lending decisions and calculating the risks of doing so. Market and financial institutions and legislative frameworks are often under-developed, and property rights – essential for robust lending activity – are not always well defined. Data on specific firms, as well as the sectors and general business environment in which they function, also tends to be unavailable or unreliable. Furthermore, many banks and private firms are newly established and have little history of working with each other. Thus, conventional risk management techniques employed to assist in lending, such as credit scoring or pricing for higher risk, are of limited use in such business environments. Also, these business contexts pose additional uncertainties for lenders, as they are rapidly evolving, prone to intermittent crises and the regulatory framework that guides them are often 'works in progress' as for the authors, what may be impossible today may be permitted tomorrow, and vice versa.

Nguyen *et al.* seek to understand how – in the absence of the kinds of institutions that legitimate markets, contracts, and private property, and a lack of robust business data – commercial banks in developing and transitional economies make loan decisions to SMEs operating in the private sector. More specifically, the authors explore the question of how banks go about lending to private sector SMEs within a business environment characterized by relatively high business uncertainty levels, and whether different types of banks employ different strategies in this regard. To do this, the authors seek to answer four questions. First, how do bankers perceive risk and uncertainty when lending to private sector SMEs? Second, what are their chosen strategies to cope with this uncertainty? Third, what trust-building strategies do they adopt, if any, when dealing with new potential borrowers? Fourth, do bankers from state-owned commercial banks differ from their counterparts in private banks in both their uncertainty coping and trust building strategies?

The results of Nguyen *et al.*'s research suggests that, in the absence of effective market institutions and business data, banks in Vietnam face considerable uncertainties (rather than conventional lending risks) in extending loans to private businesses. As a consequence, banks tend to first, employ a combination of uncertainty avoidance strategies and second, place a heavy reliance on trust development mechanisms when lending to their private business clients. The authors also found that a strong association exists between the type of banks (either state or privately owned) and the uncertainty strategies they adopt, as well as a strong relationship between the types of banks and the trust development mechanisms they employed. These areas are further detailed in the authors' contribution. One of the conclusions emanating from this study is that an exclusive reliance on conventional risk management techniques, as used by most banks in industrialized countries, is probably not appropriate for banks operating in transitional and developing economies like Vietnam, particularly when lending to private SMEs. Rather, bank officers in such countries also need to be adept in developing and adopting uncertainty management techniques that are more pertinent to the highly uncertain business environment in which they operate.

Conclusions

Our collection, we hope, contributes to the somewhat less covered, but important, *geographical focus* of South East Asia and also *key issues* (for example, from SARS to banking, risk and lending) and *organizational forms* (for example, NGOs, SMEs) found within this region. These categories cannot be seen in isolation. We thus have here an interesting *interplay* of geographical, thematic and organizational factors, each vying to shape the outcomes of the unit of analysis in question. Together, they point to a novel set of business and management responses that our authors discuss and comment on in detail. They each point to elements of *'convergence'* and *'divergence'* found in Asia as a whole (see Rowley & Benson, 2002, 2004; Warner, 2003; Rowley *et al.*, 2004), an issue we will return to in the 'Conclusions' to this collection.

After having set out above the contributions of each study presented in this collection and after presenting the contributions themselves, their findings and conclusions, we will finally attempt, at the end of this collection, to generalize about business and management in South East Asia.

Acknowledgement

We acknowledge data collection for Thailand by Siliphone Sisavath of AIT.

Note

[1] We covered mainland countries rather than Cambodia, Brunei, Burma, Indonesia, Laos and the Philippines for a number of reasons. One is conceptual, they are more outside the South East Asia mainstream than the four we used; second, pragmatic, we were not able to find academic specialist contributors available there.

References

Burton, J. (2005) Singapore labour law 'fails to protect foreign maids', *Financial Times*, 7 December, p. 13.

Burton, J. (2006) Prospects for Proton look gloomy, *Financial Times*, 14 January, p. 19.

Burton, J. & Milne, R. (2006) VW dumps its plans to seek alliance with Proton, *Financial Times*, 13 January, p. 31.

Dunning, J. H. (1993) *Multinational Enterprises and the Global Economy* (Workingham: Addison-Wesley).

Economic Planning Unit (2005) *The Malaysia Economy In Figures 2005*, Prime Minister's Department.

Economist, The (2005a) Race in Malaysia: failing to spread the wealth, 27 August, pp. 49–50.

Economist, The (2005b) Reinventing Thailand: glow in the dark, 10 December, p. 76.

Hofstede, G. (1980) *Culture's Consequences: International Differences in Work Related Values* (Beverly Hills, CA: Sage).

Hofstede, G. (2002) *Culture's Consequences: Comparing Values, Behaviours, Institutions and Organisations Across Nations* (Beverly Hills, CA: Sage).

Kazmin, A. (2006a) Rapid Vietnam growth 'likely to continue', *Financial Times*, 4 January, p. 10.

Kazmin, A. (2006b) Dairy company doubles value of Vietnam Bourse, *Financial Times*, 20 January, p. 20.

Kazmin, A. (2006c) Relatives left to tot up $1.9bn tax-free windfall, *Financial Times*, 24 January, p. 24.

Rowley, C. & Benson, J. (2002) Convergence and divergence in Asian HRM, *California Management Review*, 44(2), pp. 90–109.

Rowley, C. & Benson, J. (Eds) (2004) *The Management of Human Resources in the Asia Pacific Region* (London: Frank Cass).

Rowley, C., Benson, J. & Warner, M. (2004) Towards an Asian model of HRM: a comparative analysis of China, Japan and Korea, *International Journal of HRM*, 15(3/4), pp. 236–253.

Rowley, C. & Bhopal, M. (2005) The role of ethnicity in employment relations, *Asia Pacific Journal of Human Resources*, 43(3).

Rowley, C. & Bhopal, M. (2006a) Ethnicity as a management issue and resource: examples from Malaysia, in: H. Dahles & W. Loh (Eds) *The Remaking of Boundaries in Asian Multicultural Organisations* (London: Routledge).

Rowley, C. & Bhopal, M. (2006b) The ethnic factor in state-labour relations: the case of Malaysia, *Capital and Class*, 88, pp. 87–116.

Warner, M. (Ed.) (2003) *Culture and Management in Asia* (London: RoutledgeCurzon).

Conflicting Cultural Imperatives in Modern Thailand: Global Perspectives

PHILLIP NIFFENEGGER*, SONGPOL KULVIWAT** &
NAPATSAWAN ENGCHANIL[†]
*College of Business and Public Affairs, Department of Management and Marketing, Murray State
University, KY, USA, **Department of Marketing and International Business, Frank G. Zarb
School of Business, Hofstra University, NY, USA, [†]Hofstra University, NY, USA

Introduction

Thailand represents an important culture and economy from both the commercial
and the academic standpoints. Prior to the 1900s, Thailand existed for centuries
with little cultural change, and was never colonized by another Asian or western
power. But the twentieth century brought the introduction of new western
technology, values and capital flows. Their devaluation of the Baht in July 1997
triggered the Asian currency crisis, from which the global economy is still
recovering. The advanced and developing nations are interdependent, and cannot
enjoy stable, positive growth without access to the markets, natural resources and
capital of others. Thailand represents an attractive market for investment and trade
because of its location, market size and minimal interference from the government
(Pornpitakpan, 2000). The United States of America is Thailand's single largest
trading partner with a 1998 two-way trade of US$18 billion. Thailand provides a
cost-effective regional manufacturing and distribution base for the Mekong region
(Thailand, Laos, Cambodia, and Burma or Myanmar) which has a combined

population of over 125 million people. And yet Thailand is struggling to incorporate the modern forces of western technology and capitalism into its traditional eastern based Buddhist culture, to form a workable synthesis which may, in fact, become a model applicable to other developing Asian countries (Klausner, 1998). Thailand has made a moderate economic comeback since the 1997 crisis, but progress has been slow as indicated by the summary of key economic indicators in Appendix 1. The quality of debt restructuring (for example, public debt and non-performing loans or NPL) appears to be relatively weak. The overall level of investment including consumer and government spending has not yet fully recovered.

This work examines the conflicting cultural imperatives between Thailand and western cultures (specifically the United States), as well as some potential avenues for future Thai economic growth and development. Specifically, it mainly surveys the literature review the effects of 'national culture' i.e., a nations cultural beliefs, on the existing business values/practices and the restructuring approaches. A brief summary of some of these conflicting cultural imperatives is shown in Table 1.

Table 1. A comparison of conflicting cultural imperatives

Thai culture	*Western culture*
A tradition of spiritualism as based on Buddhism; to give more than one takes; to resist material attachments.	A need for achievement and material rewards as a sign of success.
A desire to have trust in business relationships, through traditional, social business networks, built over time.	Need for new regulatory procedures and enforcement agencies, with modern and public (transparent) reporting of data.
Need to take care of employees, avoid lay-offs and protect investors from 'taking a haircut' (loss), thus suffering a loss of face.	Need to speed up restructuring of insolvent institutions, cutting the high ratio of non-performing loans through implementing modern (chapter 11) bankruptcy laws.
Desire to keep the unemployment rate down, by preserving low skilled jobs in labour-intensive export industries.	Need to see rapid progress in the restructuring of insolvent companies, lay-offs, elimination of non-performing loans, greater reliance on high-tech production methods.
Desire for face-to-face business contacts, based on trust and confidentiality.	Need to utilize the increased productivity of e-commerce via the Internet, with public display of data.
Encouragement by the king (Rama IX) to be a more self-sufficient country, to produce what one needs, become less dependent on imports.	A desire by Thais to possess western goods as symbols of success and status; a new culture of profligacy among young consumers, students and business people.

Literature Review

Despite possessing its own uniqueness, Thailand resembles most Asian countries in terms of its cultural roots – it is collectivistic and has uncertainty avoidance, power distance and long-term orientation (Scarborough, 1998). Hence, Thai management styles and practices are relatively similar to those of Asian countries. On the other hand, the differences between Thailand and most western countries (for example, the United States) are well evidenced in the literature as cultural differences. Table 2 shows and compares four dimensions of culture in Thailand, the USA, UK, Canada and Switzerland. These are individualism-collectivism, power distance, masculinity-femininity, uncertainty avoidance (Hofstede, 1980, 2003); and the fifth dimension: long-term orientation (Frank *et al.*, 1991). These core cultural values affect society in general and individuals in particular. Besides resembling other Asian countries as based on Hofstede's culture theory, Thailand possesses its own uniqueness which rests on the essence of Thai Buddhism (Appendix 2). However, assessing any culture using only Hofstede's cultural dimensions seems insufficient for truly understanding the national culture, especially, a country like Thailand that is rooted in Buddhism. Culture is a complex phenomenon and much cultural theory is overly general and still developing. Thus, this research aims to add some insights to this important area.

There are three main reasons to investigate and study the role of cultural challenges of Thailand in managing economic crises. First, Thailand is known as the centre of the recent international economic crisis. From mid-1997, the fall of Thai Baht quickly spread to weaken other South East Asian currencies. Second, Thailand represents a non-Western nation that possesses a different set of cultural values compared with the United States and other western countries. Specifically, it has the unique Buddhist culture. Finally, Thailand has been the regional headquarters of many multinational companies in South East Asia and recently there is an increasing interest in Thailand in the business literature (Pornpitakpan, 1999; Andrews & Chompusri, 2001; Grewal & Tansuhaj, 2001).

Table 2. Hofstede's cultural dimensions for selected countries

Country	IDV	PDI	MAS	UAI	CONDYN
Thailand	20	64	34	64	56
USA	91	40	62	46	29
United Kingdom	89	35	66	35	25
Canada	80	39	52	48	23
Switzerland	68	34	70	58	N/A

Note: IDV = individualism; PDI = power distance; MAS = masculinity; UAI = uncertainty avoidance; CONDYN = long-term orientation (or Confucian dynamism) (Scores range from 0 = low, 100 = high)
Sources: Hofstede (1980, 2003)

Hofstede's Cultural Theory

The topic of how different cultures foster varying beliefs and values, and the resulting impact on people's behaviours has long been of academic interest. Culture has been defined as 'the collective programming of the mind that distinguishes the members of one category of people from those of another' (Hofstede, 1991: 5). Hofstede's research identified culture as four quantifiable dimensions. The first dimension, individualism versus collectivism, of which the degree of individualism in a country correlates with that country's wealth, is reflected in the extent to which a society is integrated. Individualism is the degree to which people in a culture prefer to act as individuals rather than as members of groups. The contrast between collectivism and individualism is one of the most important cultural differences in social behaviour (Triandis, 1995).

Power distance, the second dimension, is the degree to which inequality among people in the population of a culture is considered normal. It is often applied to explain the inequality within an organization and is reflected by the degree of centralization and autocratic leadership within its structure. The third dimension is called 'uncertainty avoidance'. Uncertainty avoidance is the degree to which people in a culture feel uncomfortable with uncertainty and ambiguity. It sometimes relates to the degree to which people in a country prefer structured over unstructured situations. Uncertainty avoidance is exemplified by risk management within organizations; members' behaviour and work ethic reflect their acceptance or fear of an uncertain future. Masculinity, the fourth dimension, is the degree to which values like assertiveness, performance, success, and competition prevail among people of a culture over gentler values like the quality of life, maintaining warm personal relationships, service, and care for the weak. Masculinity versus femininity manifests through the division of roles within a society or an organization.

A fifth dimension, Confucian dynamism, identified in later research, has generally been described as an indicator of whether a particular culture has a short-term versus a longer-term perspective (Hofstede & Bond, 1988). Confucian dynamism is the degree to which people accept the legitimacy of hierarchy and the valuing of perseverance and thrift, all without undue emphasis on tradition and social obligations which could impede business initiative. High Confucian dynamism characterizes individuals who place more importance on values associated with Confucian teachings that are future oriented (persistence, status-ordered relationships, thrift, and a sense of shame). The first two dimensions have the most impact on the leadership roles of management, while the third and fourth dimensions apply to organizations as distributors of power. The fifth dimension is often applied to economic performance and reform.

Key Differences of Conflicting Cultural Imperatives: Research Propositions

Spiritualism as a Sign of Success

Over 90 per cent of Thais are Buddhist, a religion that stresses the notion of giving more than one takes, and avoiding a strong attachment to material things (Klausner, 1998). Since infancy, Thais are always taught to be humble and *Kreng Jai* others. The concept of *Kreng Jai* (to be considerate of others' feelings) has a

Table 3. A conflict between new and old values

Old values
- Respect for elders
- Tolerance and emotional distance
- Compassion
- Strong family ties, respect for parents
- A strong sense of hierarchy in government, civilian society and business; 'knowing one's place'
- Emotional neutrality and avoidance of confrontation

New transitional values
- Individualism, with its emphasis on individual rights
- Egalitarianism
- Emotional commitment and engagement
- Critical questioning and challenging of authority
- Confrontation and argumentation
- Open, frank and direct expression of feelings and opinions; participatory democracy
- Achievement orientation
- Materials as a sign of success

Source: Klausner (1998)

strong root in Thai Buddhism which teaches to care for others more than to care for oneself (giving more than one takes). Besides Hofstede's culture theory, it is always said that to truly understand the Thai culture, one must be familiar with the essence of Thai Buddhism consisting mainly of the four sublime states of consciousness and the four noble truths (Appendix 2). Consistent with the four states (Metta, Karuna, Mudita and Ubekkha), Buddhism is generally considered to be a religion that emphasizes coexistence, tolerance and individual initiative (Wongtada *et al.*, 1998). An understanding of these four states is useful in dealing and doing business with Thais.

The four noble truths expressed in Thai Buddhism stress that human suffering stems from craving and that the end of craving will be achieved through following the Eightfold path; at the end of the path lies nirvana or a sense of complete detachment and oneness with the universe. This is in strong contrast to the western values of achievement and materialism, where success earns one the right to material rewards. Although emerging values of materialism are increasingly seen as the sign of success by new generations, this represents conflict between old and new values (Table 3). Successful western enterprises are rated by how well they reward their investors (growth, profitability and return on investment). Success flows from individuals' hard work, which justifies their acquisition of goods ('You deserve it') (Peter & Olson, 2005). This contrasts with the concept of *Kreng Jai* applied in a business sense 'whereby an individual seeks to avoid potentially traumatic or discomforting situations even where his or her own interests may be compromised' (Andrews & Chompusri, 2001: 87). However, often western enterprises will not be willing to compromise, especially in business situations. This conflict is expressed in Proposition 1.

> **Proposition 1.** There exists a conflicting cultural imperative of a tradition of spiritualism based on Buddhism (rooted mainly in the four

sublime states of consciousness and the four noble truths) which is statistically different from the western culture's need for achievement and material rewards as a sign of success.

Different Approaches in Building Business Relationships

The Thais also desire to develop trust in business relationships, which are built over time through personal social contacts and networks (Klausner, 1998). From their childhood, Thais are taught to depend on each other and to help one another, or to show 'collectivism' instead of 'individualism' as demonstrated by many western countries (see Table 2). Buddhism teaches that if you do good deeds to others, you receive good in return (*Tam Dee, Dai Dee*); thus, help others so that in the event you need assistance, you will be helped in return. This is captured in the saying *Nam Phung Ruea Suea Phung Pa* (water relies on boats; tigers rely on jungles) (Pornpitakpan, 2000). Most of the business relations in Thailand are based upon the concept of *Buun Kuhn*. *Buun Kuhn* means if someone helps or favours one's counterpart, there is an obligation on the counterpart to return the favour. It somewhat resembles *Nam Phung Ruea Suea Phung Pa*, mentioned above. Consistent with these, Thai people (for example, employees or business partners) are generally expected to be treated fairly. Thus, these two concepts are considered important building blocks for Thai people and businessmen alike.

Conversely, western economists and investors see the need for new regulatory procedures and enforcement agencies, accompanied by more public (transparent) reporting of financial data. Potential investors see a lack of basic regulatory infrastructure (laws and agencies to enforce them) which hinders the confidence necessary for long-term investment (Tam, 1999). Although new agencies have been created and new laws are on the books, enforcement is still a 'work in progress' as detailed next. Further, contrary to the Thais, western culture stresses an aggressive business approach focusing on swift results. This approach will prove ineffective as Thais rely more on a long-term orientation and business relationships that have to be developed over time. This leads to Proposition 2.

> **Proposition 2**. There exists a conflicting cultural imperative in the form of building business relationships through traditional, social business networks, built over time which is statistically different from western culture's need for new regulatory procedures and enforcement agencies, with modern and public reporting of data.

Conflicts in the Restructuring Approaches: Lay-offs

Thai culture stresses both social and interpersonal harmony (Pornpitakpan, 1999). Rooted in the four sublime states of consciousness, Thais often develop affection arising from the affinity. As shown in Table 2, Thailand scores low in masculinity ranking. This low level indicates that Thailand is considerd a feminine society. This femininity emphasizes quality of life and interpersonal relationships. As such, Thai employers feel a need and responsibility to take care of their employees, avoiding lay-offs, especially because the majority of employees receive no unemployment benefits. This action is rooted in the value of showing empathy to others. This is consistent with the Thai popular concept of *Ruam Hau Jom Tai*, meaning sharing gain and loss from beginning till end. This concept is consistent in some certain degree with Confucianism (for example, concern for others). This might stem from the fact that most Thai companies are family-owned businesses. Most businesses wish to stay in business, even when marginal, to prevent their investors from incurring a loss ('taking a hair cut'), and thus suffering a loss of face (Knecht, 1998). In the same way, it fosters strong feelings of belonging to groups, organizations, or businesses. For example, in 1998, the Siam Cement Group reported a loss of 52.5 billion Baht (US$1.9 billion), but did not lay off a single one of its 35,000 employees. Instead of pursuing lay-offs when facing economic decline, the Thai government chose the strategy of investment and job creation aimed at alleviating the social impact of the economic crisis (Shari, 2003). Further, the Thai government negotiated with entrepreneurs in order to request that they did not lay off employees. In fact, at least 20 billion Baht have been allocated for the job creation programmes. The main purpose of investment is to alleviate the impact on the poor; while that of job creation is to help unskilled workers who account for the majority of the workforce in Thailand. Private companies (except the foreign subsidiary companies, for example, CitiBank, Nestlé, P&G, etc.) are not required to pay unemployment benefits, unless the employee has it written into his contract (which only a small proportion do). Those unfortunate workers who are laid off, are expected to be innovative and self-reliant in finding alternative jobs, some through government public works projects (Theparat, 1999).

Western investors see a need to speed up the restructuring of insolvent institutions, cutting the high ratio of NPL (currently about 11 per cent), by implementing relatively swift court-supervised workings out of debt repayment procedures similar to America's chapter 11 proceedings. For instance, in 2003 Kmart (a US-based organization) avoided bankruptcy by laying off 57,000 of its more than 2 million workers and closed one-third of its stores. In other words, they wanted to make the use of invested capital more productive and efficient and less impeded by outdated customs and bureaucratic procedures. Although western-style bankruptcy laws have been passed in Thailand, the government was forced by interest groups to weaken the insolvency provisions, to prevent the large banks from using the law to bankrupt small individual debtors. In Thailand, under the current law, corporations that have debts of more than five million Baht ($US 120,000) are presumed to be bankrupt. However, they can still argue that their assets are greater than their liabilities, and thus avoid the imposition of a strict debt repayment schedule. If the debtor is not declared insolvent, the creditor is forced to use the civil court processes, which can take years to complete. This weak bankruptcy law is a major reason why Thai financial institutions remained burdened with non-performing loans in excess of 17 per cent five years after the outbreak of the crisis. Concerns have also been voiced about the new policy of government intervention in the form of direct cash injections to selected firms of their choice, as opposed to a market-driven approach to the solving of debt (Crispin, 2003). This is summarized in Proposition 3.

> **Proposition 3**. There exists a conflicting cultural imperative in the form of a need to take care of employees and avoid lay-offs (rooted mainly in high power distance) that is statistically different from western culture's need to speed up restructuring of insolvent

institutions, cutting the high ratio of NPL through implementing modern bankruptcy laws.

Conflicts in the Role of Technology in Restructuring Approaches

Thai culture stresses an empathy with others. Thus, Thais like to avoid confrontation at all costs. Thai style management is autocratic and paternalistic. As such, Thai companies desire to preserve the low-skilled jobs in labour-intensive export businesses, which constitute about 36 per cent of Thailand's total export value. This helps to keep the unemployment rate low, given that only about 69 per cent of workers finish their first six years of education (Chareonwongsak, 2000a). Consistent with Hofstede's collective orientation, Thai Buddhism's four sublime states of consciousness (especially Metta, Karuna and Mudita) stress sharing the feeling of pity or sorrow for the distress of others. For example, the approach of TOA (a Thai paint manufacturer) in shaking off the difficulties during the financial crisis was to keep a low level of unskilled employees with plans to double its domestic capacity as well as expand its overseas businesses (Changsorn, 2003). It can be said that Thai management desires social harmony with empathic relationships between owners of the businesses or superiors and subordinates or employees. A high power-oriented culture (see Table 2), as in Thailand's case, tends to create respect for the superiors or leaders of the companies through paternalism and dependence. Hence, subordinates often respect and are more willing to accept authority from superiors or business owners than from a low power-oriented culture likes western societies (Scarborough 1998). As noted earlier, most Thai companies are family-styled businesses which tend to feel obligated and operate as 'father' and thus tend to take care of others who work for the company. There often exists no formal written rule or organizational chart. Rather, management style rests on a traditional style of treating their workers just like members in the family. Thus, the owner's or superior's role is almost like the role of a parent in a family who has an obligation to take care of the children (Komin, 1990).

In contrast, western countries belong to an individualistic culture which emphasizes independence, and lack of concern for others (Hofstede, 1980, 2003). Stemming from this cultural background, western economists see the need to eliminate the non-performing loans, freeing up assets to be invested in high-tech manufacturing methods, thereby boosting productivity and international competitiveness (Frank, 2000). For instance, Delta Air's restructuring plan in fighting to avoid bankruptcy was to cut 6,000–6,900 jobs over 18 months, to cut pay 10 per cent across the board, and to reduce employee benefits in 2004. Of course, the shift from an intensive labour-based system to a higher technology-based production system will require workers with skilled expertise, most often trained overseas. Creating sufficient numbers of technically literate workers will take time, as unskilled labourers currently account for three-quarters of Thailand's workforce (Chareonwongsak, 2000b) which leads to Proposition 4.

Proposition 4. There exists a conflicting cultural imperative in the form of the desire to keep the unemployment rate down by preserving low skilled jobs in labour-intensive export industries (rooted mainly in low masculinity) which is statistically different from western culture's

need to see rapid progress in the restructuring of insolvent companies, lay-offs, and greater reliance on high-tech production methods.

Business Contacts

High uncertainty avoidance, as for Thailand (Table 2), is the degree that members of a society feel uncomfortable with uncertainty and ambiguity. As such, it could affect technology acceptance and usage in a business sense. Specifically, it could affect the media choices for communication tasks.

Thai business people prefer dealing face to face, often relying on long-term relationships based on trust and confidentiality. From childhood, they are taught the importance of achieving social harmony (a collective orientation) in their relationships through sensitivity and empathy for the needs and desires of others (Pornpitakpan, 1999). Moreover, business contacts 'Thai style' are often associated with *Kreng Jai* (consideration towards others' feelings and a reluctance to impose upon another person) and *Buun Kuhn* (indebted goodness often used for the relationship between two people doing favours for each other on a continuous basis). Compared to contacting businesses via the Internet, face-to-face contacts can influence the other business party's feelings of obligation and consideration. In addition to *Kreng Jai*, the degree of *Buun Kuhn* can be evoked more with face-to-face contacts. Contrary to the Internet's way of business contact, face-to-face contacts are more personal. This is consistent with Thai culture's high uncertainty avoidance that often seeks to reduce uncomfortable feelings from uncertainty and ambiguity.

Avoiding uncertainty as much as possible (see Table 2), the majority of Thai business transactions still involve cash or letters of credit, and written receipts are often required. More than 90 per cent of the e-commerce activities in Thailand during 1999 were in the form of electronic data interchange and electronic money transfers between retailers and consumers (Niffenegger & Hood, 2000). Although Thailand's business-to-business e-commerce revenues are projected to grow rapidly, most businesses still rely on the traditional use of paper and pencil, instead of electronic methods (Einhorn, 2000). Western technology is needed to speed up and improve the efficiency of business-to-business e-commerce. Thai companies are reluctant to outsource functions like accounting and billing which are key elements of e-commerce. And the adoption of modern supply chain management programmes which require users to open their procurement and inventory processes to suppliers and customers, is hindered by a reluctance to put such sensitive information online (Moore, 1999). Based on this argument, the following is proposed:

> **Proposition 5**. There exists a conflicting cultural imperative in the form of a desire for face-to-face business contacts, based on trust and confidentiality (rooted mainly in high uncertainty avoidance) which is statistically different from the western cultural need to utilize the increased productivity of e-commerce via the Internet.

A Self-reliance Approach

Upon seeing the disastrous effect in 1997 of becoming an export-driven economy, at the mercy of capricious overseas investment inflows and outflows, Thailand's king recently called for a slower growth approach, using the nation's human and natural resources in a way that would allow the country to control its destiny through a return to basic Buddhist principles based mainly on four noble truths following the Eight fold path. He recognized that modernization and the widespread embracing of materialistic values, and adoption of a money-centred strategy as the national development paradigm, could have a destructive result. In 1998, the Rama IX king (King Bhumibol Adulyadej Maharaj), challenged the country to become a self-sufficient economy. This follows the Buddhist concept of self-reliance as embodied in the slogan 'Produce enough to live on while preserving the integrity of the environment' which is the universal life-support system for sustainable living. In the Buddhist view, the key to self-sufficiency lies in the eradication of greed, in knowing what is enough. Thus, the self-reliance approach advocated by the Rama IX King is consistent with Hofstede's fifth cultural dimension or Confucian dynamism (see Table 2) which stresses a long-term perspective (future orientation).

Conversely, western modernization has encouraged people to seek to receive more than they give, collecting for their own benefit. During the 1990s, urban Thais have been among the world's most voracious consumers, quadrupling their monthly credit spending between 1991 and 1997, fuelling a boom in luxury imports from Mercedes Benz cars to the latest cell phones (Waldman & Shere, 1997). During the 1990s, Thailand became second only to Japan as the largest Asian import market for Mercedes Benz cars, and seventh worldwide in import sales of the prestigious German status symbol (Klausner, 1998). Thus, this discussion leads to Proposition 6.

> **Proposition 6**. There exists a conflicting cultural imperative in the form of a self-reliance approach (rooted in the long-term orientation of Confucian dynamism) which is statistically different from an emerging new culture of profligacy among young consumers who seek to receive more than they give.

Discussion on a Future Economic Development Approach

An emerging consensus of Thai economists and some western observers is that the ultimate economic model that will succeed in Thailand will result from constructive confrontation of a both external and internal nature that will evolve over time. External conflict will occur with forces outside Thai society such as foreign investors, trade partners, and world regulatory agencies. Internal conflict will occur between Thais following the old values versus those adopting new transitional values (see Table 3). Thailand has faced the threat of external confrontation and control NBsplong before the current crisis. In the eighteenth century, Siam under King Chulalongkorn (Rama V) confronted the threat of European imperialism in order to preserve the independence of Thailand. He achieved this through strategic compromises.

Now Thailand is facing the same dilemma that confronted nineteenth-century Siam. But this time the threat comes in the form of globalization brought about by the revolution in information technology and the liberalization of world trade, resulting in the conflict of old and new values (see Table 3). New transitional values are emerging from the liberalization of the media which has a significant effect on the new generation. Put into a different context, the new generation of Thais absorbs more and more western values. Furthermore, technological change (especially in the form of the Internet) has come so rapidly that Thailand is finding it difficult to adapt. Still reeling from the pain of economic crisis, modern Thailand is not yet in the best position to confront the dilemma of having to deal with globalization. Thailand is still struggling to find a workable balance among the cited cultural conflicts. The financial crisis has forced the government, under the guidelines of the World Bank and the International Monetary Fund (IMF), to undertake what are perceived by the Thai society as some rather radical structural reforms: new regulations governing the bank system, bankruptcy laws, and pressures on government policies regarding taxation, spending and interest rates. While progress has been made, Thailand has still suffered, and views many of these policies with suspicion; it does not desire to become economically colonized, dependent upon external factors and agencies for survival. For example, Thai citizens see their banks gradually falling into the hands of foreign banks as the restructuring proceeds (Waldman & Shere, 1997).

The Thais recognize that they lack expertise in the areas of global capital flows, information technology and global financial services. However, they cannot directly confront these forces that seem at once, both friendly and predatory. The solution may be in Rama V's third option of constructive engagement. Thailand can continue to open up its economy through liberalization and structural adjustments, giving up the sectors in which it is not competitive and building up the sectors in which it has strengths. Thailand cannot afford to commit the past mistake of trying to excel in every business sector; it can use a selective approach, promoting development in those sectors where it can excel, such as tourism, agri-business, agronomic engineering, light manufacturing and selected services. Income created from these competitive sectors can then be used to purchase the goods and services for which Thailand cannot compete, perhaps assuring its independence well into the twenty-first century.

But how will the necessary *internal* economic reorganization be accomplished without social upheaval? A possible scenario has been put forth by William Klausner, a respected author and retired expatriate Yale anthropologist who has lived in Thailand for some 40 years. He sees a positive outcome from constructive confrontation between the established government bureaucratic policy makers and the newly empowered and emboldened civilian activists that will gradually lead to a peaceful and creative transformation of Thai society and the economy from within (Frank, 2000). Klausner (1998) sees a workable approach for successfully combining the conflicting mandates of capitalization and Buddhism through the teachings of Buddhadasa, Thailand's respected but controversial philosopher monk who sought to explain the relevance of Buddhist principles to an educated but sceptical urban elite some 30 years ago. His thesis was that laymen and laywomen can have access to the same spiritual attainment as formal Buddhist monks, even though they live very different lifestyles.

Buddhadasa (now deceased) saw the present as more important than the past or future lifetimes in the potential for meritorious existence with positive Karma for the individual. The actions of past lives have been completed, while those of the future are yet to be determined. In his view, suffering can be eliminated because suffering is the product of external conditions. Termination of suffering involves the adoption of *jit waang* or the 'freed mind'. This means letting go of attachments to material and non-material objects of desire. Achieving a mind freed of self-centredness, craving and aggrandizement. An individual who achieves this state of *jit waang* is reborn, in the sense of achieving a state of mental calm and equilibrium, which imbues every action of their present existence (and in the Buddhist view represents significant progress towards the ideal state of nirvana). This view can be compatible with economic growth and development as long as it has *socially positive outcomes*. In other words, one must not retreat from the world with its suffering and chaos, but instead, seek to overcome and alleviate poverty and social injustice through the mechanisms available including the tools of western technology and capitalist approaches. Economic activity, guided by a lack of self-centredness can lead to spiritual attainment as long as it promotes the removal of poverty, sickness and injustice. For example, Klausner notes how the rural 'development monks' of northern Thailand seem to have been successful in merging spiritual and material development. Their approach is to teach the native farmers self-sufficiency, moderation, frugality, appropriate technology, mutual help and cooperative patterns of behaviour (Klausner, 1998: 162).

It should be noted that many Thai business managers of Chinese origin practice a form of Buddhism (Mahayana) which does view material involvement as a positive developmental force, and are thus somewhat in agreement with the views espoused by Buddhadasa. However, this form of Buddhism is practised less in comparison to the more widely practised, inward looking form of Thai Buddhism (Theravada) discussed in this work.

For modern Thai society, Klausner (1998) sees the need for and possible development of new mechanisms for cooperative, collaborative partnerships, at all levels of society. These may be created through experimentation in areas such as legal and political reform, natural resource management and rational security, resulting in new policies and innovative programmes. The confrontation of the civil society versus the bureaucracy can be made productive through the development of mechanisms to promote coordination, cooperation and accommodation to foster a creative partnership that ultimately results in good governance, stability and progress. To achieve this new synthesis, data must be shared and policy formation must be public and cooperative. By doing this, this new partnership can ultimately help to resolve the political, economic, social and cultural problems facing Thai society.

The authors recognize that some observers would envision a different possible scenario for successful Thai economic development, namely that of dominance and control by a powerful autocratic leader (prime minister). This leader would maintain a stable government, through imposed measures to produce continued economic progress, ensuring re-election by a voter majority every four years. Unfortunately present-day Thai political history (eight different governments, including one by military coup) preceding the existing one, casts some doubt on this prospect (*Economist*, 2005). Unless the Thai leadership can keep voters satisfied by producing growth in real incomes, job opportunities at all levels, accompanied by signs of material progress and feelings of participation (see Table 3), they are likely to become another transitory event in Thai political history.

How can this sustained, long-term growth be achieved? In today's global marketplace it will require the successful adoption of western technology, capital investment, and management expertise, which leads back to the proposed model of cooperation through confrontation and compromise. Experimentation and adoption of new practices will be necessary at all levels of Thai society (and in other Asian cultures as well) over time, in order to achieve sustainable economic progress.

Theoretical Contributions and Managerial Implications

While the literature on culture in general is large, the scholarly literature on culture in Thailand is relatively thin, specifically, the scholarly literature that deals with the unique essence of Thai Buddhism and the implications for business practices. This work is important in that it represents the first scholarly attempt to document the cultural conflicts between the strongly Buddhist-based economy of Thailand, one that has resisted outside influence since before Rama V, and a capitalist economy. By doing this, the research contributes an added perspective to the existing literature. This work has attempted to take Hofstede's *general* dimensions of culture to a deeper, more specific level of explanation, using Thailand, and the added *specific* dimension of cited Thai Buddhist principles. It has attempted to be more culture-specific. While culture is widely recognized as an important criterion in planning and conducting global business operations, much work remains in identifying and explaining its impact in specific countries and geographic regions. Some scholars have argued in the past that cultures embrace collective groups of nations, such as the Middle East, Asia, and Africa (Hill, 2005). Yet it remains essential to go beyond this general view, by concentrating on the uniquely defined cultures of specific countries. Thailand represents one such (Buddhism dominated) culture; significant proportions of other Asian countries also practise this religion. Thus, this work may yield added insights into certain business approaches that conflict with western practices in other Asian countries. Specifically, our work contributes to fill a partial void in theory by providing a more complete picture when combined with Hofstede's cultural dimension theory. In particular, we propose that the cultural dimension theory can be enhanced to add explanatory and predictive powers to Asian countries (specifically Thailand) by adding the fundamental teachings of Buddhism which is a core belief of all citizens. This, thus, represents an enhancement of Hofstede's more general theory.

Understanding these cultural differences/conflicts can be useful for multi-national corporations (MNCs) that conduct business practices and relationships with Thai counterparts (for example, negotiations, doing business overseas, executives' decisions, and cross-cultural buyer-seller interactions). Specifically, these cultural differences are shown to play a significant role in shaping managers' strategic decision making when dealing with international business arenas. Locally-based values and norms are strong elements in the 'corporate-societal' interface influencing organizational restructuring approaches and values especially for the Thai national economy.

Foreign organizations doing business in Thailand must understand Thai culture and business practices. Specifically, foreigners need to understand the meaning of terms such as *Kreng Jai, Mai Pen* Rai and *Tam Dee, Dai Dee*. One of Thailand's best qualities is the loyalty and devotion of its people. When doing business in Thailand, the key thing is to develop personal trust. The organization will suffer if mistrust exists. Further, with the core concepts of *Kreng Jai* and *Mai Pen R*ai, businesses have to learn to treat people the way they desire to be treated themselves and also to make sure they prevent a loss of face for their organization. Other concepts of *Nam Phung Ruea Suea Phung Pa* and *Buun Kuhn* stress the importance of using a long-term (rather than short-term) orientation to create a successful business relationship in Thailand. Patience and persistence are essential in Thai business negotiations.

As an important base for regional business distribution and global business, the resolving of Thailand's current economic difficulties is likely to depend on an increase in global demand accompanied by an adjustment to these conflicting cultural/ideological identities. The evolving Thai model can provide insights into potentially successful international business strategies for foreign companies which operate in the other countries of South East Asia. This work proposes that successful Thai economic development will incorporate both confrontation and compromise in the attempt to integrate Buddhist and capitalist principles, to create a more competitive and self-reliant Thailand.

Conclusion and Future Research Directions

As one of the emerging countries in South East Asia, Thailand is said to have enjoyed the world's highest growth rate from 1985 to 1996. The mid-1997 Asian crisis started with the fall of the Thai Baht that quickly spread to weaken other Asian countries' economies such as those of Korea, Japan, the Philippines, Malaysia, Taiwan, and Indonesia. Economic crises are complex phenomena and to successfully manage them one needs not only to understand the economic structure, but also the cultural roots that are a major influence in a nation's business decisions. Thailand is dominated by the Buddhist culture and its values pervade every part of a Thai's daily personal and business activities. Thailand is similar to most Asian countries but clearly different from western countries. Although managers of Thai firms and those in other Asian countries have begun to adopt some US business practices in recent years, the conflicting cultural imperatives as outlined still exist.

Based on Hofstede's culture theory (individualism vs. collectivism; power distance; uncertainty avoidance; masculinity; and Confucian dynamism) and the essential component beliefs of Thai Buddhism (e.g. the practice of loving kindness and compassion, achieving freedom from suffering by letting go of attachments, and achieving material progress by helping others to escape poverty by building a positive, and sustainable environment), this work surveys the conflicting cultural imperatives between Thai and western cultures. It aims to construct a theory by laying a theoretical foundation rather than to test or confirm a theory. Specifically, we present a set of research propositions that aim to guide future research studies. Further empirical studies can be undertaken to prove the proposed thesis. Future research could also incorporate other cultural theories from business (see, for example, Trompenaar, 2004), anthropology (see, for example, Geertz, 1973; Keesing, 1974, 1994; Hall, 1976; Hall & Hall, 1987) as well as from other fields (for example, psychology – see Triandis, 1980) to add more insights which could ultimately enrich existing cultural studies.

It is worth noting that the thesis presented in this research reflects the contrast primarily between typical Thai and western behaviour and norms. It is not intended to capture every nuance of cultural differences or details even in the illustrated example (Thailand). Given that the world economy is becoming increasingly integrated and globalized, host and home countries from different nationalities will need to employ a range of different strategies to adapt to developing and changing global business practices. Additionally, future research could utilize different theories (for example, role theory) to explain why some businesses can deal successfully with their international business counterparts, while others sometimes do not.

References

Andrews, T. & Chompusri, N. (2001) Lessons in 'cross-vergence': Restructuring the Thai subsidiary corporation, *Journal of International Business Studies*, 32(1), pp. 77–94.

Bank of Thailand, http://www.bot.or.th/bothomepage/databank/EconData/EconData_e.htm. Accessed 28 December 2001.

Changsorn, P. (2003) Paint giant recovers: TOA set for growth at home and aboard, *The Nation*, 11 September.

Chareonwongsak, K. (2000a) Thailand's transition traumas, *Bangkok Post*, 9 July.

Chareonwongsak, K. (2000b) Thailand's transition traumas, *Bangkok Post*, 30 April.

Crispin, S. (2003) Thailand plans fund to aid key companies, *Wall Street Journal*, 25 June, A10.

Economist, The (2005) Thaksin's way, p. 23, 5 February.

Einhorn, B. (2000) Asia's internet deficit, *Business Week E. Biz*, 23 October, EB106.

Frank, R. (2000) Asia: perception vs. reality, *Wall Street Journal*, 8 May, R7.

Frank, R., Hofstede, G. & Bond, M. (1991) Cultural roots of economic performance: a research note, *Strategic Management Journal*, 12, pp. 165–173.

Geertz, C. (1973) *The Interpretation of Cultures* (New York: Basic Books).

Grewal, R. & Tansuhaj, P. (2001) Building organisational capabilities for managing economic crisis: the role of market orientation and strategic flexibility, *Journal of Marketing*, 65 (April), pp. 67–80.

Hall, E. (1976) *Beyond Culture* (Garden City, NY: Doubleday).

Hall, E. & Hall, M. (1987) *Hidden Differences: Doing Business with the Japanese* (Garden City, NY: Anchor/Doubleday).

Hill, C. (2005) International Business: Competing in the Global Marketplace, (New York: McGraw-Hill/Irwin).

Hofstede, G. (1980) *Culture's Consequences: International Differences in Work Related Values* (Sage: Beverly Hills, CA).

Hofstede, G. (1991) *Cultures and Organizations: Software of the Mind* (London: McGraw-Hill).

Hofstede, G. (2003) *Culture's Consequences: Comparing Values, Behaviours, Institutions and Organisations across Nations* (Beverly Hills, CA: Sage).

Hofstede, G. & Bond, M. (1988) The Confucius connection: from cultural roots to economic growth, *Organisational Dynamics*, 16(4), pp. 5–21.

Keesing, R. (1974) Theories of culture, *Annual Review of Anthropology*, 3, pp. 73–97.

Klausner, W. (1998) *Thai Culture in Transition* (Bangkok: The Siam Society).

Knecht, G. (1998) Signs of recovery in Thailand look hard to sustain, *Wall Street Journal*, 21 October, B3.

Komin, S. (1990) Culture and work-related values in Thai organizations, *International Journal of Psychology*, 25, pp. 681–704.

Ministry of Finance, http://www.apecsec.org.sg/apec/member_economies/key_economic_indicators.htm/. Accessed 2 January 2002.

Moore, J. (1999) A business-to-business e-boom, *Business Week*, 25 October, p. 62.

Niffenegger, P. & Hood, D. (2000) Asia's limping tiger: The state of Thailand's e-commerce, *Proceedings of the Academy of Business Disciplines*, November, pp. 573–587.

Peter, J. & Olson, J. (2005) *Understanding Consumer Behaviour* (New York: Irwin/McGraw-Hill).

Pornpitakpan, C. (1999) The effects of cultural adaptation on business relationships: Americans selling to Japanese and Thais, *Journal of International Business Studies*, Second Quarter, 30(2), pp. 317–338.

Pornpitakpan, C. (2000) Trade in Thailand: a three-way cultural comparison, *Business Horizons*, March–April, pp. 61–70.

Scarborough, J. (1998) Comparing Chinese and Western cultural roots: why 'East is East and ...', *Business Horizons*, November–December, pp. 15–24.

Shari, M. (2003) Thaksin's Thailand, *Business Week*, 28 July, pp. 48–50.

Tam, P. (1999) Will scudder's Cornell return to Asia?, *Wall Street Journal*, 6 July, p. R29.

Theparat, C. (1999) Spending progress defended, *Bangkok Post*, 31 May, B1.

Triandis, H. (1995) *Individualism and Collectivism* (Boulder, CO: Westview Press).

Triandis, H. (1980) Introduction, in: Triandis (Ed.), *The Handbook of Cross-cultural Psychology*, Vol. 1, pp. 1–30.

Trompenaar, F. (2004) *Managing People Across Cultures* (Oxford: Capstone).

Waldman, P. & Shere, P. (1997) The Go-Go years in Bangkok keep going and going, *Wall Street Journal*, 26 September, A2.

Wongtada, N., Leelakulthanit, O. & Singhapakdi, A. (1998) Thailand: Consumer behaviour and marketing, in: Anthony Pecotich & Clifford J. Shultz II (Eds) *Marketing and Consumer Behaviour in East and Southeast Asia*, pp. 667–713 (New York: McGraw-Hill).

Woo, K. (2000) New bankruptcy law: insolvency laws need amending, *The Nation*, 18 March.

Appendix 1.   Thailand's key economic indicators

Year	GDP Change at Constant 1988 price %	Unemployment %	Inflation %
1996	5.9	5.9	1.54
1997	−1.4	5.6	1.51
1998	−10.8	8.1	4.37
1999	4.2	0.3	4.17
2000	4.4	1.6	3.7
2001	1.8	1.8	3.3
2002	3.9	0.9	2.4
2003	5.8	0.8	2.2
Source:	(1)	(1)	(2)

Year	Exchange Rate (Baht/Dollar)	NPL Ratio (% of total loans)	Change in Investment %
1996	25.3	N/A	7.4
1997	31.4	8 to 9	−21.7
1998	41.4	45.4	−44.2
1999	37.8	47.7	−4.8
2000	40.1	38.5	−2.24
2001	44.4	17.9	0.5
2002	44.0	36.0	6.7
2003	41.5	11.1	5.2
Source:	(1)	(3)	(2)

Year	Public Debt as a % of GDP	Consumer Spending (%)	Government Spending (%)
1996	14.8	6.8	11.9
1997	35.5	−1.1	−3
1998	43.7	−11.5	11.06
1999	53.9	4.0	11.52
2000	59	3.4	11.43
2001	57.6	2.6	11.63
2002	55.1	3.7	11
2003	49.7	5.1	−3.5
Source:	(4)	(2)	(5)

Sources:
1) Bank of Thailand
2) Ministry of Finance

Appendix 2. The essence of Thai Buddhism – the Four Sublime States of Consciousness:

1. *Metta*: loving kindness
2. *Karuna*: compassion
3. *Mudita*: sympathetic joy
4. *Ubekkha*: equanimity

The Four Noble Truths (these capture the essence of Buddhism)
1. All is sorrow and suffering.
2. Suffering stems from craving.
3. The end of suffering is achieved by the end of craving.
4. The way to end craving is by following the Eightfold Path of:

    4.1 Right View: Having an understanding of the four Noble Truths.

    4.2 Right Thought: Freedom from lust, ill will, and cruelty.

    4.3 Right Speech: Abstention from lying, gossiping, harsh language and vain talk.

    4.4 Right Action: Proscription of killing, stealing and sexual misconduct.

    4.5 Right Livelihood: Requires that an individual's sustenance be learning in a way that is not harmful to living things.

    4.6 Right Effort: Good thoughts are encouraged and bad thoughts are avoided or overcome.

    4.7 Right Mindfulness: Close attention to all states of the body, feeling and mind.

    4.8 Right Concentration: Concentration on a single object to bring about a special state of consciousness in meditation.

Source: Klausner (1998)

Accruals Accounting in Government – Developments in Malaysia

ZAKIAH SALEH* & MAURICE W. PENDLEBURY**
*Faculty of Business and Accountancy, University of Malaya, Malaysia, **Cardiff Business School, Cardiff University, UK

Introduction

Although there has been much debate over the use of accruals accounting for the accounts of national governments, the actual take up has been limited. Since the adoption of accruals accounting by the New Zealand government in 1990 only a small number of additional countries (including Australia, Canada, the UK and the USA) have made the change. This is in spite of the strong encouragement for accruals accounting by the public sector committee of the International Federation of Accountants (IFAC) – the body responsible for developing international public sector accounting standards. An obvious benefit of accruals accounting is that it focuses on the resources consumed in each accounting period in providing services, rather than simply the cash paid and therefore attempts to reflect the full cost of service provision. This, it is argued, leads to improved performance measurement and accountability and control, encourages the more efficient use of resources and provides a better basis for comparison with alternative service providers.[1]

On the other hand there are significant difficulties associated with the introduction of accruals accounting. Not least of these is that of identifying and valuing the wide range of assets that exist in the public sector. The difficulty is not restricted to cultural and heritage assets such as art and museum collections, public monuments, national parks, and so on but also to infrastructure assets such as roads.[2] The subjectivity that affects asset valuation and depreciation expenses in business accounting is likely to be significantly more pronounced in governmental accounting. Compared to cash accounting the accounting and administrative costs associated with accruals accounting will be much higher and it is not at all clear whether the additional costs are justifiable in terms of the additional information benefits that accruals accounting might provide.

In the private sector it is assumed that there is a strong user need for decision-relevant information which provides a periodic measure of an entity's financial performance (profit and loss account) and financial position (balance sheet) and this can only be satisfied by the use of accruals accounting. However, most government services are not evaluated in terms of profits earned or loses incurred and there is no equivalent to the private sector's need for information for investment decision purposes. In fact, whichever basis is used for preparing the ex-post financial accounts of governments and local governments, there is little evidence that these highly aggregated accounting statements are actually used by any of the potential external user groups for accountability and performance evaluation purposes, or even for any purpose. Rutherford (1992: 270), for example, argues that 'the difficulty of identifying in practice external users of public sector financial statements tends to confirm the *a priori* conclusion reached earlier that there are no rational reasons why such parties should wish to use these financial statements'. Similarly, Jones (1992: 262) states, somewhat trenchantly, that 'the publication of financial statements is not in the public interest because the public has no interest'. This theme is developed further in the context of local government accounting by Jones and Pendlebury (2004), who argue that the only purpose of local authority accounts is to provide an implicit assurance to external users that proper accounting is in place. This does not mean that the published financial accounts of governments are not required. Their publication is an essential part of accountability because they provide an audited record of the financial transactions of the period. Even though there is no evidence of any widespread public interest in this information the fact that it is placed on record means that it can be scrutinized if the need arises. However, if this is the main purpose of the ex-post financial statements of governments then it seems unlikely that this alone would justify the significant effort involved in changing to accruals accounting. It is likely, therefore that more compelling reasons exists to explain the growing support for the use of accruals accounting by governments.

One author who is closely associated with attempts to explain why changes in governmental accounting take place is Professor Klaus Lüder. Lüder's contingency model, first outlined in Lüder (1992) and subsequently modified in Lüder (1994) and Godfrey *et al.* (1996), suggests that accounting innovation can be traced to stimuli which affect the attitudes and behaviour of users and producers of accounting information (including politicians, administrators and the public). Offsetting these positive forces for change are the implementation barriers. Examples of stimuli for change in Lüder (1994) are fiscal stress, financial scandal or some dominant doctrine and implementation barriers include the legal system, the size of jurisdiction and availability of qualified staff. Although the contingency models were based on a study of developed economies they do offer a starting point for assessing the potential for a switch to accruals accounting by less developed economies.

Malaysia offers a typical example of a less developed economy. It is a fast growing, politically stable economy with government expenditure running at approximately 40 per cent of gross domestic product. This study examines the potential for the introduction of accruals accounting by the Malaysian government and attempts to answer the following research questions:

1. Are there similarities between the development of governmental accounting in the UK and developments in Malaysia?
2. What is the perception of government accountants in Malaysia towards current governmental accounting and reporting practices?
3. What is the opinion of government accountants in Malaysia on the likely developments in governmental accounting and reporting practices?

The first stage of this examination is to trace the origins of the move to accruals accounting in the UK[3] and to compare this with developments in Malaysia. This is discussed in the next section (section 2). The third section contains a discussion and analysis of the views and perceptions of government accountants in Malaysia that were obtained by means of a 2001 questionnaire. The final section discusses the conclusions that can be drawn from this examination.

Accruals Accounting in Government

In the UK the attempts to implement the recommendations of the 1968 'Fulton Report' (H.M. Government, 1968) for the introduction of accountable management have had a far-reaching effect. The Fulton Committee was set up in 1966 to 'examine the structure, recruitment and management... of the Home Civil Service, and to make recommendations' (H.M. Government, 1968: 2). The report recommends (51) that the executive activities of government departments should be organized 'in such a way that the principles of accountable management can be applied'. The report defines accountable management as: 'holding individuals and units responsible for performance measured as objectively as possible' (51), and goes on to point out that this requires accountable units to be identified within government departments so that 'output can be measured against costs or other criteria and where individuals can be held personally responsible for their performance'. The Fulton Report recognized that for accountable management to work properly there needed to be improvements in the accounting system in use and provided an early recognition of the limitations of traditional vote accounting, which was criticized for being incapable of identifying 'complete cost figures for the work and expenditure of individual divisions and branches or for particular activities...' (51). The limitations of traditional governmental accounting, and in particular cash accounting, were once again recognized in the 1982 Financial Management Initiative (FMI). The FMI developed further the Fulton Committee's call for the introduction of accountable management and stated that managers at all levels were to have:

(a) a clear view of their objectives and the means to assess and, whenever possible, measure outputs or performance in relation to those objectives;

(b) well-defined responsibility for making the best use of their resources including a critical scrutiny of output and value for money; and

(c) the information (particularly about costs), the training and the access to expert advice that they need to exercise their responsibilities effectively. (H.M. Government, 1982: 5)

A key requirement of these principles of good financial management is that of information about costs and outputs. The FMI criticized existing governmental accounting systems on two grounds. In the first place management accounting was restricted to measuring the cost of inputs rather than relating inputs to activities or outputs. Secondly the cash-flow focus of input calculation was seen as too narrow because good financial management requires that a manager 'should be concerned with his total costs and not simply with his annual cash flow' (25). The FMI goes on to point out that costs 'such as the accruing liability for superannuation, are relevant to decisions which involve a choice between staff and other resources' and that sometimes a 'manager uses resources which include capital items like buildings and stocks acquired in the past, and these can be a major factor in the costs of his operation' (p.25). This clearly indicates a recognition of the need for the principles of accruals accounting to be used, not for financial reporting purposes but to meet the aims of management control by permitting the full cost of resources consumed to be clearly shown. Accruals accounting has therefore not been introduced to satisfy the needs of external users because external users have no needs. It is essentially serving a management accounting function by helping departments manage resources and to be accountable for the full costs of the resources consumed. This then raises the question, articulated by Jones (1998: 13), of 'why the whole framework of resource accounting is built upon GAAP, which is a financial accounting framework, rather than on a management accounting framework'. Likierman (2000), who is closely associated with the introduction of resource accounting and budgeting in the UK central government, distinguishes between its use for public accountability purposes and its use internally within government departments for decision taking and discusses the potential for resource accounting and budgeting to improve management. The management accounting purpose of accruals accounting is also supported by Robinson (1998: 22) who argues that a key claim for the need for information on the full cost of services that accruals accounting provides is that this is essential for the purposes of:

● performance monitoring, including benchmarking and analysis of performance trends; and

● the costing of in-house bids for competitive tendering purposes, and the specification of in-house purchase provider contracts.

Although Robinson goes on to point out the flaws in the use of accruals accounting for these purposes, there seems little doubt that the reason for the introduction of accruals accounting in the UK government was primarily to serve

the managerial requirements of improved cost measurement, resource management and performance evaluation and control. This is what Lüder (1994: 10)
describes as a managerialism driven approach:

> The managerialism-driven approach is mainly stimulated by fiscal stress
> and in the first place aimed at contributing to more efficient and effective
> public sector management. This approach therefore is primarily
> concerned with reforming governmental internal (managerial)
> accounting but improvements in financial accounting and reporting
> sometimes is [*sic*] a by-product of the innovation process.

Malaysia offers a further example of a country which has focused on
management accounting initiatives for the development of governmental
accounting. An early initiative was the reform of the budgeting process. Prior to
1968 Malaysia adopted a line item budget focusing on inputs. The system
emphasized 'control, conformity with rules, and the legality of expenditure'
(Dean, 1989: 43). In 1968 public sector financial management underwent a major
reform with the introduction of a new budgeting system called the Programme
Performance Budgeting System (PPBS).

PPBS was implemented in 1969 with a former controller of the United States
General Services Administration acting as budget adviser. The system was
envisaged to 'help government administrators to think and plan in terms of
programme objectives and the most efficient and economical way of attaining
them [and] to establish budget priorities between competing programmes' (Dean,
1989: 64). However, the success of the system was limited by lack of skills in
human resources, incompatibilities between accounting and budgeting systems,
lack of management commitment and difficulties in determining programme
structures and performance measurement (Dean, 1989).

In the 1980s, as a result of problems associated with PPBS, particularly on the
implementation of the performance measurement and programme evaluation, a
Modified Budgeting System (MBS) was devised. MBS was premised on the
PPBS, with the main objective being to increase the efficiency in the financial
management of government, specifically, to increase accountability among
controlling officers and programme and activities managers. Controlling officers
were given authority to manage financial resources under the principle of 'let
managers manage' (MAMPU, 2000). MBS was introduced on a pilot basis in
1990. The system was implemented in all Federal Agencies in five phases between
1992 and 1995. The implementation of MBS was expedited when the government
set up computer networking in 1994. The change in budgeting system required a
change in information. In order to assess the cost-effectiveness of a programme
under MBS, full cost information was required. The introduction of the Micro
Accounting System (MAS) in 1992, which is similar to activity-based-costing,
supplemented the information produced by the cash-based accounting system for
MBS.

Financial management in the government includes planning processes,
implementation and control on the use of assets and public financial resources.
In an attempt to increase efficiency in financial management, the Malaysian public

service has taken the following steps:

(a) Strengthened the implementation of the micro accounting system.
(b) Strengthened the implementation of a standard computerized accounting system in statutory bodies.
(c) Ensured follow up actions on the Auditor General's Report.
(d) Improved the assets and stores supplies management systems. (MAMPU, 2000)

MAS was also introduced to enhance the financial management and performance of public sector organizations and was designed to achieve the following objectives:

- facilitate the collection, processing and preparation of cost information;
- prepare information on cost efficiently and in a more flexible manner;
- produce reliable cost information;
- contribute to the optimization of the use of resources.

The emphasis of the Malaysian government on management accounting is clearly stated in the Manual of MAS:

> [MAS] is another step towards strengthening management accounting at the department level. Its implementation would further improve the strategic planning process and engender the optimal utilisation of resources. In general, the implementation of [MAS] would further enhance accountability in the Public Service. (MAMPU, 1992: 1)

A further implementation of MAS is the need to record assets and depreciation so that a measure of asset utilization can be obtained. As stated in the Manual of MAS, 'the cost of utilising capital assets should be determined by taking into consideration depreciation, maintenance and the cost of operations' (MAMPU, 1992: 10).

The latest developments in the Malaysian governmental accounting system are the business reengineering process and information technology (IT) strategic plan. Both of these are geared towards developing a new and integrated federal government accounting system. The objectives of these efforts are to improve efficiency in accounting and financial planning, improve management of government funds and improve the monitoring mechanism. According to a circular issued by the Accountant General's Department (AGD), the new system is 'expected to be flexible and in compliance with accounting standards based on cash or accrual basis, or a hybrid of both' (AGD, 2003a: 1). The AGD had also put forward the accrual accounting migration conceptual plan in which it is planned that the government would adopt accrual accounting by 2008. The accrual accounting system will be part of the support system for the Government Financial Management Accounting System (GFMAS) (AGD, 2003b).

Information technology has played a major part in the development of governmental accounting and has been a key factor in the introduction of the MBS and MAS. Accounting innovation in Malaysia has focused on management accounting and fits the managerialism driven approach outlined by Lüder. If, as a

Table 1. Opinion on objectives of financial reporting in Malaysia

Objectives	Analysis		Level of Importance						
	n	x	1	2	3	4	5	6	7
1. To indicate whether resources were obtained and used in accordance with legally adopted budget	26	6.77	–	–	–	–	–	6 26 (100%)	20
2. To indicate whether resources were obtained and used in accordance with legal and contractual requirements, including financial limits established by appropriate legislative authorities	26	6.65	–	1 (4%)	1	–	–	5 25 (96%)	20
3. To provide information about the sources, allocation and uses of financial resources	26	6.62	–	–	–	1	1	5 25 (96%)	19
4. To provide information about how the entity financed its activities and met its cash requirements	25	5.64	3	3 (12%)	–	1	5	3 21 (84%)	13
5. To provide information that is useful in evaluating the entity's ability to finance its activities and to meet its liabilities and commitments	26	4.96	4	1 7 (27%)	2	–	6	4 19 (73.%)	9
6. To provide information about the financial condition of the entity and changes in it	26	5.15	3	4 (15%)	1	3	7	5 19 (73%)	7

Level of importance on a scale of:
1 = not at all important   2 = not important   3 = slightly unimportant   4 = neutral
5 = slightly important   6 = important   7 = very important

Table 2. Opinion on whether financial reports should be improved

	Analysis		Level of Agreement												
			1		2		3		4		5		6		7	
	n	x	no.	%	no.	%	no.	%	no.	%	no.	%	no.	%	no.	%
Total	25	4.92	1	4	3	12	2	8	4	16	4	16	3	12	8	32
Disagree vs. agree						6 (24%)								15 (60%)		

Level of agreement on a scale of:
1 = strongly disagree   2 = disagree   3 = slightly disagree   4 = neutral
5 = slightly agree   6 = agree   7 = strongly agree

by-product of this, attention is turned to the use of accruals accounting for external financial accounting and reporting then the information technology developments would support this.

Method and Results

In an attempt to obtain views and opinions on current financial accounting and reporting practices as well as opinions on the likely developments and innovations in external financial reporting by the Malaysian government, a questionnaire survey of a sample of government accountants was undertaken[4]. The Accountant General of Malaysia's department provided the names and addresses of 77 federal and state government accountants and the questionnaire was mailed to them in April 2001. A total of 27 completed questionnaires were returned, a usable response rate of 35 per cent. An analysis of the job category of the respondents revealed that 6 were directors, 2 were deputy directors, 4 were state treasurers, 12 were accountants and 3 were assistant accountants.

Because of their close involvement with the preparation of governmental accounting information, the respondents were in a position to provide informed and expert opinions on the objectives of financial reporting by the Malaysian government and the factors that they felt to be important in the development of government accounting. Table 1 provides an analysis of the opinions of the questionnaire respondents on the objectives of financial reporting. The objectives listed in this question are those identified in International Public Sector Accounting Standard No 1 (IFAC, 2000) and the respondents were asked for their opinion on the importance of each objective on a scale ranging from 1 (not at all important) to 7 (very important).

The accounting basis used by the federal and state governments in Malaysia is that of modified cash accounting (a cash basis of accounting throughout the year but modified to include those transactions that relate to the financial year that occurred within one month of the year end). The first three of the objectives in Table 1 are consistent with a cash basis of accounting and it is therefore not surprising to see that these objectives scored mean responses of close to 7 (very important). The distribution of responses confirms this, with at least 92 per cent of the respondents stating that each of these objectives was important or very important. A more surprising result is that objectives 4, 5 and 6, although clearly regarded as less important than the first three objectives, still scored a mean of close to 5 (slightly important). These objectives, particularly the last two, are more closely associated with the information provided by accruals accounting. This would seem to suggest that many of those closely involved with the preparation of governmental accounts in Malaysia see a need for the use of accruals accounting rather than modified cash.

The questionnaire survey also sought to elicit opinions on whether the financial reports of the Malaysian government should be improved. As shown in Table 2, overall, 60 per cent of the respondents agreed that financial reports should be improved whilst 24 per cent disagreed.

The question on which Table 2 is based invited respondents to indicate the kinds of improvements they felt should be introduced and space was provided in the questionnaire for this information to be written in. Many respondents took the opportunity to write in comments and it was clear from these that it was generally felt that the current government accounting system is sufficient for providing financial information about government activities. Even so, there was also a clearly felt need for a movement towards accruals accounting. Among the suggestions offered for improvements in financial reports were: the need to have information on cost of output, the need to report performance measurement, the need for more reliable and transparent reports, the need to report based on accruals accounting and the need to provide separate reports for each Ministry.

The factors that the questionnaire respondents felt to be important in the development of government accounting are reported in Table 3. The factors included in this table are adapted from Lüder (1992, 1994).

The results show that 'increased professionalism' is regarded as the most important factor, with a mean score of close to 7. Also 96 per cent of the respondents felt this to be an important or very important factor. The questionnaire sought background information about the respondents and this revealed that only 9 of the 27 respondents were professionally qualified. It may well be that as the proportion of accountants employed by the Malaysian government that are professionally qualified increases then this will lead to even stronger support for changes in the accounting basis. This is because accruals accounting dominates the training and qualification requirements of professional accountancy bodies and obviously dominates accounting practices in the business sector. In an era in which many governments of developed economies have shown a preference for the adoption of private sector practices into the management of government services then it is likely that a profession such as accounting, which is dominated

Table 3. Important factors in the development of governmental accounting in Malaysia

Factors	Analysis		Level of Importance						
	n	x	1	2	3	4	5	6	7
Increased professionalism	27	6.63	–	–	1	–	–	6	20
				1 (4%)				26 (96%)	
Technological change	27	6.22	1	–	–	1	2	8	15
				1 (4%)				25 (92%)	
Demand from general public	25	5.57	–	2	1	1	6	8	7
				3 (12%)				21 (84%)	
Financial crisis	25	5.40	1	2	–	3	3	9	7
				3 (12%)				19 (76%)	
Political incentives	25	4.73	2	–	3	7	3	2	8
				5 (20%)				13 (52%)	
Demand from creditors	24	4.29	1	4	2	5	5	6	1
				7 (29%)				12 (50%)	

Level of importance on a scale of:
1 = not at all important   2 = not important   3 = slightly unimportant   4 = neutral
5 = slightly important   6 = important   7 = very important

by private sector practice, would encourage the use of this in the public sector. Also, the role of consultants in developments in the financial management practices of the Malaysian government is likely to be influential in this regard. Consulting firms often draw heavily on private sector experiences and these would also tend to support the use of accruals accounting. The question on which Table 3 is based also offered the opportunity for respondents to write in additional comments. An analysis of these reveals further support for a change to accruals accounting, with 6 of the respondents specifically mentioning this as a necessary development in governmental accounting.

It can also be seen from Table 3 that technological change is perceived to be an important factor in the development of governmental accounting, with 92 per cent of the respondents recording this as important or very important. This is perhaps unsurprising given the important role that technology has already played in the introduction of MBS and MAS. On the other hand the level of importance attached to demand from the public, with 84 per cent perceiving this to be important or very important, is more surprising given the discussion earlier of the lack of interest in the financial accounts of governments that has been found in other studies. However, the public presumably do have a concern over the value for money that is being achieved on their behalf and perhaps the respondents here were contemplating developments in performance reporting by the government. There was reasonably strong support for financial crisis as a factor affecting accounting development. Financial crisis does focus attention on priorities and support the need for full cost information and the deficiencies of cash based accounting in providing this.

Discussion

When assessed against the stimuli for change in governmental accounting and the barriers to change as outlined in Lüder (1992 and 1994) it seems clear that it is a managerialism driven stimulus that best explains the UK government's change to accruals accounting. The desirability identified in the Fulton report and developed further in the 1982 Financial Management Initiative of holding managers to account for the full cost of resources consumed and the output achieved from those resources has been a key feature of attempts to improve the efficiency and effectiveness of public sector management. Cash accounting was obviously deficient for this purpose because of its failure to measure the full cost of resources consumed and so accruals accounting, which is the method widely used by the private sector, was eventually implemented. This is entirely consistent with the UK's acceptance of what Olson *et al.* (1998: 18) describe as the reforms of 'new public financial management'. Olson *et al.* identify five categories of new public financial management reforms and these include: the use of 'accruals-based financial statements across government departments and sectors'; 'commercially-minded, market oriented management systems and structures to deal with the pricing and provision of public services'; an emphasis on performance measurement and the use of financial and non-financial performance indicators; the use of budget delegation 'coupled with the attempted integration of both financial and management accounting systems and also economic-based information sets'; and the involvement of internal and external audit with monitoring service delivery and examining value for money. Over the past 30 years or so all of these reforms have been firmly embraced by the UK public sector.

The situation in Malaysia is very similar. An analysis of the stimuli for change would reveal very little support for a need to change to accruals accounting for external financial reporting purposes. However, Malaysia does seem to have accepted the doctrine of the superiority of the private sector's management practices. Administrative reforms have led to the use of such private sector developed practices of total quality management and quality circles and these have led to the implementation of the micro accounting system, which draws heavily on the activity based costing approach devised in the private sector. The willingness in Malaysia to adopt private sector solutions, including many of the reforms of new public financial management, combined with the pressures facing any government of achieving the best value from the resources available, suggest that accrual accounting's ability to provide a measure of the full cost of resources consumed, rather than simply the cash payments, might be an attractive option.

However the implementation barrier of qualified staff availability is likely to be of more importance in Malaysia than the UK. As in many developing economies, there is a shortage of professionally qualified accountants and the demand for these from the private sector bids up the price beyond public sector salary levels. The government would need to overcome the problem of recruiting and retaining qualified accounting staff and although developments in the use of IT might help to alleviate this problem, it is likely that a significant and expensive reliance on consultants would be needed. The Malaysian government does provide incentives for its accounting staff to obtain professional qualifications. These incentives include the reimbursement of the annual fees of professional bodies and scholarships for government accountants to undertake courses that lead to professional accounting qualifications.

Implications

This work used an exploratory approach to understand accounting developments in the Malaysian government. The study could be extended by broadening the categories of respondents to include, for example, the users of governmental financial information and professional accountants. Their views would be a useful contribution to the debate concerning any changes that might be needed to the governmental accounting system in Malaysia. Increasing the range and number of respondents might also enable a more positivist approach to be adopted and allow for the statistical testing of hypotheses. There is also a need to ascertain the extent to which accruals accounting is already used in the various bodies and organizations that make up what is broadly thought of as the Malaysian government. This would provide a useful basis for identifying the efforts likely to be needed to bring about a comprehensive change. For many parts of the Malaysian government the efforts and associated costs are likely to be significant. Because of the obvious difficulties facing any attempt to measure the *actual* benefits this rules out a conventional cost-benefit analysis and so it would seem essential to obtain as broad a range of opinions as possible on the *perceived* benefits. This provides further support for the need to extend the scope of the survey.

If accruals accounting is introduced by the Malaysian government then the experience from other countries points to the need for a comprehensive and well-planned training programme. This will obviously be required for the preparers of accounting information but will also be particularly important for the users of the information. Many of the benefits of accruals accounting will be lost if the information it provides is not used effectively.

Conclusions

An examination of recent developments in Malaysian governmental accounting reveals a clear willingness to embrace many of the features of new public financial management. This is very similar to the experience of the UK. However one key difference between the two countries is that the UK government has now completed the lengthy switch to full accruals accounting and budgeting for all aspects of government activity. It is argued in this study that the main impetus for this reform was the need for improved information for financial management and control. This survey of Malaysian government accountants reveals that although the current accounting and reporting system was generally felt to have been able to meet its main objectives there was also a clearly felt need for improvements, including a move to accruals accounting. Such a move is now under active consideration and given that the costs are likely to be significant it would seem sensible to extend the scope of this survey and seek as broad a range of authoritative opinions on the likely benefits as possible.

Notes

[1] For a summary of the benefits of accruals accounting see, for example, H.M. Government (1994); Evans (1995); Guthrie (1998).

[2] For a discussion of the accounting treatment of cultural and heritage assets and infrastructure assets see, for example, Mautz (1988); Pallot (1990); Stanton & Stanton (1998); Barton (1999); McGregor (1999).

[3] In the UK the term used for the accruals accounting system used in central government is 'resource accounting and budgeting'. Resource accounting essentially follows the techniques of accruals accounting and resource budgeting involves the planning and controlling of public expenditure on a resource accounting basis. The first set of published resource accounts was for the 1999/2000 financial year.

[4] The actual questionnaire used in this survey covered a broad range of questions about the accounting practices and procedures of the Malaysian government and also sought perceptions about the purpose, quality and potential for the improvement of government accounting. Many of the issues covered in the full questionnaire were not relevant to the aims of this study. The questions that were relevant are as follows:

   • A question which asked respondents to indicate the importance they attached (on a 7-point scale) to the financial reporting objectives of the Malaysian government. The responses are reported in Table 1.
   • A question which asked respondents to indicate their level of agreement (on a 7-point scale) with the statement that 'the financial reports provided by government to external users should be improved'. The responses are reported in Table 2. This question also provided space for examples of areas for improvement to be 'written in' by respondents.

• A question which asked respondents to indicate the importance they attached (on a 7-point scale) to factors which might affect the development of Malaysian governmental accounting. The responses are reported in Table 3. This question also provided space for respondents to 'write-in' other factors that they felt to be important in the development of governmental accounting.

The questionnaire also asked for background information on the respondents covering their experience, qualifications, and so on. The complete anonymity of all respondents was assured.

References

AGD (Accountant General's Department) (2003a) *AGD Circular, Issue No. 1*. Available at http:// www.anm.gov. my/BM_Perakaunan/CircularReengineering.html (accessed 7 September 2004).

AGD (2003b) *AGD Circular, Issue No. 5*. Available at http:// www.anm.gov.my/BM_Perakaunan/reengineering_ files/isu5.htm (accessed 3 March 2005).

Barton, A. (1999) Public and private sector accounting – the non-identical twins, *Australian Accounting Review*, 9(2), pp. 22–31.

Dean, P. N. (1989) *Government Budgeting in Developing Countries* (London: Routledge).

Evans, M. (1995) *Resource Accounting and Budgeting* (London: CIPFA).

Godfrey, A. D., Devlin, P. J. & Merrouche, C. (1996) Governmental accounting in Kenya, Tanzania and Uganda, *Research in Governmental and Nonprofit Accounting*, 9 pp. 193–208.

Guthrie, J. (1998) Application of accrual accounting in the Australian public sector – rhetoric or reality?, *Financial Accountability and Management*, 14(1), pp. 1–19.

Government, H. M. (1968) *The Civil Service, Volume 1, Report of the Fulton Committee*, Cmd 3638 (London: Stationery Office).

Government, H. M. (1982) *Efficiency and Effectiveness in the Civil Service: Government Observations on the Third Report from the Treasury and Civil Service Committee, Session 1981–82*, Cmnd 8616 (London: Stationery Office).

Government, H. M. (1994) *Better Accounting for the Taxpayer's Money: Resource Accounting and Budgeting in Government*, Cmd 2626 (London: Stationery Office).

IFAC (International Federation of Accountants) (2000) *International Public Sector Accounting Standard No. 1 – Presentation of Financial Statements* (New York: IFAC).

Jones, R. (1992) The development of conceptual frameworks of accounting for the public sector, *Financial Accountability and Management*, 8(4), pp. 249–264.

Jones, R. (1998) The conceptual framework of resource accounting, *Public Money and Management*, 18(2), pp. 11–16.

Jones, R. & Pendlebury, M. (2004) A theory of the published accounts of local authorities, *Financial Accountability and Management*, 20(3), pp. 305–325.

Likierman, A. (2000) Changes to managerial decision-taking in U.K. central government, *Management Accounting Research*, 11(2), pp. 253–261.

Lüder, K. G. (1992) A contingency model of governmental accounting innovations in the political administrative environment, *Research in Governmental and Nonprofit Accounting*, 7, pp. 99–127.

Lüder, K. G. (1994) The 'Contingency Model' reconsidered: experiences from Italy, Japan and Spain, in: E. Buschor & K. Schedler (Eds) *Perspectives on Performance Measurement and Public Sector Accounting*, pp. 1–15 (Berne: Haupt).

MAMPU (Malaysian Administration Modernisation and Management Planning Unit) (1992) Manual on Micro Accounting System, *Development Administration Circular No. 3/1992*, Malaysia.

MAMPU (2000) *The Civil Service of Malaysia: Moving into the New Millennium*, (Kuala Lumpur: MAMPU).

Mautz, R. K. (1988) Monuments, mistakes and opportunities, *Accounting Horizons*, pp. 123–128.

McGregor, W. (1999) The pivotal role of accounting concepts in the development of public sector accounting standards, *Australian Accounting Review*, 9(1), pp. 3–8.

Olson, O., Guthrie, J. & Humphrey, C. (1998) *Global Warning – Debating International Developments in New Public Financial Management* (Oslo: Cappeln Akademisk Forlag).

Pallot, J. (1990) The nature of public assets: a response to Mautz, *Accounting Horizons*, June pp. 79–85.

Robinson, M. (1998) Accrual accounting and the efficiency of the core public sector, *Financial Accountability and Management*, 14(1), pp. 21–37.

Rutherford, B. A. (1992) Developing a conceptual framework for central government financial reporting: intermediate users and indirect control, *Financial Accountability and Management*, 8(4), pp. 265–280.

Stanton, P. & Stanton, J. (1998) The questionable economics of governmental accounting, *Accounting, Auditing and Accountability Journal*, 11(2), pp. 191–203.

Telecommunication Industry in Malaysia: Demographics Effect on Customer Expectations, Performance, Satisfaction and Retention

NORIZAN MOHD KASSIM

Department of Management and Marketing, College of Business and Economics, University of Qatar, Qatar

Introduction

Many demographic characteristics and service quality studies have been carried out in western countries (for example, Webster, 1989; Gagliano & Hatchote, 1994; Webb, 1998;), but not in a developing country like Malaysia. These studies revealed that demographic characteristics are important when determining the expected service quality (Webster, 1989; Gagliano & Hatchote, 1994) but further demographic studies about predicting customers' expectations and their relationship with service performance perceptions, satisfaction and retention cannot be identified. Moreover, customers' demographic characteristics may be potent forces in the global business environment in the future (Webb, 1998). For example, the multi-ethnic and multicultural mix of the population of a country like Malaysia may cause local demographic characteristics to influence expectations, performance perceptions, satisfaction and retention in service contexts (Aliah, 1999). In other words, what leads to expectations, performance formations and their relationship with satisfaction and retention, and to demographics as a segmentation basis, could provide useful insights to a service provider.

This study was done within the context of the cellular telephone service market in Malaysia because the above issues have not been empirically investigated in a developing country environment before. It is hoped that the findings from this study will be useful to other countries with a similar environment and level of economic development as Malaysia. Malaysia has a population of 22.36 million and is a relatively large economy that has an important role in South East Asia. Telecommunications are critical for a rapidly growing economy and Malaysia's deregulated cellular telephone market is one of the most competitive in the world, and was forecasted to grow at 26 per cent in the year 2000 (Kahaner, 1996).

Literature Review

First, consider the role of expectations in the construction of satisfaction. The extent to which a service fulfils a person's desires may play a role in shaping his or her feelings of satisfaction because of the impact of disconfirmation of expectations on satisfaction (for example, Westbrook, 1980; Spreng *et al.*, 1996). Failure to consider the extent to which a service fulfils a person's desires has led to logical inconsistencies, such as predicting that a customer who expects and receives poor performance will be satisfied (LaTour & Peat, 1979; Spreng *et al.*, 1996). Hence, expectations appear to be important in formulating levels of satisfaction, and so how these standards of expectation influence satisfaction formation are important for managers when determining customers' needs and wants. There are different ways in which expectations have been investigated and defined in customer satisfaction/dissatisfaction literatures.

Moreover, it is generally argued that if customers are satisfied with a particular product or service offering after its use, then they are likely to engage in a repeat purchase and to try line extensions (East, 1997). Satisfied customers are likely to tell others of their favourable experiences and thus engage in positive word-of-mouth advertising (Richins, 1983; File & Prince, 1992). On the other hand, dissatisfied customers are likely to switch brands and engage in negative word-of-mouth advertising. Thus the significance of customer satisfaction and customer retention in strategy development for a market-oriented and customer-focused firm cannot be underestimated (Kohli & Jaworski, 1990).

However, there is a debate as to whether attribute-level performance should affect customer satisfaction/dissatisfaction and customer retention through repurchase intentions or loyalty differently, because they are qualitatively different constructs (Ostrom & Iacobucci, 1995). That is, performance of a certain attribute may become critical for repurchase intentions but not for satisfaction. For example, a customer may be satisfied with all aspects of the service provided by his or her cellular phone service operator, but he or she may relocate to another area far from the cellular phone service operator's office. This customer might indicate high overall satisfaction with the cellular phone service operator, but he or she may still choose another service operator because performance on a critical attribute has changed. In brief, although the performance on 'distance of cellular phone service operator's office from home' had a negative impact on repurchase intention, it may have had a small or no impact at all on overall satisfaction. Such a discrepancy could be explained by the attribution theory (Folkes, 1988).

In other words, attribute-level performance may have a separate and distinct impact on overall satisfaction and on repurchase intentions or loyalty (Oliva *et al.*, 1992; Mitall *et al.*, 1998). For example, Oliver (1993) suggests that customer satisfaction and dissatisfaction have different affective outcomes that may be related differently to repurchase intentions, that is, 'the probability of repurchase was not isomorphic with either positive or negative service experiences' (Feinberg *et al.*, 1990: 113).

In turn, surrogate measures of customer retention are normally used because of the constraint involved in longitudinal studies (Levesque & McDougall, 1996). These measures relate to attitudes or future intentions towards the service provider. Moreover, there is sufficient evidence to suggest that customer satisfaction can and should be viewed as an attitude (Yi, 1990). For example, in a cellular phone service there is an ongoing relationship between the service provider and the customer. In brief, customer satisfaction is based on an evaluation of multiple interactions.

This study comprehensively defined customer retention in the form of behavioural outcome. The five favourable measures of future intentions used in this study – recommending to others, express preference, continuing using the service, increased usage and propensity not to switch – are used to measure retention (Boulding *et al.*, 1993: 27; Heskett *et al.*, 1994; Danaher & Rust, 1996; Levesque & McDougall, 1996; Zeithaml *et al.*, 1996).

Nevertheless, while other standards have been suggested in the literature, the predictive standards that do not include desired levels of service at the same time have received the widest attention. Indeed, because customers might still be satisfied even when the service provider did not fulfil their expectations (Yuskel & Rimmington, 1998), an examination of a model about the minimum or adequate level of service may be fruitful. Adequate service level is partly based on the customer's assessment of predictive service level, which can change over time and from one service encounter to the next for the same customers (Zeithaml *et al.*, 1993). There is also empirical evidence that confirms the impact of desired expectations in shaping satisfaction (for example, Westbrook & Reily, 1983; Spreng *et al.*, 1996). Thus, I developed a model of how demographics may affect expectations, perceptions of performance, satisfaction and retention based on dimensions developed in stage one of the studies described below.

In turn, demographic segments may have different expectations. The concept of market segmentation remains a central tenet of modern marketing and is linked to the marketing concept itself. The concept attempts to reconcile differing customer needs with limited company resources, and allows product and marketing groups' offerings to be adjusted to suit different customers (Assael & Roscoe, 1976; Blattberg & Sen, 1976; Wind, 1978). That is, it involves the grouping of customers with similar needs and buying behaviour into segments, each of which can be reached with a distinct marketing programme. It would therefore seem likely that personality and people differences will produce different service requirements (Scott & Shieff, 1993).

This type of perception has been confirmed by marketers to some extent by using demographic characteristics to segment markets (for example, age, gender, education, occupation, income, family size, family lifecycle, ethnic, social class, religion). These characteristics can be associated with needs, wants, preferences, and usage rates, and therefore, with consumption and purchasing habits of consumers (Hair, Lamb & McDaniel, 2000; Kotler, 2000; McColl-Kennedy & Kiel, 2000). A list of some variables within the demographic base that have been identified by some representative writers is shown in Table 1.

The effects of demographic characteristics are found in both service quality and customer satisfaction/dissatisfaction literatures. Previous study has shown that demographic variables are related to service quality expectations. Examples of demographic variables include income in retailing stores (Gagliano & Hatchote, 1994), age, gender and income for professional services (Webster, 1989) and income and ethnic groups in local government services (Scott & Shieff, 1993). Further, the effects of demographics at both the desired and predictive standards of expectations are found in non-profit organizations (Webb, 1998). Therefore, these characteristics are important when developing marketing efforts (Levesque & McDoughall, 1996; Zeithaml, 2000) and quality improvements (Scott & Shieff, 1993; Stafford, 1996; Edvardsson, 1998).

Finally, the effects of demographics on service quality expectations (Gagliano & Hatchote, 1994; Stafford, 1996; Webb, 1998; Webster, 1989), perceptions of performance (Herbig & Genestre, 1996: 30), and satisfaction (Bryant & Cha, 1996; Varki & Rust, 1997) have been empirically investigated. However, the literature concerns the impact of demographics in western countries (Aliah, 1999). Moreover, it has not addressed what specific demographics lead to service retention and to the interrelationship between expectations, perceptions of performance and satisfaction. Thus, the generalizability of the findings in the Malaysian context is questionable. How relevant are these demographics for this study in particular?

Hypotheses

The above discussions lead to the study issue: *How do demographics affect satisfaction and retention?* To find answers to this issue, three hypotheses were examined:

H1.1: Demographics of a customer affect his or her:

(a) perception of performance,

(b) desired expectations, and

(c) expectations of adequate service.

H1.2: Demographics of a customer affect his or her overall satisfaction.

H1.3: Demographics of a customer affect his or her overall retention.

Table 1. Variables within the demographic segmentation base, in order of citations

	Age	Gender	Education	Income	Ethnic	Occupation	Family size	Family lifecycle	Social class	Religion	Total
Boone & Kurtz (1992)	✓	✓		✓							3
Hair, Lamb & McDaniel (2000)	✓	✓		✓	✓						4
Keegan & Green (2000)	✓	✓	✓		✓			✓		✓	6
Kotler (2000)	✓	✓	✓	✓	✓	✓	✓	✓	✓	✓	10
McCarthy *et al.* (1994)	✓	✓	✓	✓	✓	✓	✓	✓	✓		9
McColl-Kennedy & Kiel (2000)	✓	✓	✓		✓	✓	✓	✓	✓	✓	9
Schwartz (1981)	✓	✓	✓	✓		✓	✓		✓	✓	8
Total	7	7	5	5	5	4	4	4	4	4	

Source: Kassim (2001), Boone & Kurtz (1992), Keegan & Green (2000), McCarthy *et al.* (1994) and Schwartz, D.J. (1981).

Methodology

The study was done in two stages. In *stage one*, a preliminary questionnaire was constructed from discussions with five executives from each of the five telecommunications operators in Malaysia, two Malaysian authorities, two professors in management and 15 users who were experts on the issues (Edvardsson, 1998; Hayes, 1998). Five dimensions of satisfaction were developed – customer service, service coverage, billing integrity, quality of line and customer service outlets – and a draft questionnaire was then developed for pre-testing and further interviews with the respondents.

The scale used was a forced response, 6-point Likert-type scale. The possible explanations for using a forced response type of scale could be that prior knowledge through exploratory study suggested a high likelihood of favourable responses to the attitude under study (Wong, 1999; Burns & Bush, 2000; Zikmund, 2000); the survey was conducted in a conservative market where respondents were more guarded in offering praise (Wong, 1999).

Conceptualization and Operationalization of Variables

The conceptualization of each construct in this study is listed in Appendix A. For example, 'Customer Satisfaction' is a construct about an accumulated experience of a customer's purchase and consumption experiences. Further, because the amount of customer satisfaction varies between service dimensions, customer satisfaction is measured by the five dimensions of questions 5, 10, 15, 20 and 25 in the questionnaire.

In turn, the operationalization is the process of precisely delineating how a construct is to be measured (Hair *et al.*, 2000). That is, the variables have to be specified in such a manner as to be potentially observable or manipulative.

Questionnaire Design

The questionnaire consisted of four parts. The first part consisted of general information about the respondents' cellular phone operators. This general information was useful as a guide and support for the findings, which will be discussed later.

The second part was designed to assess the quality of services provided by the cellular phone operators. The respondents were asked to indicate their opinions about their level of expectations and service performance perceptions on the 6-point scale from extremely poor to extremely good. Each of the quality dimensions will be discussed in turn.

Dimension one: service coverage. A cellular phone operator's service coverage area is an important component of a cellular phone service, especially for subscribers who frequently travel beyond their local metropolitan area, or subscribers in areas that are not well covered by a competitor's network. Limitations in service coverage are one of the reasons why cellular phone service subscribers have switched services (Kahaner, 1996).

Dimension two: billing integrity. This dimension concerns the reliability of the company's ability to fulfil its commitment such as price agreements to be fulfilled, time limits to be kept and the service to be carried out correctly from the beginning (Parasuraman *et al.*, 1985, 1988). Sweeney *et al.* (1992) suggest that price sets expectations for the quality of service when other cues to quality are not available. Although the prices of registration fees are controlled and fixed by the Malaysian government, airtime prices are not, and vary considerably between operators.

Dimension three: quality of line. This dimension concerns the quality of the signal (Kahaner, 1996). Digital services have become popular in Malaysia because of the clarity of their signals and are another component of a cellular's phone service.

Dimension four: customer service. Customers' perception of service is often associated with some personal interaction with the employees (Kandampully, 1993; Avkiran, 1999). Services management literature has emphasized the importance of the human element in the delivery of superior service (Parasuraman *et al.*, 1985; Solomon, *et al.*, 1985; Crosby & Stephens, 1987; Gronroos, 1990b). Thus, the first three items of this dimension are about employees' willingness and readiness to carry out the service punctually and quickly (Solomon *et al.*, 1985), being there for the customer and being available when the customer needs assistance.

In many service situations the service personnel's interaction with the customer has been recognized as a critical determinant of satisfaction (Surprenant & Solomon, 1987). Some customers prefer personalized and close relationships with service providers (Zeithaml *et al.*, 1996). Hence, the fourth to seventh items about customer service measure the behaviour and decorum of the company employees. Next, nine items measured the employee's knowledge and competence and their ability to inspire reliance and trust (Parasuraman *et al.*, 1988). Finally, two items measured the employees' interest in the customer (Brown & Swartz, 1989; Parasuraman *et al.*, 1988) and their paying attention to the customer (Bitner *et al.*, 1990).

Dimension five: customer service outlet. This dimension concerns the service atmosphere – what it is easy for customers to observe and enjoy – including the physical environment in the service organization: premises, equipment, personnel and dress code as well as the spatial layout and functionality (Parasuraman *et al.*, 1988; Bitner, 1992). Five items were identified during the exploratory research (in stage one) which comprise convenient location, convenient business hour, modern looking equipment, visually appealing materials and ease of making payment.

Next, there were three *dependent* measures: levels of service (performance, desired and adequate), overall satisfaction, and overall retention. Two of these measures are single-item measures (overall satisfaction and retention) and in this study the reliability test for these measures is acceptable (0.64–0.84) and thus for this reason, I believe the measures are adequate (Mittal *et al.*, 1998). The respondents were asked to rank the importance of the services offered by the cellular phone operators. This ranking of services was also used to define the population (Edvardsson, 1998).

The third part of the questionnaire addressed the issue of retention. Only the favourable measures established in the literature were used (for example, Boulding *et al.*, 1993; Heskett *et al.*, 1994; Danaher & Rust, 1996; Levesque & McDougall, 1996; Zeithaml *et al.*, 1996) because retention in the telecommunications industry should be similar to retention in other industry.

Three reasons were considered for asking respondents questions pertaining to retention. First, recommending the service to others will attract new customers through the mechanism of positive word-of-mouth comments that will subsequently reduce the marketing costs the company must expand its efforts to get additional customers (Parasuraman *et al.*, 1988; Danaher & Rust, 1996; Zeithaml *et al.*, 1996; Zeithaml, 2000). Second, preferring the service to others (Woodside *et al.*, 1989; Zeithaml, 2000) indicates that the experiences that customers had with the service provider influenced their decisions not to defect or switch to others (Bhote, 1997). Finally, continuing to use the service, usage rate and no intention to switch indicates that these customers will have the strongest levels of retention intentions and the are the least likely to switch (Danaher & Rust, 1996; Zeithaml *et al.*, 1996).

Finally, the fourth part of the questionnaire consisted of a series of respondents' demographic and socio-economic characteristics such as ethnicity, gender, age, marital status, education, occupation and income.

Pre-test, Revise and Final Draft

The pre-testing involved a group of respondents selected on a convenience basis, (Sekaran, 2000; Zikmund, 2000). A total of 100 sets of questionnaires were distributed to cellular phone users and this resulted in 60 usable completed questionnaires. The questions provided high Cronbach alpha scores for each latent construct selected (above 0.80). Further discussion with three marketing experts was held to identify any content validity problems. As a result of this only two items from question 13 were dropped and there were some modifications in relation to some wordings: 'cellular', 'adequate', 'expectation' and 'experience' were changed to 'mobile', 'tolerable', 'reasonable' and 'received', respectively.

Questionnaire Administration

In *stage two*, the most appropriate survey method used (in the Malaysian context) was a personally administered survey. The databases containing addresses and telephone numbers (both home and office) of a total population of 600,000 individuals were obtained from the five telecommunication operators. Using systematic sampling method, every 1000th individual was selected until the required sample size was reached. Each respondent was given the questionnaire personally by the interviewer so that any doubts could be clarified immediately and the questionnaire could take a significantly shorter time to complete (Aaker *et al.*, 2000; Sekaran, 2000). Of the 425 questionnaires distributed, 120 cases of the completed questionnaires were found to be unusable due to missing responses and unexplained outliers (Bollen, 1989; Hooley & Hussey, 1994; Hair *et al.*, 1995; Tabachnick & Fidell, 1996). Thus, the response rate of 71.8 per cent was achieved.

Multivariate covariance analysis (MANCOVA) was used to test the hypotheses about the categorical demographic variables. In brief, MANCOVA assesses whether there are group differences (for example, gender, ethnic, marital status, age, income and education) across a set of dependent variables and is an extension of multivariate analysis of variance (Tabachnick & Fidell, 1996; Varki & Rust, 1997). The Spearman rho rank correlation coefficient was used to calculate the strength of the relationship between the rank ordered demographic variables (Triola & Franklin, 1995).

Most of the demographic variable relationships reported in Table 2 were correlated in the expected direction. These correlations fitted the expected patterns in Malaysia, for example, income and ethnic were significantly correlated, age and marital status were significantly correlated, and marital status and ethnic were not significantly correlated. Thus, further analysis could proceed even if the data had a non-normal distribution (Biddle & Marlin, 1987).

Table 2. Relationships amongst the demographic variable – Spearman Rho rank correlations

		1	2	3	4	5	6
1	Gender	1.00					
2	Ethnic	0.03	1.00				
3	Age	**− 0.19**	*0.13*	1.00			
4	Marital	**− 0.19**	0.03	**0.39**	1.00		
5	Education	*0.11*	**0.20**	**0.43**	0.00	1.00	
6	Income	**− 0.17**	**0.15**	**0.70**	**0.26**	**0.64**	1.00

Covariate variables (age, education and income)
$P < 0.05$; **$P < 0.01$**); two-tailed (N = 305)

Next, the usual validity and reliability measures were addressed. For example, content or face validity and construct validity were established from the experts in stage one, the literature review, the pre-testing of the questionnaire and the confirmatory factor analysis.

Results

Preliminary Test

Preliminary data analysis was undertaken to examine the psychometric properties of the scales via measures of central tendency, dispersion, bivariate Pearson correlation, and principal components analysis with varimax rotation, reliability estimates and confirmatory factor analysis (CFA). AMOS software was used to test the CFAs. To evaluate the fit of the CFAs, two common model goodness-of-fit indicators were examined: Root mean square residual (RMR) and comparative fit index (CFI) (Chau & Hu, 2002). Chi square statistic was not used because of its inherent problems with sensitivity to sample size (Kassim, 2001; Chau & Hu, 2002).

Descriptive statistics such as means and standard deviation were obtained for the interval-scaled independent and dependent variables (see Table 3).

Next, the five dimensions of overall satisfaction were tested with confirmatory factor analysis (CFA). The 42 indicators used to measure the five dimensions in the survey questionnaire were then reduced to 28 appropriate indicators (see Table 4).

Table 3. Summary of descriptive statistics of variables

Construct	Expectations		Performance	Overall Satisfaction	Overall Retention
	Adequate level	Desired level			
Mean	3.70	3.97	4.02	3.96	4.09
Std. Dev.	0.58	0.57	0.78	0.42	0.58

The confirmatory factor analysis adequately reflects a satisfactory fit to the data, $P = 0.001$ with RMR ranged from 0.01 to 0.02 and CFI ranged from 0.90 to 0.95 (Baumgartner & Homburg, 1996). The RMR and CFI indicated that the five-factor model is valid. The results indicated that the factor loadings ranged from 0.58 to 0.98, thus supporting the models. Admittedly, two of the overall satisfaction variables had beta coefficient of less than 0.50: (i) Overall satisfaction → customer service (0.32) and (ii) Overall satisfaction → customer service outlet (0.45). However, these variables were retained because they were significantly different than zero and thus could be considered as acceptable for this exploratory study (Hair *et al.*, 1995; Tabachnick & Fidell, 1996; Kline, 1998; Kassim, 2001). These preliminary results also indicated that the constructs proposed were being tapped by the measurement instrument developed for the five forms of overall satisfaction. The results of the preliminary analyses of the instrument indicated acceptance of the psychometric properties of the scales (Anderson & Gerbing, 1998; O'Cass, 2000).

Respondent Profile

The respondents were almost evenly split by ethnic groups (56.1 per cent non-Malays and 43.9 per cent Malays) and marital status (48.2 per cent single and 51.8 per cent married). Most of the respondents (64.6 per cent) were male. Most of the respondents were 27 years of age, followed by the age groups of 22 and 32 years at 24.6 per cent and 23.3 per cent, respectively. These three groups contributed approximately 76 per cent of the overall total in term of age. About 32.5 per cent of the respondents had spent at least 13 years in education and earned between RM10,000 to RM40,000 per annum (87.5 per cent of the income) (see Table 5).

Profile of Service Operators

The information given by the respondents had to be treated as confidential, and so the names of the service operators were disguised as Telco 1 to Telco 5, as shown in Table 6.

Testing the Hypotheses

The results which show the effect of demographic variables on levels of service, overall satisfaction and overall retention, are summarized in Table 7. The

Table 4. Standardized confirmatory factor loadings

		Results				
		Level of services				
		Adequate	Desired	Performance	Overall Satisfaction[1]	Overall Retention[2]
	Service coverage				0.61	0.69
1.	On-street coverage	**0.96**	**0.98**	**0.89**		
2.	In-building coverage	**0.86**	**0.94**	**0.86**		
3.	Nation-wide coverage	**0.69**	**0.88**	**0.69**		
	Cronbach alpha	*0.87*	*0.95*	*0.84*		
	RMR	N/A	N/A	N/A		
	CFI	N/A	N/A	N/A		
	Billing integrity				0.54	0.78
4.	Promptness in billing	**0.58**	**0.61**	**0.64**		
5.	Unauthorized charges	**0.97**	**0.99**	**0.96**		
6.	Unexplained charges	**0.92**	**0.92**	**0.96**		
	Cronbach alpha	*0.86*	*0.87*	*0.88*		
	RMR	N/A	N/A	N/A		
	CFI	N/A	N/A	N/A		
	Quality of line				0.57	0.75
7.	Interruptions	**0.93**	**0.88**	**0.91**		
8.	Line disconnection	**0.92**	**0.92**	**0.92**		
9.	Echoes	**0.89**	**0.88**	**0.91**		
10.	Noise	**0.88**	**0.91**	**0.91**		
11.	Service restoration	**0.69**	**0.77**	**0.66**		
12.	One way connection	**0.72**	**0.82**	**0.71**		
	Cronbach alpha	*0.93*	*0.95*	*0.93*		
	RMR	0.01	0.01	0.02		
	CFI	0.95	0.90	0.95		
	Customer service				0.32	0.71
13.	Time taken for staff to respond	**0.79**	**0.81**	**0.74**		
14.	Knowledgeable staff	**0.83**	**0.89**	**0.81**		
15.	Staff who care about customer's problem	**0.82**	**0.92**	**0.83**		
16.	Having best interest in customer's problem	**0.83**	**0.93**	**0.84**		

Table 4. *Continued*

		Results				
		Level of services			Overall Satisfaction[1]	Overall Retention[2]
		Adequate	Desired	Performance		
17.	Staff who instils confidence in me	**0.88**	**0.93**	**0.86**		
18.	Staff who provide service at the promised time	**0.88**	**0.95**	**0.87**		
19.	Speedily resolve complaints	**0.92**	**0.94**	**0.86**		
20.	Performing service right the first time	**0.92**	**0.95**	**0.86**		
21.	Maintaining error-free record	**0.89**	**0.93**	**0.83**		
22.	Reliability in handling problem	**0.92**	**0.94**	**0.87**		
23.	Readiness to respond to a request	**0.91**	**0.94**	**0.87**		
24.	Staff's willing-ness to help	**0.91**	**0.95**	**0.85**		
25.	Providing service as promised	**0.90**	**0.96**	**0.85**		
	Cronbach alpha	*0.98*	*0.99*	*0.97*		
	RMR	0.01	0.01	0.02		
	CFI	0.90	0.90	*0.91*		
	Customer service outlet				**0.45**	**0.68**
26.	Convenient business hour	**0.68**	**0.81**	**0.58**		
27.	Modern looking equipment	**0.97**	**0.93**	**0.96**		
28.	Visually appeal-ing materials	**0.87**	**0.92**	**0.87**		
	Cronbach alpha	*0.87*ch	*0.92*	*0.84*		
	RMR	N/A	N/A	N/A		
	CFI	N/A	N/A	N/A		

Note: All factor loadings [in bold] are significant at $P < 0.01$
[1]Cronbach alpha $= 0.64$
[2]Cronbach alpha $= 0.84$

Table 5. Frequency table of the respondent's profile

N = 305	No. of respondents	%	Cumulative %
1. Gender			
Male	197	64.6	64.6
Female	108	35.4	100.0
2. Ethnic			
Non-Malay [Chinese, Indian and Others]	171	56.1	56.1
Malay	134	43.9	100.0
3. Marital status			
Single	147	48.2	48.2
Married	148	51.8	100.0
4. [1]Age			
17 years [< 20 years]	23	7.5	7.5
22 years [20–24 years]	75	24.6	32.1
27 years [25–29 years]	86	28.2	60.3
32 years [30–34 years]	71	23.3	83.6
37 years [35–39 years]	25	8.2	91.8
42 years [40–44 years]	13	4.3	96.1
47 years [45–49 years]	5	1.6	97.7
52 years [50–54 years]	6	2.0	99.7
57 years and above [5 years and above]	1	0.3	100.0
5. Education			
7 years [Primary school]	1	0.3	0.3
10 years [LCE/SRP/PMR]	6	2.0	2.3
12 years [MCE/SPM/SPVM]	99	32.5	34.8
13 years [HSC/STP]	25	8.2	43.0
14 years [Certificate/Diploma]	59	19.3	62.3
15 years [Bachelor's Degree]	85	27.9	90.2
17 years [Master's Degree]	28	9.2	99.3
19 years [Doctorate]	2	0.7	100
6. [1]Annual Income			
RM10,000 [Under RM10,000]	75	24.6	24.6
RM15,000 [RM10,000–19,999]	46	15.1	39.7
RM25,000 [RM20,000–29,999]	77	25.2	64.9
RM40,000 [RM30,000–49,999]	69	22.6	87.5
RM57,500 [RM50,000–64,999]	12	3.9	91.5
RM65,000 and above	26	8.5	100.0

Note: [1] The mean values of age group and annual income respectively

following paragraphs summarize the general trend across adequate, desired and performance levels of service, and overall satisfaction and overall retention for each demographic variable (however, the result of the overall MANCOVA was not available from the SPSS programme. Therefore, only the successive individual results were reported here without further post hoc test or post hoc adjustment because of the limited number of groups for most of the demographic variables).

Table 6. The frequency table of the service providers

N = 305	No. of Respondent	%	Cumulative %
1. Current operators			
Telco 1	87	28.5	28.5
Telco 2	52	17.1	45.6
Telco 3	28	9.2	54.7
Telco 4	72	23.6	78.3
Telco 5	66	21.6	100.0
2. No. of years subscribed			
Less than a year	58	19.0	19.0
1 year but less than 2 years	112	36.7	55.7
2 years but less than 5 years	109	35.7	91.5
5 years but less than 7 years	23	7.5	99.0
7 years but less than 10 years	2	0.7	99.7
10 years or more	1	0.3	100.0
3. Previous operators			
Telco 1	58	19.0	19.0
Telco 2	49	16.1	35.1
Telco 3	39	12.8	47.9
Telco 4	87	28.6	76.5
Telco 5	72	23.6	100.0
4. Reason for switching because of the unresolved problem			
Yes	75	24.6	24.6
No	230	75.4	100.0
5 Do you complain			
Yes	234	76.7	76.7
No	71	23.3	100.0

Demographic One: Gender

Table 7 summarizes the respondents' adequate, desired and performance levels of service, by gender. There is a significant difference for customer service, at the desired level of service, and the quality of line for performance. This finding suggests that males desired more efficient approaches when dealing with customers than did females. However, these respondents experienced better performance in quality of line dimension.

Demographic Two: Ethnic

Respondents by ethnic group were almost evenly split and categorized as either 'Malay' or 'non-Malay' [Chinese, Indian and Others] as shown in Table 5. Table 7 shows that there is a significant difference between ethnics for the customer service dimension, at the performance level of service. This finding suggests that non-Malay respondents experienced more efficient performances from the staff of the operators than the Malay respondents. This seems to indicate that Malay respondents were more casual in accepting or receiving the service. In other words, they seemed to be more tolerant with the services they received.

Table 7. Multivariate analysis of covariance of expectations, performance and satisfaction and retention

Dependent variable/dimension	Gender	Ethnic	Age	Marital	Education	Income
Adequate						
Service coverage						
ONSTR	3.785	3.783	3.770	3.769	3.770	3.770
INBLDG	3.694	3.702	3.689	3.689	3.689	3.689
NWIDE	3.712	3.705	3.695	3.695	3.695	3.695
Wilks' Lambda	0.158	1.070	**4.079**	1.143	**3.194**	**1.665**
p value	0.924	0.362	**0.007b**	0.332	**0.024b**	**0.053b**
Billing integrity						
PROMP	3.640	3.647	3.643	3.641	3.643	3.643
UNAUT	3.231	3.240	3.236	3.237	3.236	3.236
UNEXP	3.151	3.165	3.157	3.158	3.157	3.157
Wilks' Lambda	0.922	1.625	**2.924**	0.690	**1.542**	**1.510**
p value	0.431	0.185	**0.035b**	0.559	**0.058a**	**0.097a**
Quality of line						
INTERR	3.852	3.882	3.869	3.868	3.869	3.869
DISCO	3.799	3.837	3.826	3.825	3.826	3.826
ECHOE	3.806	3.853	3.836	3.836	8.836	3.836
NOISE	3.839	3.869	3.859	3.859	3.859	3.859
RESTOR	3.891	3.897	3.892	3.892	3.892	3.892
1DISCO	4.109	4.135	4.125	4.124	4.125	4.125
Wilks' Lambda	1.849	0.836	0.824	0.314	0.817	1.036
p value	0.121	0.504	0.511	0.868	0.757	0.417
Customer service						
RESPN	3.803	3.803	3.797	3.795	3.797	3.797
KNOW	3.829	3.823	3.816	3.814	3.816	3.816
CARE	3.805	3.814	3.810	3.808	3.810	3.810
BEST	3.781	3.793	3.787	3.785	3.787	3.787
CONFI	3.806	3.808	3.807	3.805	3.807	3.807
ATMISE	3.768	3.771	3.767	3.764	3.767	3.767
SOLVE	3.731	3.733	3.731	3.729	3.731	3.731
RIGHT	3.739	3.745	3.741	3.738	3.741	3.741
FREE0	3.686	3.692	3.689	3.686	3.689	3.689
RELIB	3.716	3.713	3.708	3.705	3.708	3.708
READY	3.765	3.768	3.764	3.761	3.764	3.764
WILLG	3.758	3.760	3.757	3.756	3.757	3.757
ASMISE	3.787	3.788	3.787	3.785	3.787	3.787
Wilks' Lambda	0.693	0.607	1.085	0.401	0.925	0.980
p value	0.768	0.846	0.270	0.968	0.528	0.502
Customer service outlets						
BUSHR	3.913	3.922	3.915	3.913	3.915	3.915
MODEQ	3.988	3.998	3.987	3.986	3.987	3.987
APPEAL	3.996	3.998	3.987	3.986	3.987	3.987
Wilks' Lambda	0.452	1.272	0.848	**3.388**	1.344	0.257
p value	0.716	0.285	0.675	**0.019b**	0.141	0.856

Table 7. *Continued*

Dependent variable/dimension	Gender	Ethnic	Age	Marital	Education	Income
Desired						
Service coverage						
ONSTR	3.908	3.892	3.892	3.891	3.892	3.892
INBLDG	3.895	3.888	3.889	3.888	3.889	3.889
NWIDE	3.877	3.860	3.862	3.861	3.862	3.862
Wilks' Lambda	0.215	0.516	**1.495**	0.963	1.236	0.468
p value	0.886	0.672	**0.073a**	0.411	0.215	0.705
Billing integrity						
PROMP	3.895	3.878	3.875	3.875	3.875	3.875
UNAUT	3.895	3.885	3.875	3.875	3.875	3.875
UNEXP	3.878	3.862	3.856	3.856	3.856	3.856
Wilks' Lambda	0.955	1.405	1.646	0.462	0.425	0.747
p value	0.415	0.243	0.180	0.709	0.990	0.738
Quality of line						
INTERR	3.962	3.954	3.954	3.953	3.954	3.954
DISCO	3.950	3.940	3.941	3.940	3.941	3.941
ECHOE	3.967	3.959	3.954	3.952	3.954	3.954
NOISE	3.955	3.948	3.948	3.946	3.948	3.948
RESTOR	4.000	3.990	3.987	3.985	3.987	3.987
1DISCO	3.989	3.985	3.984	3.982	3.984	3.984
Wilks' Lambda	1.129	1.211	1.047	1.415	0.868	0.892
p value	0.347	0.302	0.397	0.211	0.710	0.635
Customer service						
RESPN	4.061	4.051	4.046	4.046	4.046	4.046
KNOW	4.061	4.047	4.046	4.045	4.046	4.046
CARE	3.979	3.972	3.970	3.969	3.970	3.970
BEST	3.973	3.971	3.970	3.969	3.970	3.970
CONFI	3.989	3.981	3.984	3.982	3.984	3.984
ATMISE	4.003	3.987	3.990	3.988	3.990	3.990
SOLVE	3.989	3.978	3.980	3.978	3.980	3.980
RIGHT	3.996	3.986	3.987	3.985	3.987	3.987
FREE0	4.019	4.004	4.003	4.003	4.003	4.003
RELIB	4.023	3.999	4.000	3.999	4.000	4.000
READY	4.022	4.007	4.007	4.005	4.007	4.007
WILLG	4.010	4.000	4.000	3.998	4.000	4.000
ASMISE	3.991	3.975	3.977	3.976	3.977	3.977
Wilks' Lambda	**1.705**	1.428	0.955	1.299	1.110	1.101
p value	**0.059a**	0.145	0.497	0.258	0.350	0.358
Customer service outlets						
BUSHR	3.991	3.982	3.977	3.977	3.977	3.977
MODEQ	4.048	4.031	4.030	4.031	4.030	4.030
APPEAL	4.070	4.051	4.052	4.054	4.052	4.052
Wilks' Lambda	1.547	1.814	1.167	0.426	**1.439**	0.611
p value	0.204	0.146	0.324	0.735	**0.10a**	0.867

Table 7. *Continued*

Dependent variable/dimension	Gender	Ethnic	Age	Marital	Education	Income
Performance						
Service coverage						
ONSTR	*3.871*	*3.907*	*3.895*	*3.892*	*3.895*	*3.895*
INBLDG	*3.770*	*3.809*	*3.800*	*3.799*	*3.800*	*3.800*
NWIDE	*3.646*	*3.680*	*3.672*	*3.668*	*3.672*	*3.672*
Wilks' Lambda	1.030	1.361	**1.527**	0.128	1.395	**5.049**
p value	0.381	0.256	**0.005b**	0.943	0.114	**0.002b**
Billing integrity						
PROMP	*4.044*	*4.069*	*4.062*	*4.062*	*4.062*	*4.062*
UNAUT	*3.741*	*3.785*	*3.770*	*3.771*	*3.770*	*3.770*
UNEXP	*3.701*	*3.740*	*3.725*	*3.724*	*3.725*	*3.725*
Wilks' Lambda	0.484	0.689	**1.924**	**4.115**	1.511	**4.659**
p value	0.694	0.560	**0.006b**	**0.007b**	**0.068a**	**0.004b**
Quality of line						
INTERR	*3.327*	*3.336*	*3.331*	*3.331*	*3.331*	*3.331*
DISCO	*3.336*	*3.348*	*3.344*	*3.344*	*3.344*	*3.344*
ECHOE	*3.343*	*3.357*	*3.354*	*3.354*	*3.354*	*3.354*
NOISE	*3.318*	*3.329*	*3.325*	*3.325*	*3.325*	*3.325*
RESTOR	*3.511*	*3.513*	*3.508*	*3.509*	*3.508*	*3.508*
1DISCO	*3.634*	*3.648*	*3.646*	*3.645*	*3.646*	*3.646*
Wilks' Lambda	**1.969**	1.344	**5.941**	0.526	**1.728**	**1.522**
p value	**0.070a**	0.238	**0.001c**	0.619	**0.001c**	**0.036b**
Customer service						
RESPN	*4.121*	*4.129*	*4.118*	*4.117*	*4.118*	*4.118*
KNOW	*4.255*	*4.279*	*4.272*	*4.268*	*4.272*	*4.272*
CARE	*4.186*	*4.200*	*4.200*	*4.197*	*4.200*	*4.200*
BEST	*4.167*	*4.185*	*4.184*	*4.180*	*4.184*	*4.184*
CONFI	*4.153*	*4.175*	*4.170*	*4.166*	*4.170*	*4.170*
ATMISE	*4.102*	*4.125*	*4.118*	*4.113*	*4.118*	*4.118*
SOLVE	*4.060*	*4.078*	*4.075*	*4.072*	*4.075*	*4.075*
RIGHT	*4.116*	*4.124*	*4.118*	*4.114*	*4.118*	*4.118*
FREE0	*4.157*	*4.177*	*4.170*	*4.168*	*4.170*	*4.170*
RELIB	*4.104*	*4.124*	*4.121*	*4.117*	*4.121*	*4.121*
READY	*4.187*	*4.212*	*4.207*	*4.203*	*4.207*	*4.207*
WILLG	*4.207*	*4.239*	*4.203*	*4.225*	*4.203*	*4.203*
ASMISE	*4.157*	*4.159*	*4.157*	*4.155*	*4.157*	*4.157*
Wilks' Lambda	0.441	**1.632**	**1.537**	0.838	**1.728**	**2.475**
p value	0.951	**0.08a**	**0.001c**	0.619	**0.001c**	**0.004b**
Customer service outlets						
BUSHR	*4.070*	*4.068*	*4.066*	*4.063*	*4.066*	*4.066*
MODEQ	*4.282*	*4.304*	*4.292*	*4.291*	*4.292*	*4.292*
APPEAL	*4.323*	*4.326*	*4.315*	*4.314*	*4.315*	*4.315*
Wilks' Lambda	0.811	0.903	0.566	1.493	1.191	**4.367**
p value	0.489	0.441	0.953	0.218	0.253	**0.005b**

Table 7. *Continued*

Dependent variable/dimension	Gender	Ethnic	Age	Marital	Education	Income
Satisfaction						
Overall satisfaction						
SATCOV	3.924	3.936	3.934	3.933	3.934	3.934
SATBILL	3.923	3.928	3.928	3.929	3.928	3.928
SATLINE	3.889	3.899	3.895	3.894	3.895	3.895
SATCUST	4.082	4.084	4.082	4.081	4.082	4.082
SATLET	3.971	3.971	3.970	3.970	3.970	3.970
Wilks' Lambda	0.441	0.551	**1.346**	1.088	**1.676**	1.821
p value	0.819	0.737	**0.077a**	0.369	**0.009b**	0.111
Retention						
Overall retention						
RECOMM	4.104	4.125	4.121	4.119	4.121	4.121
PREFER	4.161	4.172	4.170	4.167	4.170	4.170
CONTD	4.206	4.208	4.210	4.207	4.210	4.210
USAGE	4.017	4.029	4.036	4.032	4.036	4.036
SWITCH	3.877	3.893	3.895	3.890	3.895	3.895
Wilks' Lambda	1.337	0.397	1.207	0.817	1.128	**2.316**
p value	0.251	0.850	0.181	0.539	0.283	**0.04b**

a = $p<0.10$; b = p value<0.05; c = $p<0.01$
Figures in italic are the mean values

Demographic Three: Age

Table 7 indicates that age has a significant effect in service coverage and billing integrity dimensions, at an adequate level of service. The findings suggest that the respondents would have less tolerance for failure of service coverage and billing integrity. There was also a significant difference in service coverage, at the desired level of service. This finding suggests that younger people desire similarly efficient service coverage in other services, for example, banking services (Stafford, 1996).

There were also significant age differences in service coverage, billing integrity, quality of line and customer service dimensions, at the performance level of service. These findings suggest that younger respondents experienced better performance from these service provisions. Moreover, younger respondents were more satisfied. One possible explanation for this could be due to the fact that more than 50 per cent of the respondents were young (from 24 to 34 years old).

Demographic Four: Marital Status

Table 7 reveals that marital status only affects one dimension of the *performance* level of service. A significant difference is evident in the dimension of billing integrity. This finding suggests that single respondents experienced receiving prompt, clear and accurate bills from their service provider. One possible explanation could be that the single respondents were young and had low incomes and hence were more concerned with accurate bills so that they would not have to pay more than they should.

Demographic Five: Education

There were significant differences for education in only two dimensions of in-service coverage and billing integrity, at the *adequate* level of service. These findings suggest that respondents who spent many years in education (12–17 years) are less tolerant when dealing with these service provisions, presumably because their education had exposed them to a wider level of service. Differences also show that these respondents also *desired* more customer service outlets, convenient business hours, and modern equipment when processing their payments.

Finally, for performance, these educated people also experienced receiving clear and accurate bills and prompt billing processed, clear quality of line and better customer service. The findings also suggested that they were more *satisfied* overall.

Demographic Six: Income

Finally, Table 7 reveals the effect of income on an *adequate* level of service. Respondents in the lower and middle earning categories (between RM10,000 to 40,000) were less tolerant when dealing with the service coverage and the accuracy and promptness of the billing. However, they experienced better *performance* across the five dimensions: service coverage, billing integrity, quality of line, customer service and customer service outlets. The findings in Table 7 also suggest that the respondents were retained by their service operators.

Discussion and Implications

Overall, the findings from Table 7 suggested that some demographic variables have significant effects for some dimensions involved in expectations, performance and satisfaction and retention with income having the most effects, and gender, ethnic and marital status have the least effects.

Levels of Service and Satisfaction

This study found significant demographic effects on some dimensions involved in expectations, perceptions of performance and satisfaction, with income having the most effect. That is, this research shows that some demographic variables do have significant effects on some dimensions involved in adequate, desired and perceptions of performance levels of service and satisfaction. Thus, this Malaysian study supports the literature about demographics being related to expectations (gender, age, education and income) (Gagliano & Hatchote, 1994; Stafford, 1996; Webb, 1998; Aliah, 1999; Kassim & Bojei, 2002), and to perceptions of performance (ethnic, age, marital status, education and income) of level of service (Herbig & Genestre, 1996; Kassim & Bojei, 2002) and to satisfaction (age and education) (Bryant & Cha, 1996; Varki & Rust, 1997).

Retention

This study also found for the first time a relationship between demographics and retention, especially for income (see Table 7). Thus, this analysis supports the non-demographic literature about building customer retention and about loyalty efforts that are not necessarily targeted at *all* customers (Dowling & Uncles, 1997; Ganesh *et al.*, 2000). Thus, this research makes a *contribution* to knowledge about demographics' effects on overall retention. Therefore, the study hypotheses were confirmed and disconfirmed through MANCOVA in order of their presentation as summarized in Table 8. The results indicate that the hypotheses were partially supported.

The findings of this study have some implications for managerial decision making in the area of customer satisfaction and retention, especially for managers of telecommunications services. An understanding of how customer groups differ demographically might provide insights for managers in designing and implementing effective customer acquisition and retention strategies. For example, the findings in this study indicate that customers with different levels of income perceive dimensions of cellular phone service differently. However, standard and quality considerations are not generally affected by income (Stafford, 1996), but they are important when building customer retention and loyalty efforts because customers with lower incomes are too costly to do business with and have little potential to be profitable (Zeithaml & Bitner, 2000).

Many service providers may also find the findings in this analysis useful. Many services are primarily employee-driven businesses requiring high levels of employee/customer participation (Stafford, 1996). For such businesses, findings from this study suggest that perceptions of performance pertaining to level of service vary between gender, ethnic identity, age, marital status, education and income. Therefore, this investigation provides information that marketing managers can use to target a particular demographic. In brief, it is important for marketing managers to be sensitive to different demographic groups in terms of service when developing corresponding marketing and advertising strategies.

Admittedly, *further research* could repeat this study in other countries' telecommunication industries to validate and generalize the findings to broader settings. The findings in this analysis are delimited to the telecommunications industry and to Malaysia, but cultural differences between Malaysia and, for example, western countries could hinder the generalizability of the findings of this

Table 8. Summary of results of hypotheses

Dependent variables		Hypotheses	Supported
Levels of service	H1.1	Demographics affect each dimension of expectations and performance for levels of service	Some demographics were supported
Overall satisfaction	H1.2	Demographics affect each dimension of overall satisfaction	Only two demographics were supported
Overall retention	H1.3	Demographics affect each dimension of overall retention	Only one demographic was supported

study. Nevertheless, the findings of this research could be generalized to services that share some common characteristics with this industry. The model proposed and tested in this research might apply to services where customer involvement with the service is high or the relationship between the customers and the service provider are continuous, for example, retail banking, postal services, business to business context. Moreover, the findings could apply to many other countries in Asia.

Next, although the sample size was 305, after disaggregation into demographic categories, a few of the subgroups were somewhat small in number, for example, age and education. However, a cross-sectional sample was used, and age and education are not the only characteristics on which marketing efforts should be based and hence other demographic variables might be considered when making generalizations (Stafford, 1996). It should be noted that there were no data about the population of cellular phone users available or published apart (or other than the sampling) from the sampling frame used in this research, and this precluded testing for non-response. Although the study findings suggest demographics are related to overall retention, further analysis should attempt to measure the lifetime value of the customer groups while their demographics, such as age and income, change (Ganesh, Arnold & Reynolds, 2000; Zeithaml, 2000). An examination of the differences in the profitability of the groups may offer concrete guidelines for the firms in their quest for acquiring and retaining the right customers.

Conclusion

In conclusion, this study on customer satisfaction and retention in the Malaysian cellular phone service industry has value since the findings from this research provide a direction to determining the service attributes to focus on in enhancing customer overall satisfaction and overall retention. Although some of the dimensions of cellular phone service are similar in nature to those encountered in other service sectors (for example, billing integrity, customer service), there are additional dimensions which are important to subscribers, namely, quality of line, service coverage and customer service outlet of cellular phone service operators. These operators need to understand that such services are important to the individual users of cellular phone service that they serve and that good communications in respect of these areas of services are important aspects of service quality enhancement. Obviously, regulators and telecommunication managers recognize the importance of these dimensions but are not sure how to incorporate them into their decision making since a diverse set of customer needs and markets has evolved, which has resulted in customers switching services. Further, this analysis is one of the few studies to demonstrate empirically the effects of demographics, especially income, on customer retention.

Acknowledgement

The author would like to express her sincere gratitude to the three anonymous reviewers who have provided very constructive comments and suggestions for improvement to this essay.

References

Aaker, D., Kumar, V. & Day, G. (2000) *Marketing Research* (New York: John Wiley).

Aliah, H. M. S (1999) Measuring Service Quality for Malaysian Financial Services and Suggestion for Future Research, in *Reinvesting Asian Management for Global Challenges*, Malaysia: 3rd Asian Academy of management Conference, 16–17 July, pp.75–95.

Anderson, J. C. & Gerbing, D. W. (1988) Structural equation modelling in practice: a review and recommended two-step approach, *Psychological Bulletin*, 103(3), pp. 411–423.

Assael, H. & Roscoe, A. M. (1976) Approaches to market segmentation analysis, *Journal of Marketing*, 40 (October), pp. 67–76.

Avkiran, N. K. (1999) Quality customer service demands human contact, *International Journal of Bank Marketing*, 17(2), pp. 61–71.

Baumgartner, H. & Homburg, C. (1996) 0 Application of structural modeling in marketing and consumer study: a review, *International Journal of Research in Marketing*, 13, pp. 139–161.

Bhote, K. R. (1997) What do customer want, anyway?, *American Management*, March, pp. 36–40.

Biddle, B. J. & Marlin, M. M. (1987) Causality, confirmation, credulity, and structural equation modeling, *Child Development*, 58, pp. 4–17.

Bitner, M. J. (1992) The impact of physical surroundings on customers and employees, *Journal of Marketing*, 56(2), pp. 57–72.

Bitner, M. J., Booms, B. H. & Tetreault, M. S. (1990) The service encounter; diagnosing favorable and unfavorable incidents, *Journal of Marketing*, 54 (January), pp. 71–84.

Blattberg, R. C. & Sen, S. K. (1976) Market segments and stochastic brand choice models, *Journal of Marketing Research*, 13 (February), pp. 34–45.

Bollen, K. A. (1989) *Structural Equations with Latent Variables* (New York: John Wiley).

Boone, L. E & Kurtz, D. L. (1992) *Contemporary Marketing* (Orlando: Harcourt Brace Jovanovich).

Boulding, W., Kalra, A., Staelin, R. & Zeithaml, V. A. (1993) A dynamic process model of service quality; from expectations to behavioral intentions, *Journal of Marketing Research*, 30 (February), pp. 7–23.

Brown, S. W. S. & Swartz, T. A. (1989) A gap analysis of professional service quality, *Journal of Marketing*, 53, pp. 92–98.

Bryant, E. B. & Cha, J. (1996) Crossing the threshold, *Marketing Study*, 8 (Winter), pp. 21–28.

Burns, A. C. & Bush, R. F. (2000) *Marketing Research* (Upper Saddle River, NJ: Prentice Hall).

Chau, P. Y. K. & Hu, J. H. (2002) Investigating healthcare professionals' decisions to accept telemedicine technology: an empirical test of competing theories, *Information and Management*, 39(4), pp. 297–311.

Crosby, L. A. & Stephens, N. (1987) Effects of relationship marketing on satisfaction, retention and prices in the life insurance industry, *Journal of Marketing Research*, 26 (November), pp. 404–411.

Danaher, P. J. & Rust, R. T. (1996) Indirect benefits from service quality, *Quality Management Journal*, 3(2), pp. 63–85.

Dowling, G. R. & Uncles, M. (1997) Do customer loyalty programs really work?, *Sloan Management Review* (Summer), pp. 71–82.

East, R. (1997) *Consumer Behaviour: Advances and Applications in Marketing* (London: Prentice Hall).

Edvardsson, B. (1998) Service quality improvement, *Managing Service Quality*, 8(2), pp. 142–149.

File, K. M. & Prince, R. A. (1992) Positive word-of-mouth: customer satisfaction and buyer behaviour, *International Journal of Bank Marketing*, 10(1), pp. 25–29.

Feinberg, R. A., Widdows, R., Hirsch-Wyncott, M. & Trappey, C. (1990) Myth and reality in customer service: good and bad service sometimes leads to re-purchase, *Journal of Consumer Satisfaction, Dissatisfaction, and Complaining Behaviour*, 3, pp. 112–114.

Folkes, V. S. (1998) Recent attribution research in consumer behaviour: a review and new directions, *Journal of Consumer Research*, 14 (March), pp. 548–565.

Gagliano, K. B. & Hatchote, J. (1994) Customer expectations and perceptions of service quality in apparel retailing, *Journal of Service Marketing*, 8(1), pp. 60–69.

Ganesh, J., Arnold, M. J. & Reynolds, K. E. (2000) Understanding the customer base of service providers: an examination of the differences between switchers and stayers, *Journal of Marketing*, 64 (July), pp. 65–87.

Gronroos, C. (1990b) Relationship approach to the marketing function in service contents: the marketing ad organizational behaviour interface, *Journal of Business Research*, 20(1), pp. 3–12.

Hair, J. F., Anderson, R. E., Tatham, R. L. & Black, W. C. (1995) *Multivariate Data Analysis with Readings* (Englewood Cliffs, NJ: Prentice Hall).

Hair, J. F., Bush, R. P. & Ortinau, D. J. (2000) *Marketing Research: A Practical Approach for the New Millennium* (New York: McGraw-Hill).

Hair, J. F., Lamb, C. W. & McDaniel, C. D. (2000) *Marketing* (Cincinnati, OH: South-Western Publishing).

Hayes, B. E. (1998) *Measuring Customer Satisfaction: Survey Design, Use and Statistical Analysis Methods* (Milwaukee, WI: ASQ Quality Press).

Herbig, P. & Genestre, A. (1996) An examination of the cross-cultural differences in service quality: the example of Mexico and the USA, *Journal of Service Marketing*, 13(3), pp. 43–53.

Heskett, J. L., Jones, T. D., Loveman, G. W., Sasser, W. E. & Schlesinger, L. L. (1994) Putting the service-profit chain to work, *Harvard Business Review*, March-April, pp. 165–174.

Hooley, G. J. & Hussey, M. K. (1994) *Qualitative Methods in Marketing* (London: The Dryden Press).

Kahaner, D. K. (1996) *Cellular Telephony in Malaysia*. Available at http://www.cs.arizona.edu/japan/atip/public/atip.reports/atip96.098.htm. (accessed 31st October 2000).

Kandampully, J. (1993) Service quality to service loyalty: a relationship, which goes beyond customer services, *Total Quality Management*, 96, pp. 431–443.

Kassim, M. N. (2001) Determinants of customer satisfaction and retention in the cellular phone market of Malaysia. Unpublished doctoral dissertation, Southern Cross University.

Kassim, M. N. & Bojei, J. (2002) Service quality: gaps in the Malaysian telemarketing industry, *Journal of Business Research*, 55(10), pp. 845–852.

Keegan, W. & Green, M. C (2000) *Global Marketing Manager* (Upper Saddle River: Prentice-Hall).

Kline, R. B. (1998) *Principles and Practice of Structural Equation Modeling* (New York: Guilford Press).

Kohli, A. K. & Jaworski, B. J. (1990) Market Orientation: the construct, research propositions, and managerial implications, *Journal of Marketing*, 54 (April), pp. 20–35.

Kotler, P. (2000) *Marketing Management, The Millennium* (Englewood Cliffs, NJ: Prentice-Hall).

LaTour, S. A. & Peat, N. C. (1979) Conceptual and methodological issues *Advances in Consumer Research,* 6(1), pp. 431–437.

Levesque, T. & McDougall, G. H. C. (1996) Determinants of customer satisfaction in retail banking, *International Journal of Bank Marketing*, 14(7), pp. 12–20.

McCarthy, E. J., Perreault, W. D., Quester, P. G., Wilkinson, J. W. & Lee, K. Y. (1994) *Basic Marketing: A Managerial Perspective* (Singapore: R. D. Irwin).

McColl-Kennedy, J. R. & Kiel, G. C. (2000) *Marketing: A Strategic Approach* (Melbourne: Nelson Thomson Learning).

Mittal, V., Rose, W. T. & Baldasare, P. M. (1998) The asymmetric impact of negative and positive attribute-level performance on overall satisfaction and repurchase intentions, *Journal of Marketing*, 62 (January), pp. 33–47.

O'Cass, A. (2000) An assessment of consumers product, purchase decision, advertising and consumption involvement in fashion clothing, *Journal of Economic Psychology*, 21, pp. 545–576.

Oliva, T. A., Oliver, R. L. & MacMillan, I. C. (1992) A catastrophe model for developing service satisfaction strategies, *Journal of Marketing*, 56 (July), pp. 83–95.

Oliver, R. L. (1993) Cognitive affective and attribute bases of the satisfaction response, *Journal of Consumer Study*, 20 (December), pp. 15–32.

Ostrom, A. & Iacobucci, D. (1995) Consumer trade-offs and the evaluation of services, *Journal of Marketing*, 59, pp. 17–18.

Parasuraman, A., Zeithaml, V. A. & Berry, L. L. (1985) A conceptual model of service quality and its implications for future research, *Journal of Marketing* (Fall), pp. 41–50.

Parasuraman, A., Zeithaml, V. A. & Berry, L. L. (1988) SERVQUAL: a multiple-item scale for measuring consumer perceptions of service quality, *Journal of Retailing*, 64 (Spring), pp. 21–40.

Richins, M. (1983) Factors affecting the level of consumer-initiated complaints to marketing organization, in: H. Hunt & R. Day (Eds) *Consumer Satisfaction, Dissatisfaction and Complaining Behaviour*, pp. 82–85 (Bloomington, IN: Indiana University).

Scott, D. & Shieff, D. S. (1993) Service quality components and group criteria in local government, *International Journal of Industry Management*, 4(4), pp. 42–53.

Schwartz, D. J. (1981) *Marketing Today* (New York: Harcourt Brace Jovanovich).

Sekaran, U. (2000) *Research Method for Business: A Skill Building Approach* (New York: John Wiley).

Solomon, M. R., Surprenant, C., Czepiel, J. A. & Guttman, E. G. (1985) A role theory perspective on dyadic interactions: the service encounter, *Journal of Marketing*, 49 (Winter), pp. 99–111.

Spreng, R. A., MacKenzie, S. B. & Olshavsky, R. W. (1996) A re-examination of the determinants of consumer satisfaction, *Journal of Marketing*, 60 (July), pp. 15–32.

Stafford, M. R. (1996) Demographics discriminators of service quality in the banking industry, *The Journal of Services Marketing*, 104, pp. 6–22.

Surprenant, C. F. & Solomon, M. R. (1987) Predictability and personalization in the service encounter, *Journal of Marketing*, 51, pp. 86–96.

Sweeney, J. C., Johnson, L. W. & Armstrong, R. W. (1992) The effect of cues on service quality expectations and service selection in a restaurant setting, *The Journal of Services Marketing*, 64, pp. 15–22.

Tabachnick, B. G. & Fidell, L. S. (1996) *Using Multivariate Statistics* (New York: Harper Collins).

Triola, M. F. & Franklin, L. A. (1995) *Business Statistic* (Boston, MA: Addison-Wesley).

Varki, S. & Rust, R. T. (1997) Satisfaction is relative: apply analysis of variance techniques to determine if your CSM scores measure up, *Marketing Research* (Summer), pp. 15–19.

Webb, D. (1998) Segmenting police 'customer' on the basis of their service quality expectations, *The Service Industry Journal*, 18(1) (January), pp. 72–110.

Webster, C. (1989) Can consumers be segmented on the basis of their service quality expectations?, *The Journal of Services Marketing*, 51, pp. 5–17.

Westbrook, R. A. (1980) Consumer satisfaction as a function of personal competence/efficacy, *Journal of the Academy of Marketing Science*, 8(4), pp. 427–437.

Westbrook, R. A. & Reily, M. D. (1983) Value-percept disparity; an alternative to the disconfirmation of expectations theory of consumer research, in: R. P. Bagozzi & A. M. Tybout (Eds) *Advances in Consumer Research*, pp. 256–261 (Ann Arbor, MI: Association of Consumer Research).

Wind, Y. (1978) Issues and advances in segmentation research, *Journal of Marketing Research* XV(August), pp. 317–337.

Woodside, A., Frey, L. & Daly, R. (1989) Linking service quality, customer satisfaction and behavioural intentions, *Journal of Health Care Marketing*, 9 (4) (December), pp. 5–17.

Wong, T. C. (1999) *Marketing Research* (Oxford: Butterworth-Heinemann).

Yi, Y. (1990) *A critical review of consumer satisfaction*, in: Ziethaml, V. A. (Ed.) Review of Marketing Annual 1978–1990, (Chicago, IL: American Marketing Association).

Yuskel, A. & Rimmington, M. (1998) Customer-satisfaction measurement: performance Counts, *Cornell Hotel and Restaurant Administration Quarterly*, pp. 59–70.

Zeithaml, V. A. (2000) Service quality, profitability and the economic worth of customers: what we know and what we need to learn, *Journal of Academy of Marketing Science*, 281, pp. 67–85.

Zeithaml, V. A. & Bitner, M. J. (2000) *Services Marketing* (New York: McGraw-Hill).

Zeithaml, V. A., Parasuraman, A. & Berry, L. L. (1993) The nature and determinants of customer expectations of service, *Journal of Academy of Marketing Science*, 211, pp. 1–12.

Zeithaml, V. A., Parasuraman, A. & Berry, L. L. (1996) The behavioural consequences of service quality, *Journal of Marketing*, 49 (Spring), pp. 33–46.

Zikmund, W. G. (2000) *Exploring Marketing Research* (Fort Worth, TX: Dryden Press).

Appendix. Definition and measurements of the research variables

Construct/Variable	Definition	Operationalization of variables	Measurement scale
Demographic	Customers' personal demographic and socio-economic characteristics	1. Ethnic;	Nominal
		2. Age;	Ordinal
		3. Gender;	Nominal
		4. Marital status;	Nominal
		5. Education;	Nominal
		6. Occupation; and	Nominal
		7. Income	Ordinal
Customer satisfaction	An accumulated experience of a customer's purchase and consumption of experiences	In general, please indicate how satisfied are you with the service provided by your hand phone service provider? This single item was measured in terms of: 1. Service coverage 2. Billing integrity 3. Quality of line 4. Customer service 5. Customer service outlets	6-point Likert scale with anchors extremely dissatisfied (1) and extremely satisfied (6)
Customer retention	Favourable measures of future intention adapted from Boulding *et al.* (1993); Heskett *et al.* (1994); Danaher & Rust (1996); Levesque & McDougall (1996); Zeithaml *et al.* (1996)	1. I have the intention of recommending my hand phone service provider to others 2. I prefer my hand phone service provider 3. I have the intention of continuing using the service of my hand phone service provider 4. I have the intention to increase the usage of the service provided by my hand phone service provider 5. I have no intention to switch to other hand phone service providers	6-point Likert scale with anchors extremely disagree (1) and extremely agree (6)

Appendix. *Continued*

Construct/Variable	Definition	Operationalization of variables	Measurement scale
Performance level of service	The subjective evaluation made by a customer after a service encounter	What is your opinion on the level of service that you have received? This multiple items were measured in terms of: 1. Service coverage 2. Billing integrity 3. Quality of line 4. Customer service 5. Customer service outlets	6-point Likert scale with anchors extremely poor (1) and extremely good (6)
Desired level of service	The level of service the customer hopes to receive or finds reasonable	What is your opinion on the level of service that you would consider reasonable? This multiple items were measured in terms of: 1. Service coverage 2. Billing integrity 3. Quality of line 4. Customer service 5. Customer service outlets	6-point Likert scale with anchors extremely poor (1) and extremely good (6)

Appendix. *Continued*

Construct/Variable	Definition	Operationalization of variables	Measurement scale
Adequate level of service	The minimum level of service the customer will accept or tolerate	What is your opinion on the level of service that you would consider tolerable? This multiple items were measured in terms of: 1. Service coverage 2. Billing integrity 3. Quality of line 4. Customer service 5. Customer service outlets	6-point Likert scale with anchors extremely poor (1) and extremely good (6)

Implementing e-HRM: The Readiness of Small and Medium Sized Manufacturing Companies in Malaysia

LAI WAN HOOI

Introduction

Over the last few years, with the advent of intranet and Internet-based technologies, a new wave of human resource (HR) technology known as electronic human resource management (e-HRM) has emerged. It is aimed to assist with human resources administrative functions. With e-HRM, the service to management and employees is expected to improve. Though e-HRM has been identified as a catalyst towards achieving business strategies, there is little interest among local companies to adopt it. Some claim that this phenomenon will reduce the number of employees in the HR department. While some view that e-HRM would reduce costs and stimulate a more strategic approach in human resource management (HRM), others opine that the implementation and maintenance of e-HRM systems involve huge investment. Thus, to what extent has e-HRM already been implemented in local companies in Malaysia?

This study hopes to explore the readiness and feasibility of implementing e-HRM in the small and medium sized enterprises in Malaysia. Firstly, it attempts to find out if a large number of small and medium sized enterprises (SMEs) in Malaysia are practising conventional HRM than e-HRM. To what extent have SMEs in Malaysia employ e-HRM tools in the administration of its HR functions? The essay will focus on five main areas of HRM, which are believed to have a significant impact on the competitiveness of the industry, namely, recruitment, compensation and benefits, performance appraisal, communication, and training and development. Secondly, it is believed that the feasibility of implementing e-HRM is very much dependent on the availability of resources. With the availability of expertise, technological and financial resources, companies would support the emergence of e-HRM. Thirdly, e-HRM will change the role of HR. When e-HRM is introduced, employees will have to adapt to the increased responsibilities they have for HR issues. Thus, the attitude and readiness of the employees to adapt to this change would affect the implementation of e-HRM. However, as the research was constrained by time and costs, the study was limited to all the manufacturing companies listed in the Federation of Malaysian Manufacturers Directory.

Literature Review

Definition of E-HRM

By accessing the various published and unpublished sources that are available, the definition of e-HRM by the different researchers is as follows. Researchers from the Human Capital Development Division of the Ministry of Manpower, Singapore (2003) defines e-HRM as 'the use of electronic media and active participation of employees to provide technology that helps to lower administration costs, improve employee communication, provide quicker access to information and reduce processing time'. CGI Precision, a service provider designates it as 'a Web-based solution that uses "kiosks" or "portals" to assist with human resources administrative functions'(2004:1). Watson Wyatt Consulting (2002:3) defines e-HRM as 'the application of any technology enabling managers and employees to have direct access to HR and other workplace services for communication, performance reporting, team management, knowledge management, learning and other administrative applications' (Watson Wyatt Worldwide, 2002). An HR outsourcing company, CnetG (Kumar, 2002:4; 2003:4) defines e-HRM as 'leveraging of technology to deliver HR solutions that brings about convergence in human capital, processes, data and tools as a catalyst towards achieving business strategies'. Karakanian (2002) describes e-HRM as 'the overall HR strategy that lifts HR, shifts it from the HR Department and isolated HR activities, and redistributes it to the organisation and its trusted business partners old and new'.

E-HRM is basically connecting staff and managers with the HR department electronically through the HR portal. E-HRM gives employees access to information systems via the Internet. This approach of e-HRM enables all employees, partners, resellers and customers to be involved in the business processes electronically. People can now work comfortably, both within and outside the office environment.

Definition of Small and Medium Sized Enterprises (SMEs)

SMEs is the abbreviation of small and medium sized enterprises. There is no universal definition of SMEs. In Malaysia, the definitions are only based on fixed quantitative criteria such as the number of employees, amount of capital, amount of assets and more recently, sales turnover (Hashim & Abdullah, 2000c). The Small and Medium Industries Development Corporation (SMIDEC), which was established on 2 May 1996 under the Ministry of International Trade and Industry (MITI), defined SMEs as manufacturing companies or companies providing

Table 1. Definition of SMES in Malaysia

	General	Medium-sized	Small	Micro-enterprise
Max. number of employees	Max. 150	51–150	5–50	Max. 5
Max. turnover (in million ringgit)	25	10–25	0.25– < 10	0.25

manufacturing related services (MRS) with annual sales turnover not exceeding RM25 million and with full-time employees not exceeding 150. The National Small and Medium Enterprise (SME) Development Council defined it more specifically as in Table 1.

The European Commission has adopted a Recommendation concerning the definition of SMEs which now provides a clear global framework for all the measures directed towards micro-, small and medium sized enterprises (effective 1 January 2005). The adopted definition is as shown in Table 2.

To be classed as an SME or a micro-enterprise, an enterprise has to satisfy the criteria for the number of employees and one of the two financial criteria, that is either the turnover total or the balance sheet total. In addition, it must be independent, which means less than 25 per cent of it is owned by one enterprise (or jointly by several enterprises) falling outside the definition of an SME or a micro-enterprise, whichever may apply.

Different Asian countries have introduced different definitions of an SME. In general, an SME is classified by the number of employees and the amount of capital or turnover. This is as shown in Table 3.

Others have described SMEs as businesses with up to about 100 employees[1], businesses with less than 250 employees[2], small to medium sized enterprises with 20 to 500 employees[3], organizations with between 30 and 200 employees[4], under 250 employees for 'medium'; under 50 for 'small'; 'microenterprises' have less than 5 employees[5] and companies that have less than 250 employees, (50 for a small business) and are less than 25 per cent foreign owned[6].

SMEs in the Malaysian Manufacturing Sector

SMEs exist in almost all sectors of the Malaysian economy; the more common ones being the agricultural sector, basic raw materials sector, general business sector and the manufacturing sector. Of these, the SMEs in the manufacturing sector contribute significantly in terms of business units, employment opportunities and economic outputs (Hashim & Wafa, 2002). Most of the SMEs in the manufacturing sector are

Table 2. Definition of SMES by European Commission

	Medium-sized	Small	Micro-enterprise
Max. number of employees	Max. 250	Max. 50	Max. 10
Max. turnover (in million euro)	50	10	2
Max. balance-sheet total (in million euro)	43	10	2

Table 3. Definition of SMEs in various Asian countries

Country	Definition of SMEs	Measurement
People's Republic of China	Varies with industries, less than 100 employees	Employment
Indonesia	Less than 100 employees	Employment
Japan	Less than 300 employees, or ¥10 million assets. • Wholesale: less than 50 employees, ¥30 million assets • Retail: less than 50 employees, ¥10 million assets	Employment and assets
Korea	• Manufacture: less than 300 employees • Service: less than 300 employees	Employment
Malaysia	Varies, turnover: less than RM25 million and 150 employees.	Shareholders, Funds and Employment
Thailand	Less than 200 employees, less than 200 million Baht assets	Assets and Employment
Philippines	Less than 200 employees, less than P40 million assets	Assets and Employment
Singapore	• Manufacture: less than S$12 million fixed assets • Service: less than 100 employees	Assets and Employment
Chinese, Taipei	• Manufacture: less than NT$40 million paid up capital, and less than total assets of NT$120 million. • Transport and service: sales of less than NT$40 million	Paid up capital, assets and sales

concentrated in the food and food products, furniture and fixtures, chemical and chemical products and metal products sub-sectors.[7] In this sector, small businesses are involved in the activities of converting basic raw materials into useful products such as food factories, bakeries, sawmills, toy factories, shoe factories, clothing manufacturing factories, paper mills, candle factories, furniture manufacturing, job printing shops, soft drink bottling, small machine shops, ironworks, ready-mixed concrete plants, fertilizer plants, rubber gloves plant, plastic bags manufacturing plants, and electrical and electronics appliances and components. Of these, 20 per cent are in food processing, 18 per cent in the manufacture of fabricated metal products, machinery and equipment, 17 per cent in the manufacture of wood and wood products, 12 per cent in apparel manufacturing, 11 per cent in the manufacture of chemical, petroleum, plastic and rubber products and the remaining 22 per cent in the other manufacturing activities such as paper and basic metal. (Osman & Hashim, 2003). According to the National Productivity Corporation (2001), they represent 92 per cent of the total number of firms in the Malaysian manufacturing sector.

As the bulk of the manufacturing establishments in Malaysia are SMEs, their importance to the Malaysian economy is crucial. SMEs provide the critical linkage in the development of a broad-based, globally competitive industrial sector as these enterprises work in a complementary way with the larger corporations. Their support is needed by large enterprises as suppliers or subcontractors and purchasers of products and in many service capacities. Competent SMEs can be vital to the economic efficiency of large enterprises and can also contribute towards improving economic relationships between and within industries, both upstream and downstream in the various sectors (Sapuan *et al.*, 1997). To remain resilient and competitive in the era of globalization and technological advancement, it is crucial that SMEs transform from being labour intensive to that based on capital, knowledge and technology. In this regard, efforts will be undertaken to develop an efficient and responsive education and training system to meet the demand for a knowledgeable and highly skilled labour force that is equipped with positive values and attitudes. The adoption of e-HRM applications would be a step towards this goal.

E-HRM for SMEs

In the past, HRM studies primarily concentrated on large firms. SMEs rarely received a mention in the mainstream HRM literature despite the fact that SMEs in most countries contribute towards employment (Bawa *et al.*, 2001). Currently, there are about 690,000 SME establishments in Malaysia, which represent 92 per cent of the total manufacturing establishments in Malaysia. They contribute about 30 per cent of total employment and have been recognized as one of the pillars of the national economy[8]. Despite this, research involving SMEs are not extensively explored. There is limited evidence of research carried out in the SMEs in Malaysia, especially in the area of HRM. Although in recent years, SMEs in Malaysia seem to have attracted increasing attention from researchers, studies about them are still relatively limited and not integrated in nature (Osman & Hashim, 2003). Several limitations inhibit the setting up of a framework for better understanding of the sector (Sim, 1991; Hashim & Abdullah, 2000a).

Limited research carried out so far on the SMEs has focused mainly on observing and reporting the general profile of the SMEs sector in Malaysia; the demographic characteristics of owners and managers of SMEs (Sim, 1991; Hashim & Abdullah, 2000b); the demographic characteristics of SMEs; strengths and weaknesses of SMEs; and SMEs assistance programmes. Little emphasis is placed on factors that can influence their performance (Sim, 1991; Hashim & Abdullah, 2000c) and the impact and the effectiveness of the assistance programmes on small businesses (Hashim & Abdullah, 2000a). Similarly, the issue of how they differ from each other, specifically their business practices does not appear to have attracted much research attention (Hashim and Abdullah, 2000b). So far, in Malaysia, few studies have explored the issue of e-HRM in the SMEs.

Given the technological advances, the notion of e-business applications could not be ignored. To keep up with the trends, SMEs have no option but to change. However, limited research on e-HRM shows that e-HRM is not for all SMEs. Unlike large corporations, smaller companies must be able to identify a clear benefit and rationale for e-HRM initiatives. Companies need to develop and document a formal convincing strategy and business case to justify the implementation of e-HRM. Gaining the support and approval of senior management would be difficult if the cost-justification for e-HRM is ambiguous. The most cost-effective approach for SMEs would be to outsource to solution providers.

According to research done by the Ministry of Manpower, Singapore, e-HRM initiatives could be introduced with an initial investment of S$3,000 and a monthly cost of a few hundred dollars. The low cost means that most SMEs could afford to implement e-HRM initiatives. However, some SMEs have not given priority to this. SMEs that have implemented e-HRM share some similar characteristics. Are these characteristics then important factors to consider in the implementation of e-HRM in the SMEs?

One obvious characteristic is the corporate culture of the company. Companies with open and flexible corporate cultures adapt easily to new technology and changes that come with it. Employees at all levels tend to view changes positively and are willing to adapt to the changes. This is especially so if the philosophy of empowering and motivating employees prevail in the company. Though some staff may be resistant to changing to new ways, empowering them gives them a sense of involvement in a shift away from manual systems. On gaining the confidence and support of its human resources, the implementation of e-HRM initiatives would be more acceptable. Assistance during the transition period would further enhance this move.

SMEs experiencing rapid growth and resource shortages are also more committed to e-HRM initiatives. In such a situation, manual processes would cause a backlog in HR functions and would hamper further development and growth. The speed and ease at which e-HRM could handle HR functions justify its introduction. Companies cannot depend wholly on the HR staff to carry out manual processes, and a dedicated workforce in times of growth and expansion is rare. It is difficult to keep staff motivated if they are overworked and the lack of resources further aggravates the situation. The introduction of e-HRM may not be a total solution to this but it helps elevate the intensity of the situation.

Companies that have regional subsidiaries too are more positive in the approach towards e-HRM. The main reason for this is the introduction of e-HRM would save cost, as it is not necessary to set up a HR department in each subsidiary. With an HR portal, employees could access information from anywhere. Thus, employees who travel frequently and need remote access to information could easily connect and retrieve data at great speed. The hassle of rushing from one place to another just to collect certain data is much reduced. Besides this, e-HRM is also applicable to companies where their workforce is office-based.

Considering the similarities between Malaysia and Singapore in many aspects, these characteristics may be applicable to the SMEs in Malaysia as well. However, one important characteristic is the influence of firm size on the adoption of HR practices. Though research on this is inconclusive, a review of theoretical and empirical literature shows that larger corporations adopt more sophisticated and socially responsive HR practices (Bawa & Ali, 1999; Jackson & Schuler, 1995; Little, 1986; McEvoy, 1984) because they are more visible and are under more pressure to gain legitimacy (Bawa *et al.*, 2001). Personnel practices in SMEs were considered by managers to be unimportant compared with other areas such as production, finance, marketing and accounting (McEvoy, 1984). Similarly, Little (1986) found that few firms with fewer than 100 employees in the state of Louisiana, USA had a personnel department and the functions were usually carried out by the owner/manager. In addition, the increase in formalization of HRM policies and procedures as firms increase in size (Little, 1986; Hofer & Sandberg,

1987; Baron & Kreps, 1999) and the lack of use of best practices, lack of sophistication, and lack of attention to the documented relationships that have been demonstrated between HRM practices and organizational outcomes in larger firms (Hay & Ross, 1989; Huselid, 1995) helps formulate the hypothesis that *a large number of SMEs in Malaysia are practising conventional HRM rather than e-HRM*.

In view of the rapid technological changes, the adoption of e-HRM initiatives offers vast opportunities to improve on HRM practices that help today's knowledge workers meet company goals. For this, various obstacles have to be overcome. Past studies showed that the common constraints faced by SMEs range from the use of outdated technology to lack of resources and capabilities to achieve their objectives (Osman & Hashim, 2003). These problems are mainly caused by internal and external environmental factors such as lack of capabilities and resources, poor management, low technology, competition, economics, technological, socio-cultural and international factors (Hashim, 2000). A survey done in 1990 showed that the major problems faced by the SMEs in Malaysia are lack of technical knowledge, financial constraints, limited market, linkage between anchor companies and inability to penetrate the export market (Ismail, 1990). Accordingly, it is logical to formulate the hypothesis that *there is a strong relationship between the availability of resources and the feasibility of implementing e-HRM*.

Contrary to expectation, demographic characteristics such as age, level of technology, race and ethnic cultures did not have significant influence on the extent of implementing HR practices (Bawa *et al.*, 2001). In a study of 802 managers of oil palm estates of varying size and age, the findings showed that managers who work in newer estates introduce more technical HR practices than older estates. This is the same for managers who are younger, who work in private firms, and who belong to professional associations. Thus, the readiness of HR practitioners to embrace technology and apply it to HR functions is one of the key factors in the introduction of e-HRM initiatives. Given the increased emphasis in the use of information and commmunication technology (ICT) in the working environment, it is logical to formulate the hypothesis *that employees are ready and receptive to the implementation of e-HRM*.

Companies planning to implement e-HRM initiatives have a choice of in-house software or an outsourced solution. However, SMEs are likely to set a budget and look for a solution within the budget. For SMEs, with up to 500 employees, a packaged solution to e-HRM is sensible.[9] Outsourcing reduces the need for huge capital investment, in addition to providing a means for accessing and maintaining the latest technology. The implementation approach is similar to that of larger corporations though scaled down in terms of time. Typical implementation cycles are 8–12 weeks for SMEs. It is feasible to implement e-HRM in SMEs though not all modules need to be implemented. SMEs should adopt a scale-down approach, step up its implementation and go for 'quick wins'. Most of all, management teams need to walk the talk and be committed.

Theoretical Framework and Research Methodology

The collection of data for this research involved both the gathering of primary and secondary data, but the main method was primary data survey. The study began with a literature review of books, as well as articles in journals related to the research topic. Company records, newspaper articles, handbooks and magazines were other sources of secondary data. Searching the World Wide Web for information on the Internet also served as a source for secondary data. Secondary data gathered through literature review and opinions of various writers on issues relating to HRM policies gave an in-depth understanding of the study. A theoretical framework that clearly identified the variables was then developed for the research.

The implementation of e-HRM is dependent on various factors, among them, the availability of resources and the attitudes of the employees. Companies are more likely to implement e-HRM if resources are available and employees view e-HRM positively. Therefore, the implementation of e-HRM is the dependent variable, and the availability of resources and employees' attitude the independent variables. Although this relationship can be said to hold true generally, it is nevertheless contingent on the communication of e-HRM. Management's effectiveness in communicating e-HRM to the rest of the organization has a contingent effect on the independent variables and dependent variable relationship. The moderating variable in this relationship is communication effectiveness.

Primary data was collected from observations, administered questionnaires, and from individuals who provide information when interviewed. The Internet also served as a primary data source as questionnaires were administered over it. Questionnaires written in English were sent through the mail, and electronically administered. A 5-point Likert scale allowed respondents to indicate how strongly they agree or disagree with the statements relating to the research question. Before finalizing the survey questionnaires, a pilot survey was conducted with a few selected organizations and individuals. The collected raw data from the respondents was then transformed into readable information and its relation to the research hypotheses was analysed. The results of the survey only described the characteristics of Malaysian employees in the manufacturing companies at a specific point of time.

Research Findings

Questions in Section A of the questionnaire are designed to collect the demographic data of the respondents targeted in this research. The targets are the small and medium sized enterprises in Malaysia. Based on the circulation volume of 400 questionnaires, a response rate of 17.25 per cent was achieved with replies from 69 respondents. However, 9 of the questionnaires were deemed unusable, thus reducing the response rate to 15 per cent. Items that were included in the background of the sample were the profile and technology level of the organization. For the profile of the company, data was obtained for the year of establishment, staff size, ownership of the company and HR plans and programmes that are provided online. As for the technological level of the organizations, information was obtained on the use of the Internet, the company's website and the intranet.

Profile of the Company

Most of the companies that responded to the survey were established in the 1990s. More than half of the companies (51.7 per cent) were set up in or after 1990 with six

(10 per cent) relatively new ones that were set up in the new millennium. Eleven of the companies (18.3 per cent) were set up in the 1980s and seven (11.7 per cent) in the 1970s. There were eight companies (13.3 per cent) established before 1960 and three (5 per cent) in the 1960s. Thus there are respondents who represent each decade, which makes the sample representative of the population to some extent.

As SMEs are generally defined as businesses with less than 250 employees[10] the sample for this research was limited to companies with 250 employees or less. Those companies with less than 50 employees are classified as small enterprises whereas those with more than 50 employees but less than 250 employees are considered medium sized enterprises. Based on the data collected, 68.3 per cent of the companies are medium sized enterprises with more than 50 employees and the others are small enterprises. Most of the medium sized enterprises (43.3 per cent) employ 150–250 employees. Only a small percentage of the medium sized companies (6.7 per cent) have less than 100 employees.

As far as ownership is concerned, two-thirds of the respondent companies are private limited companies. 21.7 per cent of the respondent companies are public limited companies, 5 per cent are partnerships and one of the respondent companies (1.7 per cent) is a sole proprietorship.

With technology advancement and the IT explosion, it is believed that companies have to keep up with the trend to compete globally. An item in the questionnaire measures the extent to which companies have provided information on HR plans and programmes online. The aim is to find out if the respondent companies have to some extent introduced e-HRM in their practices. Aspects of human resource management practices that were included and the responses of respondent companies are as shown in Table 4 below.

A glance at Table 4 shows that there are more companies not providing HR information online than those disseminating information through the Internet or intranet. Though 30 per cent of the companies did not respond to the question, those that responded show that they still provide information the conventional way in most aspects of HRM practices. In providing online information on training and education, more companies responded 'YES' – an indication that companies may be identifying and selecting employees for training electronically or embarking on

Table 4. Provision of information on HR plans and programs online (%)

HRM practices	Yes	No	No response
Health and welfare	25	45	30
Salary, bonus and incentive plan	28.3	41.7	30
Performance appraisal	28.3	41.7	30
Labour relations	10	60	30
Recruitment and selection	35	35	30
Pension and investment plan	6.7	63.3	30
HR planning	26.7	43.3	30
Succession planning	11.7	58.3	30
Training and education	43.3	26.7	30
Payroll administration	28.3	41.7	30
Transfer and relocation	18.3	51.7	30

e-learning. Online information on pension and investment plans is comparatively much lower than the other functions followed by labour relations and succession planning. In general, other than training and education, most companies provide online information on recruitment and selection to a certain extent.

Technology Level

To assess the technology level of the respondent companies, questions on the company's website, the Internet and the intranet were included in the questionnaire. The data obtained would reveal the level of involvement of the companies in the implementation and maintenance of the company's website, the Internet and the intranet. To some extent, the degree of expertise of the employees in the use of technology in the HR practices of the company and the general interest of the company to shift from conventional HR practices to contemporary methods would be uncovered. Based on the data obtained, only one of the respondent companies (1.7 per cent) does not have the infrastructure for online information.

Accessing online using cable or ISDN seems to be the most common method used (68.3 per cent) by companies that have the Internet installed in their premises. Accessing the Internet using wireless technology is not popular among the respondent companies and only 3.3 per cent are using this technology. The rest of the respondent companies (26.7 per cent) used a dial-up modem to access the Internet. As for intranet, 81.7 per cent of the companies provide intranet facilities for its staff. 15 per cent reported that they have no intranet access while 1.7 per cent of the companies have plans to implement it soon. As to whether the intranet was created in-house, 75 per cent of those who responded to the question said that the company's intranet was created in-house. In addition, most of the companies (86.7 per cent) have had Internet access for more than a year. This shows that most of the employees have had exposure to the Internet for quite a while and if e-HRM practices were introduced to the company, employees would not face much of a problem comprehending it. Thus, the infrastructure is in place for the introduction of e-HRM and its implementation depends very much on the initiative of the management of the company.

91.7 per cent of the companies have set up the company's website on the Internet. Of these, two-thirds created the website in-house while the rest outsourced it to external providers. Most of the companies used it for advertising (50 per cent) and for the promotion of their products (48.3 per cent). It is least used for B2E with only 8.3 per cent of the companies utilizing this facility on its website. B2C e-commerce and B2B e-commerce fair much better with 23.3 per cent and 20 per cent of the companies using it respectively. 16.7 per cent of the companies used it for recruitment and 13.3 per cent for after sales service. This gives an overview of the respondent companies use of their website for day-to-day business. In part, it also reveals the capability of its employees to get work done electronically, efficiently and effectively. If employees were familiar with these activities, then the implementation of e-HRM is likely to be more feasible. As the findings showed, e-HRM is not much practised among companies that responded to the survey.

Having considered the companies' profile and the technology level of the companies, the survey proper on the feasibility of implementing e-HRM in the small and medium sized enterprises was analysed. Thirty-one items were included in this part of the survey to test the three hypotheses. For the first hypothesis three items were allocated to each variable to test if the hypothesis is substantiated. Similarly, to test the second hypothesis, three items were allocated to each of the three variables. To gauge the attitude of the employees towards the implementation of e-HRM, seven items were used in the analysis.

Findings and Discussion on Hypothesis 1[11]

The first hypothesis examines whether a large number of SMEs in Malaysia are practising conventional HRM rather than e-HRM. Five variables, namely recruitment and selection, training and development, communication, compensation and performance appraisal were used for the analysis.

Recruitment and selection. As far as recruitment and selection is concerned, the number of companies using a recruitment website (36.6 per cent) to identify potential job candidates is slightly less than those not using it (38.4 per cent). More than half of the respondent companies (51.6 per cent) do not have a hiring needs list on its website while 30 per cent agreed that the company does have a hiring needs list on its website. However, 43.3 per cent of the respondent companies state that e-recruitment initiatives are in their organization's plans over the next 12 months. As fewer companies are using a recruitment website or have a hiring needs list on its website, conventional recruitment practices are more prevalent. Besides, not that many companies are enthusiastic about e-recruitment initiatives. But more companies are expected to introduce e-recruitment practices, as it is in their plans in the next 12 months.

Training and development. Most of the training and development in the respondent companies is not done through e-learning (56.7 per cent). Only 21.6 per cent of the companies agree that e-learning is carried out while those companies that neither agree nor disagree probably use e-learning occasionally. Thus, the conventional method of training and development is still popular in most of the companies. As far as the implementation of e-learning initiatives is concerned, more than half of the respondent companies have no plans for e-learning initiatives (56.7 per cent). Only a fifth of the companies are in the process of implementing e-learning initiatives. Furthermore, half of the companies do not have e-learning capabilities. About a quarter of the respondent companies (26.7 per cent) have e-learning capabilities while 23.3 per cent are neutral as far as e-learning capabilities are concerned. This goes to show that e-learning would not be given priority as companies lack the capability as well as the initiative to introduce e-learning.

Communication. Most of the respondent companies (80 per cent) have a publicly accessible website and intranet is available to all employees in more than half of the companies (58.4 per cent). Thus, facilities are available in most of the companies for e-communication. Information on the company is readily available on its website and intranet facilities make it possible for employees to communicate online. As such a knowledge-sharing system is in place in most of the companies (46.7 per cent). Only 28.3 per cent of the companies do not have a knowledge-sharing system. As far as communication practices are concerned, most companies are doing away with conventional practices and only a small percentage of the companies (15 per cent) do not have a publicly accessible website or intranet facilities for all their employees (30 per cent). In short, e-communication is quite commonly used and is very likely to have been one of the first e-HRM initiatives introduced by most of the companies. For companies that are already communicating online, the focus would be on other aspects of e-HRM. But for those that have yet to introduce e-communication, this is likely to be the first e-HRM initiative that they will embark on.

Compensation. Only a quarter of the respondent companies have facilities for their employees to view their pay-slip online. Most of the companies (68.4 per cent) give out pay-slips in printed form. This shows that there is limited use of online facilities available for disseminating information on compensation. However, most companies agreed that salary calculation is no longer done manually (56.7 per cent). Only 28.3 per cent of the respondent companies calculate the salary manually. The use of electronic devices for salary calculation enhances speed and accuracy and it is likely that more companies will move away from conventional practices as far as this is concerned. 40 per cent of the respondent companies foresee the need to have a form of online HR Service Centre to handle the day-to-day inquiries from employees and managers regarding compensation issues such as pension plans, salary administration, bonus and incentive plan. These companies therefore see the benefits of implementing this in their system but the rest of the companies do not place much emphasis on this. In fact, a third does not foresee the need to have an HR Service Centre. Either these companies are contented with the present system, or the online system is too complex and tedious to implement. Though it is possible to outsource to solution providers, smaller companies may find it not worthwhile to introduce such a system.

Performance appraisal. As far as performance appraisal is concerned, more than half of the respondent companies (58.4 per cent) hold face-to face discussions with their employees. In a quarter of the respondent companies, the discussion of employee performance is no longer done face to face, indicating the use of contemporary methods of evaluation. However, such methods are not highly practised and companies are still using conventional practices. In addition, almost half of the respondent companies (41.7 per cent) do not store data on employees' performance in a computer that can be retrieved later on when evaluating employees. However, an equal percentage of the companies do this. Thus, though some companies are storing data on employees' performance in the computers, the conventional method of evaluation is still carried out. Similarly, not many companies (21.7 per cent) are using performance appraisal software for evaluation purposes. The majority of the companies (63.3 per cent) still stick to conventional methods of evaluating their employees, which can be tedious, time-consuming and subjective. Generally, e-performance appraisal is still not widely practised in the companies surveyed.

The mean for the five variables used to analyse if a large number of SMEs in Malaysia are practising conventional HRM rather than e-HRM are tabulated as in Table 5 below.

Table 5. Means for Hypothesis 1

Variables	Mean
Recruitment and selection	2.99
Training and development	2.48
Communication	3.62
Compensation	2.97
Performance appraisal	2.57
Average	2.92

Table 2 shows that the mean for four of the five variables is less than 3, that is towards the left side of the 5-point scale, denoting low usage of e-HRM among the respondent companies. This is especially so in training and development as well as in performance appraisal. Among the five variables, the use of electronic methods in companies' HR practices is most popular in communication, followed by recruitment and selection, and compensation.

The general decision to reject the hypothesis that a large number of SMEs in Malaysia are practising conventional HRM rather than e-HRM is if the mean for all the five variables is more than 3. As the average mean (2.91) for all the five variables is less than 3, the hypothesis that a large number of SMEs in Malaysia are practising conventional HRM rather than e-HRM is substantiated. However, as the average mean for all the five variables is close to 3, it can be concluded that SMEs in Malaysia are moving towards digitizing their HRM practices. In general, priority would be given to recruitment and selection as well as compensation.

Findings and Discussion on Hypothesis 2[12]

The second hypothesis examines if there is a strong relationship between the availability of resources and the feasibility of implementing e-HRM. There are three variables for the second hypothesis, namely, financial resources, expertise and technical infrastructure. Four items were formulated to test the feasibility to implement e-HRM. Two items examine if the implementation of e-HRM is held back by financial constraints. One item was included to find out if the respondent companies have the expertise to implement e-HRM. Another two items were used to see if the respondent companies lack suitable technical infrastructure to implement e-HRM.

Financial resources. Half the respondent companies agreed that if financial resources are available it is feasible to implement e-HRM in their organizations. However, 38.4 per cent stated that it is too costly to implement e-HRM in their organizations. Besides, 40 per cent of the companies state that the implementation of e-HRM in their organizations is held back because of a lack of funds. Thus, one of the main constraints of implementing e-HRM is the element of cost. However, there are also companies (26.7 per cent), who state that it is not feasible to implement e-HRM in their organizations even if financial resources are available. A third of the companies (33.3 per cent) do not find it too costly to implement e-HRM in their organizations. In addition, 35 per cent of the companies believed that the lack of funds is not the reason that the implementation of e-HRM in their organizations is held back. This shows that though financial resources may be a constraint, it is not the main constraint. There are other constraints as well, which impede the implementation of e-HRM.

Expertise. As far as expertise is concerned, 41.6 per cent of the respondent companies agreed that they lack the internal expertise to implement e-HRM. However, 31.7 per cent of the respondent companies disagreed, with 15 per cent strongly disagreeing. Thus, quite a percentage of the companies believed that they have the expertise and that this would not hold back the implementation of e-HRM if it were introduced in their companies. If these companies have not implemented e-HRM, then perhaps there are other constraints hindering e-HRM initiatives. More than half of the respondent companies (55 per cent) agreed that if the organization provides IT training for its staff, it is feasible to implement e-HRM, though 21.6 per cent disagreed. Therefore, expertise in IT is essential for the implementation of e-HRM. In short, companies must provide IT training for its staff if they have plans to implement e-HRM. Besides, more than half of the companies (58.3 per cent) agreed that support from e-business teams from the various functional areas within the organization is necessary in the implementation of e-HRM. Only 5 per cent strongly disagreed with this. Thus, all departments must be knowledgeable about IT for the successful implementation of e-HRM.

Technical infrastructure. As far as technical infrastructure is concerned, 31.6 per cent of the respondent companies disagreed that their organizations did not implement e-HRM because of the lack of technology. These companies have the technology though e-HRM may not be implemented, indicating that technical infrastructure is not a major constraint for these companies. But, it is a major constraint for some companies as 35 per cent of the companies believed that their organizations did not implement e-HRM because of the lack of technology. Most of the companies (45 per cent) state that if their organizations provide sophisticated enterprise resource planning (ERP) functions to the majority of its staff, it is feasible to implement e-HRM. 36.7 per cent of the companies partially support this while 18.3 per cent disagreed with it. Based on the findings, most companies placed great emphasis on IT knowledge. However, 41.6 per cent of the companies agreed that the hardware infrastructure of their organizations is suitable for the implementation of e-HRM. This shows that there are companies with suitable hardware infrastructure, which have yet to implement e-HRM initiatives while a third of the companies (33.3 per cent) do not have suitable hardware infrastructure for implementing e-HRM.

The three variables used to analyse whether a relationship exists between the availability of resources and the feasibility of implementing e-HRM are summarized in Table 6 and further discussed below.

From the above table, it can be concluded that most respondent companies agreed that it is feasible to implement e-HRM if the necessary resources such as financial resources, expertise and technical infrastructure are available. The average mean of the three variables (3.47) to the right side of the 5-point scale supports this. As far as the availability of resources is concerned, most of the respondent companies lack financial resources and expertise to implement e-HRM. The results also show that

Table 6. Means for Hypothesis 2

Variables	Means
Feasibility of implementing e-HRM:	3.47
Financial resources	3.35
Expertise	3.58
Technical infrastructure	3.38
Lack of resources:	3.01
Financial resources	3.05
Expertise	3.18
Technical infrastructure	2.88

technical infrastructure is available in most of the respondent companies and is not a hindrance in the implementation of e-HRM. Moreover, the average mean of the three variables is slightly above 3 at 3.01, indicating that the lack of available resources for the implementation of e-HRM is not at the extreme end. With measures to overcome this, it may be feasible for more SMEs to implement e-HRM in the near future.

In a nutshell, financial resources, expertise and technical infrastructure are some of the major constraints in the implementation of e-HRM. The lack of expertise and financial resources seem significant. Not all variables are a constraint to all the companies. Some variables are not a hindrance to some of the companies, yet they have failed to implement e-HRM initiatives. The analysis thus does not substantiate the hypothesis that there is a strong relationship between the availability of resources and the feasibility of implementing e-HRM. To substantiate the hypothesis, a mean of 4 and above is recommended. In short, the availability of resources alone is not enough to ensure the implementation of e-HRM. There are many other constraints that are not covered in the research, such as the mind-set of senior management, which hinders its implementation.

Findings and Discussion on Hypothesis 3

To prove the third hypothesis that employees are ready and receptive to the implementation of e-HRM, seven items were included in the survey. The aim is to gauge the attitude of the employees towards the implementation of e-HRM and their readiness to adapt to the new system. On the first item as to whether e-HRM is crucial to their organizations, 38.3 per cent of the respondent companies is of the opinion that e-HRM is not crucial as opposed to 33.3 per cent that disagreed. Those that disagreed would be more receptive if e-HRM is implemented as they feel that e-HRM is crucial. The other companies would be less receptive as they seem contented with the current HRM practices.

As to whether the advantages of e-HRM are outweighed by the cost implication, almost half (43.3 per cent) of the respondent companies neither agreed nor disagreed. 28.3 per cent of the companies agreed while an almost equal percentage of companies (28.4 per cent) disagreed. These results show that companies are unsure as to whether it is worth implementing e-HRM. While the majority chose to remain neutral, the other companies are divided. Those that disagreed would be ready and more receptive if e-HRM initiatives were introduced.

The findings show that 40 per cent of the respondent companies do not agree that their staff does not have the relevant skills for e-HRM. This shows that as far as expertise is concerned, employees have the necessary skills for e-HRM. In short, they are ready if e-HRM were implemented. However, 28.3 per cent of the companies do not have the necessary skills and are less like to be ready or receptive if e-HRM were implemented. The other companies may have some of the relevant skills but are not confident that those skills are sufficient to handle e-HRM if it were introduced.

A third of the respondent companies (33.3 per cent) agreed that their organizations lacked the technology needed for e-HRM. 43.3 per cent of the companies have the technology needed for e-HRM and are therefore more ready and receptive if e-HRM were implemented. Those that neither agreed nor disagreed would be ready and receptive if the current technology available is suitable for e-HRM. If not, the implementation of e-HRM in these companies would be more difficult as technology is one of the important factors that must be considered before embarking on e-HRM.

About a third of the respondent companies (33.4 per cent) are not too concerned about the lack of security in e-HRM. The chances of these companies accepting e-HRM if it were introduced is high. Employees in these companies are not too apprehensive about the lack of security and are more ready for e-HRM. If the companies have concerns related to the lack of security in e-HRM as in 28.4 per cent of the companies, then it is unlikely that these companies would want to implement e-HRM in their organizations. However, this low percentage shows that the majority of the companies are not too concerned about the lack of security in e-HRM.

Only a very low percentage (15 per cent) finds that e-HRM is too complex to comprehend or understand. Most of the respondent companies (48.3 per cent) disagreed that e-HRM is too complex to comprehend. Thus, if e-HRM were implemented, the majority of the companies would be able to adapt to the new system. These companies either have the relevant skills for e-HRM or a positive mind-set, which makes them ready and receptive to e-HRM. 36.7 per cent neither agreed nor disagreed – complex perhaps but not too complex. These companies would readily accept e-HRM if some form of training is provided to help them adjust to the new system. Staying neutral indicates that they are receptive to e-HRM but at the same time may not have enough relevant skills for e-HRM.

As to whether it is important that e-HRM be introduced in the next 12 months, 35 per cent of the companies agreed that it is important. The fact that it is important shows that these companies are ready and would be receptive to e-HRM if it were introduced. A quarter of the companies feel that it is not important for their organizations to introduce e-HRM in the next 12 months. For these companies, there is no urgency and they would therefore be less ready and receptive to the implementation of e-HRM. 40 per cent of the companies that neither agreed nor disagreed would introduce e-HRM as the need arises. These companies may or may not be ready and receptive now but would be well equipped if they decide to introduce e-HRM. The seven variables used to analyse if a relationship exists between the readiness and receptiveness of employees to the implementation of e-HRM and the feasibility of implementing e-HRM are summarized in Table 7.

Based on the results generated, most of the employees agreed that though e-HRM is not crucial to the organization (3.02), it is important that their organizations introduce e-HRM in the next 12 months (3.10). As it is costly to implement e-HRM,

Table 7. Means for Hypothesis 3

Variables	Means
E-HRM is not crucial to my organization	3.02
The advantages of e-HRM are outweighed by the cost implication	3.03
Our staff does not have relevant skills for e-HRM	2.85
My organization lacks the technology needed for e-HRM	2.80
I have concerns related to the lack of security of e-HRM	2.95
E-HRM is too complex to comprehend/understand	2.58
It is important that my organization introduce e-HRM in the next 12 months	3.10

many of the employees agreed that the advantages of e-HRM are outweighed by the cost implication (3.03). The mean for the other four items (B27–B30) is less than 3, indicating that the employees do not agree that there are too many constraints in the implementation of e-HRM. Most of the employees believe that relevant skills for e-HRM are available in their organizations. Technical infrastructure needed for e-HRM is in place and employees are not too concerned about the lack of security of e-HRM. The employees also believed that e-HRM would not be too complex to comprehend or understand.

To conclude, the responses of the employees are very encouraging in that most think positively on the implementation of e-HRM. They believe that e-HRM would be good for their organizations and they are capable of handling e-HRM if it were introduced in their organizations. Generally, there are not too many constraints and employees are ready and receptive to the implementation of e-HRM. The third hypothesis is thus substantiated.

Discussion and Implications

As mentioned at the start of the research, the main objective of the research was to understand HRM practices among SMEs in Malaysia and to gauge the feasibility of implementing e-HRM in these companies. Based on the results of the research, more companies are using conventional HRM as compared to e-HRM even though e-HRM has been identified as a catalyst towards achieving business strategies. Some claim that they lack financial resources, expertise or suitable infrastructure to implement e-HRM. These companies are of the opinion that the implementation and maintenance of e-HRM systems involve huge investment. On the contrary, others view that the lack of resources is not a constraint for them and opine that the advantages of e-HRM far outweigh the cost involved. As far as the respondent companies are concerned, the former is more dominant.

Except for communication purposes and salary calculation, there is not much interest among local companies to adopt e-HRM. If SMEs were to follow this trend, then it is unlikely that there would be much advancement in the use of technology in HR. Despite the rapid advancement in technology, SMEs would not be able to fully utilize it to the benefit of their organizations. Not only will employees be caught up in tedious, manual processes but they will also have the opportunity to be more technologically knowledgeable in their operations.

Organizations would be more backward in their approach and this indirectly hinders the progress of the workers as well as the organization.

The findings of the research show that as in the literature review, it is clear that there is a relationship between the availability of financial resources, the availability of expertise and the availability of technical infrastructure and the feasibility of implementing e-HRM. However, as the findings show, the lack of these resources could not be considered the main constraints in the implementation of e-HRM. Though these constraints do impede the implementation of e-HRM, other barriers such as the lack of commitment in e-HRM initiative, the lack of support from senior management, insufficient intangible benefits, the misconception that employees are not flexible enough to adapt to changes and learn new skills, the misconception that e-HRM would reduce the number of employees in the HR department and other artificial obstacles may be more significant than these resources. As long as these constraints are not checked, the transformation from conventional HRM to e-HRM will be a slow one.

Therefore, for the success of e-HRM initiatives, companies have to equip themselves with the right technology. Without this, the alternative is to outsource to solution providers but it is of the utmost importance that a committed and competent service provider is utilized. Without the right software needed for e-HRM or the technical skills to handle the various functions, the implementation of e-HRM would definitely be impeded if companies that are unfamiliar with e-HRM were left to figure out problems in e-HRM initiatives on their own. A better understanding of the relationship between the availability of resources and the implementation of e-HRM would help companies identify the best solution for their HR functions.

On the readiness of employees for e-HRM, encouraging responses from the survey show that employees are ready and receptive, which would render the implementation of e-HRM initiatives more feasible. However, survey results show that e-HRM is not given much priority. One of the main obstacles is the mind-set and lack of commitment of employees. For the successful implementation of e-HRM, it is important that companies communicate e-HRM initiatives and encourage the mind-set of employees to be more receptive to e-HRM. Support from senior management on the importance of e-HRM and its effect on the bottom line of the organization would perhaps increase the awareness of employees towards e-HRM initiatives. The encouraging factor is that employees do not think that e-HRM is too complex to comprehend, indicating that employees are ready for e-HRM, thus reducing the cost of training. Based on the results of the research, the transformation of conventional HRM to e-HRM in the near future is rather encouraging.

However, as the study was unable to cover all areas of HRM or research on all the possible constraints in the implementation of e-HRM, further study and analysis is required to give a more meaningful and specific impact in the study of e-HRM. The limited sample and variables in this study can not be generalized for the population, which has more than 20,000 companies[13] but could act as a stepping stone for more extensive research. More specific research on the constraints inhibiting the implementation of e-HRM could be carried out to identify constraints that could be overcome in the short and long run. Similarly, identifying critical success factors in the implementation of e-HRM would enhance confidence and encourage more companies to adopt e-HRM initiatives.

A comparative cost-benefit analysis between conventional HRM and e-HRM initiatives or outsourcing to solution providers would help HR practitioners to decide which practice is best for their organization. To further enhance the introduction of e-HRM initiatives, the government and private sector have to play their roles in promoting the adoption of e-HRM.

Conclusion

In a nutshell, this research shows that a large number of companies are practising conventional HRM as compared to e-HRM. The main constraints in the implementation of e-HRM among the respondent companies are the lack of financial resources and expertise. Technical infrastructure for e-HRM seems to be in place and would not be a problem if the companies decide to implement e-HRM. On the positive side, most employees are ready for and receptive towards e-HRM. The attitude of the employees would not be a stumbling block in the implementation of e-HRM. From the research, it can be concluded that it is feasible to implement e-HRM in SMEs in Malaysia provided that measures are taken to overcome certain constraints. The fact that there are more newly established companies, more private companies and more medium sized companies as compared to small size companies further supports this move. In short, the transformation from conventional HRM to e-HRM in the near future is rather encouraging.

To enhance the transformation of conventional HRM practices to e-HRM in the SMEs, the government has an instrumental role to play. So far, the government's commitment to and involvement with SMEs in the manufacturing sector can be seen in its First (1971–90) and Second (1991–2000) Outline Perspective Plans (OPP1 and OPP2) which embody the National Policy and the Malaysian Development Plans. Other programmes include the Industrial Linkage Programme (ILP), Technology Development Scheme and Acquisition, Skills Development and Upgrading, Business Planning and Development Scheme, Market Development Scheme and Infrastructure Development and Financial Support (Technology Acquisition Fund, Industrial Technical Assistance Fund, Y2K Grant, Financial Package for Small- and Medium-scale Industries, Modernization and Automation Scheme, Quality Enhancement Scheme and Rehabilitation Fund for Small- and Medium-scale Industries). To assist SMEs in implementing e-HRM, the following additional measures could be taken by the government.

The provision of financial assistance, infrastructure facilities and support services by the government is very much encouraged. More aggressive promotional efforts could be undertaken to encourage SMEs to participate in training programmes that are aligned with the adoption of e-HRM applications. The government can enhance its support by encouraging the participation of more SMEs in conferences on HR issues to keep up with current trends. Policies on aligning the development of new graduates to meet industry needs are also recommended. With the right skills, new recruits could easily adapt to the newer practices. Efforts could also be made to promote research in e-HRM applications and to encourage the development of more cost-effective solutions. It is hoped that this future research would enlighten HR practitioners in particular, and employees in general on e-HRM practices.

Notes

[1] www.muecke.com.au, www.genesisny.net
[2] www.cbsresearch.co.uk, www.dmu.ac.uk
[3] www.dolanm.com
[4] www.homercomputer.com.au
[5] www.southglos.gov.uk
[6] www.robertshawmyers.co.uk
[7] Eight Malaysia Plan (2001–2005)
[8] http://www.pmo.gov.my
[9] Human Capital Development Division, Ministry of Manpower, Singapore
[10] www.smallbusinesseurope.org, www.cbresearch.co.uk, www.southglos.gov.uk, www.dmu.ac.uk, www.robertshawmyers.co.uk
[11] If the mean is more than 3 then it can be said that respondent companies are moving away from conventional practices and adopting more technology in their recruitment and selection practices, training and development, communication, compensation practices and performance appraisal.
[12] If the mean is more than 3, then it can be said that it is feasible to implement e-HRM. However, the respondent companies lack financial resources, internal expertise and technical infrastructure to implement e-HRM.
[13] http://www.mida.gov.my/stats_man/2004/appr-table10.html

References

Ali, J. & Bawa, M. A. (1999) Human resource management in the context of labor market and union status: a review, in: D. Nasir Ibrahim, I. Ismail, M. Jantan, Y. Zainuddin & Z. Ariffin Ahmad (Eds) *Reinventing Asian Management for Global Challenges, Proceedings of The third Asian Academy of Management Conference*, pp. 333–340.

Baron, J. A. & Kreps, D. M. (1999) *Strategic Human Resources: Frameworks for General Managers* (New York: John Wiley).

Bawa, M. A. & Ali, J. (1999) Human resource management in the context of labour market and union status: a review, in: D.N. Ibrahim, I. Ismail, M. Jantan, Y. Zainuddin & Z.A. Ahmad (Eds) *Reinventing Asian Management for Global Challenges, Proceedings of the Third Asian Academy of Management Conference*, pp. 333–340.

Bawa, M. A., Jantan, M. & Ali, J. (2001) HRM practices in small, medium and large firms, *Malaysian Management Review*, 36(1). Available at http://mgv.mim.edu.my/MMR/0106/010606.htm

Business Wire, Business & Technology Editors (2002) Web self-service technology begins to deliver results in the human resource area, but full potential not yet realized, Towers Perrin study finds, 16 January. Available http://www.findarticles.com

Eighth Malaysia Plan (2001–2005). (Government of Malaysia, Kuala Lumpur: National Printing Department).

Hashim, M. K. (2000) A proposed strategic framework for SMEs' success, *Malaysian Management Review*, 35(2). pp. 32–51.

Hashim, M. K. & Abdullah, M. S. (2000a) *Development of SMEs: Research Issues and Agenda, Small and Medium Enterprises in the Asian Pacific Countries* (New York: Nova Science Publishers).

Hashim, M. K. & Abdullah, M. S. (2000b) A proposed framework for redefining SMEs in Malaysia: one industry, one definition, *Asian Academy of Management Journal*, January, 5(1), pp. 65–79.

Hashim, M. K. & Abdullah, M. S. (2000c) Developing SMEs taxonomies in Malaysia, *Malaysian Management Journal*, June/December, 4(1), pp. 43–50.

Hashim, M. K. & Wafa, S. A. (2002) *Small and Medium-sized Enterprises in Malaysia: Development Issues* (Petaling Jaya: Prentice Hall).

Hay, R. K. & Ross, D. L. (1989) An assessment of success factors of non-urban start-up firms based upon financial characteristics of successful versus failed firms, *Frontiers of Entrepreneurship Research*, pp. 148–158. *Proceedings of the Ninth Annual Babson College Entrepreneurship Research Conference*: 148–158. Center for Entrepreneurial Studies, Babson College, Wellesley, Massachusetts.

Hofer, C. W. & Sandberg, W. R. (1987) Improving new venture performance: Some guidelines for success, *American Journal of Small Business*, 2(1), pp. 11–26.

Huselid, M. A. (1995) The impact of human resource management practices on turnover, productivity, and corporate financial performance, *Academy of Management Journal*, 38(3), pp. 635–672.

Ismail, S. (1990) *Small and Medium Scale Industrialisation: Problems and Prospects* (Malaysia: ISIS (Institute of Strategic and International Studies) Publications).

Jackson, S. E. & Schuler, R. S. (1995) Understanding human resource management in the context of organisations and their environments, in: M. R. Rosenszweig & L. W. Porter (Eds), *Annual Review of Psychology*, 46, pp. 237–264 (Palo Alto, CA: Annual Reviews).

Karakanian, M. (2002) Are human resource departments ready for e-HR, *Architectures for E-business System Building The Foundation For Tomorrow's Success* (Sanjiv Purba: Auerbach Publications).

Kumar, P. R. (2002) Technology and e-HR – the catalyst in transforming HR professionals as strategic partners to business. Available at http://www.cnetg.com/about-us/news-events.htm

Kumar, P. R. (2003) Quantifying the setting up of an e-HR system. Available at http://www.cnetg.com/about-us/news-events.htm

Little, B. L. (1986) The performance of personnel duties in small Louisiana firms: a research note, *Journal of Small Business Management*, 24(4), pp. 66–69.

McEvoy, G. (1984) Small business personnel practices, *Journal of Small Business Management*, 22(4), pp. 1–8.

Ministry of Manpower, Human Capital Development Division, Singapore (2003) E-HR: Leveraging technology. Available at http://www.mom.gov.sg

National Productivity Corporation (2001) *Productivity Report*, National Productivity Corporation, Malaysia.

Osman, I. & Hashim, M. K. (2003) An evaluation of the business practices in Malaysian SMEs, *Malaysian Management Review*, 38(2). Available at http://mgv.mim.edu.my/MMR/0312/031202.htm

Sapuan, M., Abu Bakar, A. H. & Smith, D. J. (1997) The roles of small and medium enterprises (SMEs) to support the large industries in the context of Malaysia, *Malaysian Management Review*, 32(4). Available http://mgv.mim.edu.my/MMR/9712/frame.htm

Sim, A. B. (1991) Turnaround for small businesses - a synthesis of determinants for action research, with reference to Malaysia, *Malaysian Management Review*, 26(3), pp. 15–22.

Watson Wyatt Worldwide (2002) B2E/e-HR Survey results 2002. Available http://www.watsonwyatt.com/us/research/resrender.asp

Internationalization Strategies of Emerging Asian MNEs – Case Study Evidence on Singaporean and Malaysian Firms

A. B. SIM
School of Management and Marketing, University of Wollongong, Australia

Emphasis on MNEs has traditionally focused on western firms and not on Asian MNEs. Firms from Asian capital exporting countries were internationalizing and multinationalizing their business activities and have emerged or are emerging as Asian multinational enterprises (World Bank, 1993). In recent years, research interest was beginning to focus on these Asian enterprises and their direct investment activities (Ting, 1985; Ulgado *et al.*, 1994; Yeung, 1994, 1997; Pangarkar, 1998). While research on Asian MNEs is growing, knowledge of the nature, organization and operations of Asian MNEs is still in its infancy. For example, are the Asian MNEs really different from the western MNEs? Are differences in strategic traits of MNEs from different Asian countries due to differences in the levels of development in these countries (such as Newly Industrialized Countries (NICs) and Less Developed Countries (LDCs)) as predicted by the investment development path (IDP) thesis (Dunning, 1993)? van Hoesel (1999) and Dunning *et al.* (1998) contend that the MNEs from the Asian NICs constitute the second wave of FDI (Foreign Direct Investment) which differs from the first wave of the Third World Multinational Enterprises (TWMNEs). Yet the precise nature of the strategic advantages of these firms is not clear and a considerable knowledge gap about them still exists (van Hoesel, 1999). Since comparative empirical research on MNEs originating from different Asian countries is limited (Luo, 1998; Sim & Ali, 2001), further research comparing MNEs from different Asian countries at varying levels of development is worthy of attention.

The purpose of this research work is to contribute to this area by examining the internationalization strategies of emerging Asian MNEs from Malaysia, being a rapidly developing country, and Singapore, an NIC. Internationalization here focuses on the international expansion of business operations and related activities across national boundaries. Empirical data of ten matched case studies are presented and used to analyse and compare their internationalization characteristics and strategies, and to examine their position in relation to the IDP explanation from a firm-level perspective. In addition these findings will also be evaluated against other conventional theories of MNEs. Our empirical findings will be discussed in relation to prior research findings on MNEs from developed countries. The next section covers the theoretical foundations of MNEs and their relevance to Asian MNEs, followed by research methodology, findings and discussion. Implications for further research are discussed.

Theoretical Perspectives on Emerging Asian MNEs

Explanations of the internationalization of firms are largely based on theories derived from western MNEs. Vernon's (1966, 1979) Product Life Cycle model, the Uppsala model (Johanson & Weidersheim-Paul, 1975; Johanson & Vahlne, 1977) and the works of Dunning (1977, 1988, 1993, 1995) on his Eclectic paradigm and the Investment Development Path (IDP) (Dunning, 1981, 1986) were all largely based on western multinationals. More recent works examining Third World (including Asian) multinationals included Dunning (1986), Tolentino (1993), Dunning & Narula (1996), Lall (1996), Dunning *et al.* (1998). Review of all these research studies clearly indicates that further research examining MNEs from countries at different stages of development especially from Asia would be required to understand how these Asian multinationals may be different from their western counterparts (Lall, 1996).

Eclectic and IDP Explanations

A widely known explanation of international production is the Eclectic Paradigm. Drawing on received theories, Dunning's (1977, 1988, 1993, 1995) Eclectic Paradigm stated that the extent and pattern of international production is determined by the configuration of ownership advantages (for example, proprietary technology), internalization advantages (for example, transaction costs reduction), and location advantages. These OLI (Ownership Location Internalization) variables explain why internationalization occurs but neglect the dynamic process of internationalization. The Investment Development Path (Dunning, 1981, 1986) provides the Eclectic Paradigm with a dynamic dimension by relating the net outward investment of a country to its stage of economic development. At low level of economic development (stage 1), there is little inward or outward investments. As the country develops (stage 2), inward investment becomes attractive, particularly in import substitution projects. Some outward investment may take place, for example, in neighbouring countries at lower stages of development. Most developing countries with some outward investments are at this stage. With further economic development (stage 3), net inward investment declines while outward investment increases (relative to inward investment). Outward investment tends to increase to countries at lower IDP stages to overcome cost disadvantages in labour intensive industries and also to seek markets or strategic assets. The NICs (for example, Singapore, Taiwan and South Korea) are said to be at this stage. At stage 4 of the IDP, net outward investment becomes positive with production being multinationalized. Most developed countries are at this stage.

Empirical research on Third World (including Asian) multinationals has given general support to the IDP concept (Dunning, 1986; Tolentino, 1993; Dunning & Narula, 1996; Lall, 1996). Dunning and Narula (1996) acknowledge that the specific IDP pattern of a country may vary depending on country factors. Revisiting the Third World Multinational Enterprises, Dunning *et al.* (1998) found that the second wave of TWMNEs was different from the first wave described by research in the early 1980s (for example, Lall, 1983; Wells, 1983). While the first wave was from developing countries, the second wave consisted mainly of East Asian NICs. The MNEs from these countries had improved and augmented ownership advantages (for example, innovatory capabilities) and made more strategic seeking FDI (for technology and marketing) in advanced industrial countries via higher equity and control modes (for example, mergers and acquisitions (M&A)). The authors argued that the second wave was consistent with the IDP explanation (stage 3) and represented an intermediate stage between the first wave of TWMNEs and conventional (western) MNEs. Differences in the patterns of the IDP between Taiwan and South Korea were also reported by the authors. Specific studies on the IDP of Singaporean firms at the firm's level are lacking. While generally supporting the IDP concept, Lall (1996) stated that it should be extended and modified to take into account the different sub-patterns of countries.

The IDP concept still remains vague about the precise relationships between the underlying advantages (factors) and the pattern of inward and outward FDI or stage of IDP (van Hoesel, 1999). The precise nature of the ownership specific advantages of the Asian MNEs from NICs remains unclear. How do they differ from MNEs originating from less developed countries? Further research is needed in this area. In fact studies on MNEs from Asian countries less developed than the NICs are lacking. This research will examine at the micro or firm's level, the characteristics of MNEs from a fast developing country, Malaysia, and an NIC, Singapore, to provide further evidence on the applicability of the IDP for these two groups of firms. In addition, these emerging MNEs will also be assessed in relation to other explanations or theories of MNEs.

Other Explanations

A similar concept to the IDP is that relating to the internationalization of firms based on distinct patterns of national development, such as the level of economic development, resource, size of domestic market and development path pursued (Cantwell, 1997; Tolentino, 2000). An earlier model for explaining the dynamic nature of international trade and investment is the Product Life Cycle model (Vernon, 1966, 1979). The Uppsala model (Johanson & Weidersheim-Paul, 1975; Johanson & Vahlne, 1977) provides an explanation of the dynamic process of internationalization of individual firms. This model of gradual incremental steps to international business expansion is based on a series of incremental decisions, whose successive steps of increasingly higher commitments are based on knowledge acquisition and learning about the foreign market. The steps of foreign activities start with export to a country via an independent representative/agent, followed by the establishment of a sales subsidiary and eventually production in the host country. The internationalization of the firm across many foreign markets is related to psychic distance (in terms of differences in language, education, business practices, culture and industrial development). Initial entry is to a foreign market that is closer in terms of psychic distance, followed by subsequent entries in markets with greater psychic distances. Similarly, commitment in terms of the level of ownership in different markets is correlated with their psychic distance. The Uppsala model has received general support in empirical research (for example, Davidson, 1980, 1983; Welch & Loustarinen, 1986; Erramilli *et al.*, 1999) and its largely intuitive nature and evolutionary learning perspective makes it an attractive model.

Contextual Perspectives for Asian MNEs

The above theories and concepts provide an understanding and an explanation of the internationalization of MNEs from NICs and developing countries. However by themselves, they are by no means a complete explanation of MNEs, particularly Asian MNEs. The TWMNEs and Asian MNEs did exhibit characteristics, motivations and internationalization paths which varied from those of western MNEs from developed countries and which are not fully explained by extant theories of MNEs. Li (2003) contends that extant theories of MNEs need to be modified and enhanced to explain all MNEs, including Asian MNEs.

Western theories on internationalization have overlooked the active role played by the state and neglected the institutional or contextual perspective in the internationalization of Asian firms (Zutshi & Gibbons, 1998; Yeung, 1999). In the Asian context the state often plays a direct and active role in the internationalization of its MNEs. For example, the Singapore government played a key and direct role in the promotion of outward FDI, particularly from the early 1990s, in its regionalization programmes (Pang, 1995; Tan, 1995; ESCAP/UNC-TAD, 1997). Yeung (1998a) indicated that this role was taken to overcome the underdevelopment of indigenous entrepreneurship in Singapore. The state assumed the role of entrepreneur by actively opening up overseas business opportunities and setting up institutional frameworks (for example, growth triangles, industrial parks in foreign countries) for Singaporean firms to tap. Government linked corporations (GLCs) were used to push regionalization activities either on their own or in partnerships with other firms. For example, our case study firm, Keppel Corporation, a GLC, led a consortium of Singapore's firms to set up the

Singapore-Suzhou industrial township in Suzhou, China. The government also provided generous incentives and other programmes (for example, tax incentives, finance schemes, training and so forth) to foster the rapid development of local entrepreneurship in the regionalization efforts. This type of direct and active involvement in internationalization is usually not undertaken on such a scale in other Asian countries. In Malaysia, the government took a very active role in promoting the internationalization of Malaysian firms. Investment promotion missions abroad were organized and often led by the prime minister. The government provided incentives including tax abatement in 1991 and subsequently full tax exemption in 1995 for income earned overseas and remitted back to Malaysia. An overseas investment guarantee programme, an Exim bank and FDI advisory services were instituted. In the Asian context, the state has played a very active and direct role in promoting the internationalization of its national firms. This is unlike the western context where the role of the state is benign and indirect. As a result, MNEs operating in the Asian context, including those in our research, have to manage this institutional context successfully.

There is a need to examine Asian MNEs within the context of their institutional as well as socio-cultural embeddedness. While national cultural characteristics or differences have been investigated and found to have influences on different aspects of internationalization in western MNEs (for example, Johanson & Vahlne, 1977; Kogut & Singh, 1988; Shane, 1994), these cultural factors are essential in explaining Asian internationalization. Asian internationalization tends to be organised through social and ethnic networks. The 'Spirit of Chinese capitalism' (Redding, 1990) with its sets of values and beliefs underlies the way Chinese business and cross-border operations are conducted (Yeung & Olds, 2000). Personal relationships and networks (for example, Chen, 1995; Hamilton, 1996; Luo, 2000) form the basis of the internationalization of Chinese and Asian firms. Hence the internationalization of Asian MNEs needs to be seen in its contextual embeddedness (both institutional and cultural). It is our view that it is imperative to combine these contextual perspectives with the economic perspective normally used to explain the internationalization of western MNEs. Our research will endeavour to examine these characteristics and their role in the internationalization of Malaysian and Singaporean firms within the context of IDP and other explanations of MNEs.

Hence more empirical studies on Asian MNEs are required to provide further data on the applicability of extant theories on the internationalization of MNEs from Asian countries at different levels of development. van Hoesel (1999: 35) stated that 'What is seriously lacking at present, are new empirical findings that will enable us to make theoretical statements and hypotheses more concrete'. Towards this end, this research work provides further empirical data on MNEs originating from two Asian countries at different development stages, Singapore (an NIC) and Malaysia (a fast developing country). This research particularly makes an empirical contribution with such comparative research data.

Research Methodology

As this is an exploratory study, a matched case study approach was chosen. This approach was used to collect comprehensive and holistic data (Eisenhardt, 1989;

Yin, 1994) about firms that have internationalized their operations over time. This will provide data for more extensive subsequent research and testing of propositions and hypotheses as part of an ongoing research on Asian MNEs. The focus here is on MNEs from Malaysia (a fast developing country) and Singapore (an NIC) and has substantial outward FDI. The data is primarily drawn from field interviews with the chief executive officers (CEOs) or top executives responsible for the international operations of the firm at the home country in Malaysia and Singapore. As our focus is on the internationalization strategies of the parent firms, overseas subsidiaries were not interviewed. In addition to interviews, annual reports, prospectus, presentation to security analysts, news releases and other publications were requested and collected from the firms visited. Data from other published sources (for example, industry sources, published materials in business periodicals) and internet websites were used to supplement the primary material. This use of data from various sources will also allow us to cross-check, verify data and to ensure their validity.

This study focuses on the internationalization of firms from Malaysia and Singapore in five industrial sectors. These included the textiles, food, electrical, electronics and diversified sectors. Before the field visits, data on firms in these industrial sectors in Malaysia and Singapore were collected from various company listings and other sources (for example, *Dun's Asia/Pacific Key Business Enterprises* (1998), Murphy & Walsh's (1998) *Major Companies of the Far East and Australasia 1998*, Stock Exchanges and internet web sources). Only Malaysian and Singaporean firms with overseas operations were selected. This search yielded 59 firms (33 Singaporean and 26 Malaysian). They were approached (via letter, with several follow-ups by mail, email and telephone) for participation in the study. Ten firms agreed and formed the final case firms, which were matched by industrial sectors. Several of these firms requested confidentiality and anonymity as a condition of participation and are accordingly disguised in this study. The reluctance of firms to participate in the research was strongly encountered by the researcher and is a common problem of research in Asian counties. Our matched case study firms, while not randomly selected, were similiar to those MNEs from Malaysia and Singapore described in aggregative data and previous studies (Lu & Zhu, 1995; Tan, 1995; Bank Negara Malaysia, 1994, 2002; Rogayah, 1999).

Results from the fieldwork were transcribed, collated and analysed. Together with data from other sources, case notes were prepared, tabulated and analysed for each case firm. The evidence was examined case by case for replicative effects. Across-case analysis to detect similarities and differences were undertaken using various tabular displays (along the lines indicated by Miles & Huberman (1994)) of data by case firms, by country, and by industry to cover the dimensions examined.

Case Study Findings

This section presents the findings on our case studies and analysis. These findings are also discussed in relation to prior research findings on other Asian MNEs and western MNEs.

Size and International Spread

The size of our sample firms varied from small (US$26 million in sales) to large (US$2.12 billion). (See appendix for summary details of all case studies.) In general our Singaporean firms were larger (average US$797 million, range US$89million–$2.12 billion) than Malaysian firms (average US$644 million, range US$26 million–$1.8 billion), particularly in the textile, electronics and diversified sectors. The largest firms in both countries were in the diversified group. Compared to western MNEs from developed countries, our case firms are much smaller in size. They are representative of MNEs in general from Malaysia and Singapore (as well as Asian MNEs) reported in the literature.

In general, our case firms tend to concentrate in the Asian region and have fewer overseas locations (as indicated in the appendix tables). All our five Malaysian case firms have concentrations in the Asian region. The textile firm has one location (Sri Lanka), followed by the electronics firm (two countries), food firm (three countries), electrical firm (four countries) and the diversified conglomerate Lion Group with extensive operations in Asia and ventures in the USA and Germany. In the Singaporean sample firms, all the five cases have operations in the Association of South East Asian Nations (ASEAN) region, China and Sri Lanka. The number of overseas locations ranged from three to over 80 countries. The most extensive are Keppel and Creative Technology with operations worldwide. For example, Creative Technology has operations in over 80 countries, with production in several countries including Malaysia, China, Europe and the USA. Hence our Singaporean firms were more internationalized than the Malaysian firms in all the five sectors, which seems consistent with the IDP thesis. Our case firms while concentrating in the Asian region have begun to move to the developed countries. This is particularly so for our Singaporean firms in the electronics and diversified sectors with investments in the USA and Europe for mainly strategic asset seeking motives. It is interesting to note the forays, for technology acquisition, into Australia by the Malaysian electronics firm and into the USA and Germany by the Lion Group for technology reasons were all subsequently divested or restructured.

The size of our case firms as well as that of Asian MNEs in general has a constraining effect on the geographical spread of their internationalization. With limited resources, such firms tend to extend their current products and technologies to nearby countries with similar economic and cultural environments. The choice of proximate country in the initial stages of internationalization is consistent with the internationalization processes of the Uppsala School (Johanson & Vahlne, 1977). In general, our Malaysian sample firms have moved overseas later than their Singaporean counterparts. The longitudinal spread of our case firms is reflective of Asian MNEs from developing countries in general, with firms from the NICs ahead of the lesser developed Asian countries. The competitive catch-up processes become very important for Asian MNEs and some may be able to leapfrog stages in the internationalization process (Young *et al.*, 1996). Creative Technology was able to move quickly to the advanced countries and establish its own reputation and brand name. Malaysian and Singaporean MNEs have been latecomers in globalization. While these firms have gone international since the 1960s, the big impetus for internationalization only occurred during the late 1980s; but they seemed to have moved rapidly since then to capitalize on overseas manufacturing to enhance their competitiveness. This is also reflected in our sample firms.

Motives

The internationalization motivations of our sample firms in both Malaysia and Singapore were basically the search overseas for low cost bases and markets (see tables in the appendix). Cost was particularly important for the textile and food sectors. The Singaporean textile firm in fact shut down its factories in Singapore and relocated all manufacturing activities overseas in Asia for cost and quota reasons. Market expansion was the key factor for our firms in the electrical, electronics and the diversified sectors. This is particularly so for Singaporean firms that had limited domestic markets compared to the Malaysian case firms. China and the ASEAN markets were key target markets. For the two diversified firms in our sample, diversification motives (both product and geographical diversification) played a major part in their internationalization. For our Malaysian and Singaporean firms, their motivations varied by the destination of investments. While cheap local labour is the main motivator in the Asian countries, market seeking and strategic asset seeking motives prevail in the developed countries, especially for the higher technology sectors. This is particularly true for Keppel and Creative Technology. Creative Technology was very aggressive in pursuing acquisitions and alliances in the USA for these purposes. It is evident from the case studies that the more aggressive Singaporean firms (particularly in electronics) have started to move beyond their Asian bases to prepare themselves for the next stage of internationalization. This is also true for a few Malaysian firms which ventured overseas to acquire technology. However these ventures were not very successful and were subsequently disposed off.

Strategic Advantages and Traits

In general the competitive advantage of our case firms in both Malaysia and Singapore is based on cost-based competencies and adaptation to markets. However there are differences by industrial sector and country. In the textile sector, low cost input largely for OEM (Original Equipment Manufacture) manufacture underlies their internationalization advantage and strategies. Our Singaporean firm has moved all its garments manufacturing overseas to capitalize on the cost and quota advantages offered by host countries. Both the food firms in our sample relied on cost advantage and have moved vertically. The Malaysian firm started in flour milling and has grown organically to animal feeds, food products, oil processing and related business. It has a packaging plant (polypropylene bags) in Myanmar and JV (Joint Venture) with the Australian Wheat Authority and local partner in Vietnam. The Singaporean firm expanded into Sri Lanka and has since moved into agri-based businesses and retailing. It diversified into China with three JVs. In Singapore itself the firm has diversified into confectionery, franchising and food services. Both food firms in our sample have made integrative efforts as well as trying to create their own brand names (both necessary requirements to be second wave firms, stage 3 of the IDP).

In the electrical sector, both our Singaporean and Malaysian firms relied on product expertise and reputation (originally derived from overseas principals) and adaptation to local markets and niches. The Singaporean firm has an organic approach to its regionalization, growing its agents/distributors in the respective host countries to the assembly and production stages where the demand and cost justification become realizable. The Malaysian electrical firm has grown in the Asia Pacific area based on its engineering expertise, product reputation, quick and flexible after sales service and the targeting of specific market niches. It seems that both these two firms are at the same stage of internationalization (late stage 2), with the Singaporean firm slightly ahead.

There is a big variation between the Singaporean and Malaysian electronics firm. Our Malaysian electronics firm relied on its technical expertise and its ability to tailor advanced electronics displays to host market requirements. The company is conscious of its need for R & D and acquired an Australian firm for its technology and used its China's joint venture to tap technology developed and tailored to the Chinese market. It has a conservative approach to internationalization and expands when its capacity can sustain them. Creative Technology is among the most globalized of Singapore's MNEs. It has moved the most away from the low technology and cost based Asian MNE model. While cost still underlies its production bases in Malaysia and China, its competitive advantages are its niche technology leadership, brand recognition, extensive distribution network and product line-up. The founder of Creative deliberately moved to the USA in 1988 to tap the US market and technology. It has since developed a leadership position in audio-visual technology for personal computers (PCs) (its Sound Blaster technology is industry standard for PCs, with a widely recognised brand name). R&D and product development remain its main strengths. MNEs that rely on the Asian region for its business, about 80 per cent of Creative Technology's turnover in 1999 is from North America and Europe. Creative Technology resembles Acer of Taiwan (Li, 1998) and other second wave Asian MNEs.

In the diversified sector, both Keppel and Lion are very internationalized, while the former has greater global spread. Lion's emphasis is largely in Asia, particularly China. The Lion Group, one of Malaysia's largest conglomerates with businesses in steel, plantations, property, motor vehicles and components, tyres, food and beverages, retailing and financial services, has grown via diversification and internationalization. The competitive advantage of Lion in China is its intimate market knowledge and elaborate network built up over years of development in China, particularly by its CEO, who stressed the importance of patience, perseverance and a very long-term view in developing the Chinese market. In addition, a great deal of efforts was put into staff development to build a team of committed staff with shared vision and values.

The internationalization of the diversified GLC, Keppel, varied depending on its business. Keppel has five core businesses: marine; offshore, energy and engineering; property; banking and financial services and telecommunications and transportation. Internationalization started in the marine business with the establishment of a shipyard in the Philippines in 1975. The overseas locations of the offshore, energy and engineering services are very widespread, with operations going to where the market is. Hence operations have spread to the USA, Mexico, Nicaragua, Europe, the Caspian Sea, Australia, China and the Philippines. The property business is focused more in Asia but has interests in the USA, Europe and Australia. The other two core businesses are more regionalized with operations only in Asia. Keppel has also internationalized as part of the government efforts to use the GLCs to pursue regionalization. The GLC strengths and links have bolstered Keppel's internationalization and competitiveness.

Entry Strategies

Our Malaysian and Singaporean case firms exhibit a preference for joint ventures, which is similar to the behaviour of other MNEs from developing countries (Ting, 1985; Monkiewicz, 1986), which is unlike the behaviour MNEs from developed western countries. Nearly all the firms in our sample use joint ventures with the exception of our Malaysian textile and electronics firms (see appendix tables). The Malaysian textile firm used WOS (Wholly Owned Subsidiaries) in its sole overseas venture, while the Malaysian electronics firm used WOS in its Australia and Chinese ventures for technology acquisition. Creative Technology mainly used WOS in their North American and European operations, while JVs were used to a greater extent in Asia. During 1993–97, it made a series of acquisitions (WOS) in the USA to expand its product lines. The greater utilization of WOS in the electronic sector is a reflection of the need for greater control to maximize manufacturing flexibility and technology advantage. These strategic motivations and need for global synergies have been found to be among key determinants of higher equity stakes in entry modes (Rajan & Pangarkar, 2000). It is interesting to note that the Malaysian and Singaporean firms in our sample made greater use of WOS in the more culturally distant countries (USA and Europe), a finding similar to Erramilli *et al.* (1999). This is different from less equity control for more culturally distant countries indicated by internationalization theory (Johanson & Vahlne, 1977; Kogut & Singh, 1988). This difference warrants further empirical research.

Networks and Alliances

Ethnic networks strongly aided the internationalization of our sample firms in the Asian region. All our case study firms reported using their ethnic and other networks in their foreign operations (see tables in appendix). A good example is the case of our Singaporean textile firm that initially expanded overseas via its extended family network in the region and is now capitalizing on its network of ethnic associates in Asia to form an Asian grouping for all its businesses. The Malaysian textile firm is linked to a large network of suppliers and related businesses in Asia with which it has closely associated over a long period of time. Similarly all the electronics firms in our sample had ethnic networks in Southeast Asia and China that they utilize for their overseas operations. For example, our Malaysian electronics firm has ethnic partners in research and development in

China and an extensive network of Japanese and other suppliers. Our electronics case firms also make use of strategic alliances (which involve both business and ethnic partners) and licensing. In the global electronics industry, networks of subcontracting and logistics are well developed to ensure efficient and smooth supply and distribution. Hence a considerable part of the network is not necessarily ethnic based, but based on industry relationships. Creative Technology and our Malaysian electronics firm made greater utilization of strategic alliances, licensing and partnerships with companies in technologically advanced countries.

In their internationalization, all our case firms in the electrical, food, and diversified sectors benefited from their ethnic networks and connections. For example, the Singapore food firm's first overseas venture in Indonesia was ethnic based. Both Singaporean and Malaysian electrical firms as well as the Malaysian food firm were part of their respective regional groupings of associates and partners. Ethnic networks featured very prominently in the Chinese operations of the Lion Group. The company, particularly its CEO, has cultivated extensive *guanxi* (connections) and political networks in China and the region over a long period of time. The Singaporean GLC, Keppel benefited from its governmental links (particularly in China and Southeast Asia) and business associates to form JVs and strategic alliances.

Discussion

The above findings on internationalization indicated that our Singaporean firms internationalized earlier and were more internationalized than our Malaysian firms in all the five sectors. This is reflective of the general pattern in the IDP thesis. Our case firms while concentrating in the Asian region have begun to move to the developed countries, particularly to acquire technology and other strategic assets. This is particularly so for our Singaporean firms. This pattern was also observed by van Hoesel (1999) for second wave investors. In terms of scale and scope, the Singaporean case firms were ahead of the Malaysian firms in their move to the developed countries for strategic asset seeking purposes. This provided some support for the IDP concept. The chequered efforts of our Malaysian sample firms venturing into developed countries is probably a reflection that time and learning is required for such a move further along the IDP. Mathews (2003) suggested that latecomers, like our sample firms, can be successful quickly in globalization via learning and building capabilities.

The research findings showed that all our sample firms share similar competitive advantages and traits, though there are some variations, particularly by country and sectors. The majority of firms rely on advantages based on cost, responsiveness, and knowledge of the local market. Similar findings on other Asian MNEs have been reported by Luo (1998, 1999), Yeung (1994, 1997), Li (1994, 1998), and Chen (1998). In the textile sector, while both firms relied on cost-based advantages, the Singaporean firm was more internationalized and had moved towards greater vertical control of its value chain activities. The Malaysian textile firm was confined more to its cost-based OEM manufacture. Similarly in the electronics sector, the Singaporean firm had its own world class technology, own brands and logistics networks (the transaction-type ownership advantages of Dunning (1993)). Our

Malaysian electronics firm was occupied with adaptation of technology for Asian markets. Its acquisition in Australia for technology purposes was an attempt to move beyond its current situation, but was not successful and hence discontinued.

In the electrical and food sectors, our Malaysian and Singaporean firms have similar strategic traits and advantages. However both the Singaporean firms in these two sectors have longer internationalization experience. While the two firms in the food sector were attempting vertical control and product differentiation (via branding), it is doubtful whether any of them has achieved the second wave status yet. As for the diversified firms, the Singaporean firm (Keppel) have developed more of the strategic traits of the second wave MNEs with its scale and scope economies, technology and organizational skills.

The strategic characteristics of our Malaysian firms are generally consistent with the first wave (stage 2) while a majority of the Singaporean firms (particularly in the electronics and diversified sector) reflects the second wave (stage 3) of the IDP. Our more forward-looking case firms have moved to the developed countries to seek technology, strategic assets and markets, but their advantages are still different from those of advanced western MNEs which are largely based on some intangible assets. Only Creative Technology is approaching this level. Nevertheless our case firms are augmenting their competitive advantages and moving towards resembling more like western MNEs. This indicates some general support for the IDP thesis.

The utilization and role of ethnic networks in our sample firms is not unlike that of other Asian MNEs reported in the literature (for example, Kao, 1993; Yeung, 1997; Luo, 2000). These ethnic networks are characteristic features of Chinese businesses and their internationalization in Asia (East Asia Analytical Unit, 1995; Hamilton, 1996; Weidenbaum & Hughes, 1996). Cooperative activities in such networks are based on personal relationships (*guanxi*) which are usually ethnically linked. Their similar cultural attitudes and heritage fostered the development of trust and cooperative behaviour. These ethnic networks and ties provide knowledge and access to local markets, distribution systems, connections around local bureaucracy and business systems, as well as potential business partners and associates and even financing. In Southeast Asia, overseas Chinese, who share common dialects with Singaporean and Malaysian Chinese investors (all our case firms are Chinese controlled), provide valuable links to form local networks for their businesses (Chen & Liu, 1998; Sim & Pandian, 2002). Yeung (1998b) also illustrated that economic synergy is embedded in the complex business networks among the transnational enterprises from Malaysia and Singapore. Ethnic and cultural ties also result in the surge of Singaporean and Malaysian investments and operations in China, particularly in Fujian and Guangdong provinces (Lu & Zhu, 1995; Chia, 1999). Such expansion had the active encouragement and support of their respective governments.

It could be argued that our sample firms and other Asian MNEs are no different from Western MNEs which have made use of extensive global networks, particularly in the textile and electronics industries. Organizational networks have been extensively covered in the literature on organizational dynamics (for example, Oliver, 1990; Nohria & Eccles, 1992). The textile and electronics industries with their extensive system of international OEM suppliers and contractors have well-established patterns of networks, and Asian firms are usually part of this network (Ernst, 2000). Even in the internationalization literature on western SMEs, recent attention has also shifted to using networks to examine and explain their internationalization (for example, Johanson & Mattsson, 1988; Coviello & McAuley, 1999; Chetty & Holm, 2000). Dunning (1988) has also seen the need to include the influence of alliance networks in his MNE explanations. But these western networks are of a business type and not linked to the social and institutional contexts. Networks of Asian firms, including our Singaporean and Malaysian case firms, are largely based on ethnic and cultural foundations, treading similar cultural values and attitudes in the pursuit of businesses. Hence the ethnic and social embeddedness of networks and relationships (*guanxi*) is a distinguishing feature of Chinese and Asian MNEs and not well covered by conventional explanations of MNEs. In addition the direct role of the governments of Singapore and Malaysia in the promotion of the internationalization activities of its national firms, including our case firms, needs to be considered as well. Our proposition is that such ethnic, social and political contexts should be explicitly taken into account in any explanation of Asian MNEs. Our case studies point to their key role.

Implications

The above research findings have several managerial and research implications. As Singaporean and Malaysian MNEs evolve and internationalize, particular attention needs to be paid to learning and accumulating new knowledge and competencies, particularly from their experiences as evident from our sample case studies. The need to develop existing capabilities and to accumulate new knowledge is becoming critical for Asian MNEs in an increasingly global market (Pananond & Zeithaml, 1998; Tsang, 1999). The trend towards differentiation strategies based on technological and other capabilities by our sample firms seems to indicate a move towards the ownership (or firm) specific advantages specified by the Investment Development Path thesis. These findings suggest several managerial and policy implications. Asian (as well as other) firms, wishing to progress beyond their initial internationalization, need to develop their competencies and capabilities to match the contextual requirements of their target markets. For example, the migration from cost and location-based advantages to more differentiation-based competencies (for example, innovative product edge, brand building and so forth) is indicated in any such development. In addition, ethnic and other networks should be cultivated and utilized to accelerate their internationalization. There is also a general implication for both private firms and national policy makers that the IDP can provide a useful framework for developing strategies and policies to progress firms or countries further in the internationalization path over time.

From a research perspective, the findings here provide support for the IDP from a micro or firm's level. The strategies utilized in our sample reflected those indicated in the IDP, though with some variations at the national and sectoral levels. Such variations or sub-patterns can be incorporated to enrich the IDP concept, which traditionally had a macro-perspective. Whether the future strategies of our sample firms (and those of other Asian MNEs) will result in them fully resembling western MNEs remain to be seen and warrant further research and discourse. There are other observable differences between our sample Asian firms and western MNEs. In particular our findings indicate the key role government, ethnic network and relationships played in their internationalization. These elements have been neglected in conventional MNE theories. Our findings here reinforce the basic proposition that the social and institutional framework is a distinguishing feature of our firms as well as other Asian MNEs and need to be incorporated in any further development or refinement of MNE theories. Such theoretical implications can be the subject of verification by further empirical research. Further research can focus on Asian MNEs from other countries at different levels of economic development to fill some of these research gaps and to provide a more comprehensive test of the IDP and other MNE theories. Other potential areas of research include longitudinal studies of Asian MNEs to examine whether they will resemble western MNEs as they evolve, the impact of ethnic networks on the performance of Asian MNEs and the role of the state in internationalization of Asian MNEs. Li (2003) also postulated several areas for such research. Research into these and related areas will provide a better and more comprehensive understanding of Asian MNEs and contribute towards the development of MNE theories.

Conclusion

The internationalization strategies of our Singaporean and Malaysian case firms were largely founded on cost-based competencies and other location-based advantages, brought together by an extensive web of ethnic networks and aided by government encouragement and institutional framework. Some differences between our Singaporean and Malaysian case firms were found. For example, the Singaporean firms were more internationalized and developed as second wave firms than the Malaysian firms. Increasingly, these Singaporean firms are extending beyond their current competitive advantages to those that capitalize on differentiation benefits, such as technology, innovative product features and value. Our case study firm in electronics (Creative Technology) has achieved world recognition in its technology niche. Some of our sample firms are moving outside their Asian bases to North America and Europe to position themselves strategically for new markets and technologies. The Malaysian case firms were less active in all these areas and indicated a lower level of internationalization. Hence they are more reflective of the first wave investors rather than the second wave of firms described by Dunning *et al.* (1998). Our findings here are consistent with the IDP thesis and also with prior research studies on Asian MNEs. General support for the IDP concept is indicated.

This research makes an empirical contribution with comparative data and analysis of the internationalization characteristics and strategies of Asian MNEs from countries at different levels of development, namely Singapore (an NIC) and Malaysia (a fast developing country), drawing specifically from ten case studies matched by industrial sectors. The key role government, ethnic network and relationships played in their internationalization was also found. Such institutional and social contextual factors need to be incorporated in explanations and research of MNEs, particularly Asian MNEs. It should be pointed out that our empirical database is not random and hence limited accordingly. Also the use of a case method has its inherent limitations (for example, small sample size, inability to perform statistical tests and so forth). Our research did not capture the operational strategies at the level of the subsidiary or JV. Hence the findings may not necessarily be generalizable beyond our sample and need verification by further research. As indicated there is a wide empirical research gap on Asian as well as Singaporean and Malaysian MNEs to be filled to provide further evidence and answers to many of the issues raised here. Areas for further research have been suggested above.

References

Bank Negara Malaysia (1994, 2002) *Annual Reports* (Kuala Lumpur: Bank Negara Malaysia) (and other years).

Cantwell, J. A. (1997) Globalization and development in Africa, in: J. H. Dunning & K. A. Hamdani (Eds) *The New Globalism and Developing Countries* (Tokyo and New York: United Nations University Press).

Chen, H. & Liu, M. C. (1998) Non economic elements of Taiwan's foreign direct investment, in: T. J. Chen (Ed.) *Taiwanese Firms in Southeast Asia*, pp. 97–120 (Cheltenham: Edward Elgar).

Chen, M. (1995) *Asian Business Systems: Chinese, Japanese and Korean Styles of Business* (London: Routledge).

Chen, T. J. (Ed.) (1998) *Taiwanese Firms in Southeast Asia* (Cheltenham: Edward Elgar).

Chetty, S. & Holm, D. B. (2000) Internationalization of small to medium-sized manufacturing firms, *International Business Review*, 9, pp. 77–93.

Chia, O.P. (1996) *Malaysian Investment in China* (Tokyo: Tokyo Institute of Developing Economies).

Coviello, N. E. & McAuley, A. (1999) Internationalisation and the smaller firms: a review of contemporary empirical research, *Management International Review*, 39(3), pp. 223–256.

Davidson, W. H. (1980) The location of foreign direct investment activity: country characteristics and experience effects, *Journal of International Business Studies*, 11(2), pp. 9–22.

Davidson, W. H. (1983) Market similarity and market selection: implications for international marketing strategy, *Journal of Business Research*, 11, pp. 439–456.

Dunning, J. H. (1977) Trade, location of economic activity and the multinational enterprise: a search for an eclectic approach, in: B. Ohlin, P. Hesselborn & P.M. Wükm (Eds.) *The International Allocation of Economic Activity* (New York: Holmes & Meier).

Dunning, J. H. (1981) Explaining the international direct investment position of countries: towards a dynamic or development approach, *Weltwirtschaftliches Archiv*, 117(1), pp. 30–64.

Dunnings, J. H. (1985) Quarterly research review: research on third world multinationals, *Multinational Business*, 4, pp. 39–45.

Dunning, J. H. (1986) The investment development and third world multinationals, in: K. M. Khan (Ed.) *Multinationals from the South: New Actors in the International Economy* (London: Pinter).

Dunning, J. H. (1988) The eclectic paradigm of international production: a restatement and some possible extensions, *Journal of International Business Studies*, 19(1), pp. 1–25.

Dunnings, J. H. (1993) *Multinational Enterprises and the Global Economy* (Workingham, UK: Addison-Wesley).

Dunning, J. H. (1995) Reappraising the eclectic paradigm in an age of alliance capitalism, *Journal of International Business Studies*, 26(3), pp. 461–491.

Dunning, J. H. & Narula, R. (Eds) (1996) *Foreign Direct Investments and Governments: Catalysts for Economic Restructuring* (London: Routledge).

Dunning, J. H., van Hoesel, R. & Narula, R. (1998) Third world multinationals revisited: new developments and theoretical implications, in: J. H. Dunning (Ed.) *Globalisation, Trade and Investment*, pp. 255–286 (Amsterdam: Elsevier).

Dun's Asia/Pacific Key Business Enterprises 1998/1999 (1998) (Chatswood, NSW: Dun and Bradstreet Information Services).

East Asia Analytical Unit (1995) *Overseas Chinese Business Networks in Asia* (Parkes, ACT: Department of Foreign Affairs and Trade).

Eisenhardt, K. M. (1989) Building theories from case study research, *Academy of Management Review*, 14(4), pp. 532–550.

Ernst, D. (2000) Inter-organizational knowledge outsourcing: what permits small Taiwanese firms to compete in the computer industry? *Asia Pacific Journal of Management*, 17(2), pp. 223–256.

Erramilli, M. K., Srivastava, R. & Kim, S. S. (1999) Internationalization theory and Korean multinationals, *Asia Pacific Journal of Management*, 16(1), pp. 29–45.

ESCAP/UNCTAD (Economic and Social Commission for Asia and the Pacific/United Nations Conference on Trade and Development) (1997) *Competitive Business Strategies of Asian Transnational Corporations* (New York: United Nations).

Hamilton, G. G. (1996) *Asian Business Networks* (Berlin: Walter de Gruyter).

Johanson, J. & Mattsson, L. (1988) Internationalization in industrial system - a network approach, in: P. J. Buckley & P. N. Ghauri (Eds) *The Internationalization of the Firm: A Reader*, pp. 303–321 (London: Academic Press).

Johanson, J. & Vahlne, J. E. (1977) The internationalisation process of the firm – A model of knowledge development and increasing foreign market commitment, *Journal of International Business Studies*, 8(1) (Spring/Summer), pp. 23–32.

Johanson, J. & Weidersheim-Paul, F. (1975) The internationalization of the firm: four Swedish cases, *Journal of Management Studies*, 12(3), pp. 305–322.

Kao, J. (1993) The worldwide web of Chinese business, *Harvard Business Review*, 71(2), March/April, pp. 24–36.

Kogut, B. & Singh, H. (1988) The effect of national culture on the choice of entry mode, *Journal of International Business Studies*, 19(3), pp. 183–198.

Lall, S. (1983) *The Third World Multinationals: The Spread of Third World Enterprises* (Chichester: J. Wiley & Sons).

Lall, S. (1996) The investment development path: some conclusions, in: J. H. Dunning & R. Narula (Eds) *Foreign Direct Investments and Governments: Catalysts for Economic Restructuring* (London: Routledge).

Li, P. P. (1994) Strategy profiles of indigenous MNEs from the NIEs: the case of South Korea and Taiwan, *The International Executive*, 36, pp. 147–170.

Li, P. P. (1998) The evolution of multinational firms from Asia – a longitudinal study of Taiwan's ACER group, *Journal of Organizational Change*, 11(4), pp. 321–337.

Li, P. P. (2003) Towards a geocentric theory of multinational evolution: the implications from the Asian MNEs as latecomers, *Asia Pacific Journal of Management*, 20(2), pp. 217–242.

Lu, Ding & Zhu, G. (1995) Singapore foreign direct investment in China: features and implications, *Asean Economic Bulletin*, 12(1), pp. 53–63.

Luo, Y. (1998) Strategic traits of foreign direct investment in China: a country of origin perspective, *Management International Review*, 38(2), pp. 109–132.

Luo, Y. (1999) Dimensions of knowledge: comparing Asian and western MNEs in China, *Asia Pacific Journal of Management*, 16(1), pp. 75–93.

Luo, Y. (2000) *Guanxi and Business.* (Singapore: World Scientific Publishing Co).

Mathews, J. A. (2003) Competitive advantage of the latecomer firms: a resource-based account of industrial catch-up strategies, *Asia Pacific Journal Of Management*, 19(4), pp. 467–488.

Miles, M. B. & Huberman, A. M. (1994) *Qualitative Data Analysis*, 2nd edn. (Thousand Oaks, CA: Sage).

Monkiewicz, J. (1986) Multinational enterprises of developing countries: some emerging trends, *Management International Review*, 26(3), pp. 67–79.

Murphy, J. L. & Walsh, D. (Eds) (1998) *Major Companies of the Far East and Australasia 1998*, Vols 1 & 2. (London: Graham & Whiteside).

Nohria, N. & Eccles, R. G. (1992) *Networks and Organizations* (Cambridge, MA: Harvard Business Press).

Oliver, C. (1990) Determinants of interorganizational relationships: integrations and future directions, *Academy of Management Review*, 15(2), pp. 241–265.

Pang, E. F. (1995) Staying global and going regional: Singapore's inward and outward direct investments, in: Nomura Research Institute & Institute of Southeast Asian Studies *The New Wave of Foreign Direct Investment in Asia*, pp. 111–130 (Singapore: Institute of Southeast Asian Studies).

Pananond, P. & Zeithaml, C. P. (1998) The international expansion process of MNEs from developing countries: a case study of Thailand's CP group, *Asia Pacific Journal of Management*, 15(2), pp. 163–184.

Pangarkar, N. (1998) The Asian multinational corporation: strategies, performance and key challenges, *Asia Pacific Journal of Management*, 15(2), pp. 109–118.

Rajan, K. S. & Pangarkar, N. (2000) Mode of entry choice: an empirical study of Singaporean multinationals, *Asia Pacific Journal Of Management*, 7(1), pp. 49–66.

Redding, S. G. (1990) *The Spirit of Chinese Capitalism* (New York: Walter de Gruyter).

Rogayah Haji Mat Din (1999) Malaysian reverse investments: trends and strategies, *Asia Pacific Journal of Management*, 16, pp. 469–496.

Shane, S. (1994) The effect of national culture on the choice between licensing and direct foreign investment, *Strategic Management Journal*, 15(8), pp. 627–642.

Sim, A. B. & Ali, Y. (2001) Joint ventures of Asian and western multinational enterprises: a comparative analysis of western, Japanese, NIC & LDC firms, *Asia Pacific Business Review*, 8(1), pp. 37–57.

Sim, A. B. & Pandian, J. R. (2002) internationalization strategies of emerging Asian MNEs: case evidence on Taiwanese firms, *Journal of Asian Business*, 18(1), pp. 67–80.

Tan, C. H. (1995) *Venturing Overseas: Singapore's External Wing* (Singapore: McGraw-Hill).

Ting, W. L. (1985) *Business and Technological Dynamics in Newly Industrializing Asia* (Westport, CT: Quorum Books).

Tolentino, P. E. (1993) *Technological Innovation and Third World Multinationals* (London: Routledge).

Tolentino, P. E. (2000) *Multinational Corporations: Emergence and Evolution* (London: Routledge).

Tsang, E. W. K. (1999) Internationalization as a learning process: Singapore MNCs in China, *Academy of Management Executive*, 13(1), pp. 91–101.

Ulgado, F. M., Yu, C. & Negandhi, A. R. (1994) Multinational enterprises from Asian developing countries: management and organizational characteristics, *International Business Review*, 3(2), pp. 123–133.

van Hoesel, R. (1999) *New Multinational Enterprises from Korea and Taiwan* (London: Routledge).

Vernon, R. (1966) International investment and international trade in the product life cycle, *Quarterly Journal of Economics*, 80, pp. 190–207.

Vernon, R. (1979) The product cycle hypothesis in the new international environment, *Oxford Bulletin of Economics and Statistics*, 41, pp. 255–267.

Weidenbaum, M. & Hughes, S. (1996) *The Bamboo Network: How Expatriate Chinese Entrepreneurs are Creating a New Economic Superpower in Asia* (New York: The Free Press).

Welch, L. S. & Loustarinen, R. (1988) Internationalization: evolution of a concept, *Journal of General Management*, 14(2), pp. 34–55.

Wells, L. T. (1983) *Third World Multinationals: The Rise of Foreign Investment from Developing Countries* (Cambridge, MA: The MIT Press).

World Bank (1993) *The East Asian Miracle: Economic Growth and Public Policy* (New York: Oxford University Press).

Yeung, H. W. C. (1994) Transnational corporations from Asian developing countries: their characteristics and competitive edge, *Journal of Asian Business*, 10(4), pp. 17–58.

Yeung, H. W. C. (1997) Cooperative strategies and Chinese business networks, in: P. W. Beamish & P. Killing (Eds), *Cooperative Strategies Asian Pacific Perspectives* (San Francisco: The New Lexington Press). pp. 3–21.

Yeung, H. W. C. (1998a) The political economy of transnational corporations: a study of the regionalization of Singaporean firms, *Political Geography*, 17(4), pp. 389–416.

Yeung, H. W. C. (1998b) Transnational economic synergy and business networks: the case of two-way investment between Malaysia and Singapore, *Regional Studies*, 23(8), pp. 687–706.

Yeung, H. W. C. (1999) Introduction: Competing in the Global Economy: The Globalization of Business Firms from Emerging Economies, in: H. W. C. Yeung (Ed.) *The Globalization of Business Firms from Emerging Economies*, Vol. 1, pp. xiii–xlvi, (Cheltenham: Edward Elgar).

Yeung, H. W. C. & Olds, K. (Eds) (2000) *Globalization of Chinese Business Firms* (London: Macmillan Press).

Yin, R. K. (1994) *Case Study Research* (Thousands Oaks, CA: Sage).

Young, S., Huang, C. H. & McDermott, M. (1996) Internationalization and competitive catch-up processes: case study evidence on Chinese multinational enterprises, *Management International Review*, 36(4), pp. 295–314.

Zutshi, R. K. & Gibbons, P. T. (1998) The internationalization process of Singapore government-linked companies: a contextual perspective, *Asia Pacific Journal of Management*, 15(2), pp. 219–246.

Appendix

Table 1. Summary of Singapore case studies

Characteristics	Textile Firm	Electrical Firm	Food Products	Electronics (Creative Technology)	Diversified (Keppel)
Product	Garments, Property, Lifestyle	Electrical installation products	Milling & foods	Multimedia software & hardware products for PC	Diversified marine, eng., property & services
Size (1998 sales)	US$340 million	US$134 million	US$89 million	US$1.3 billion	US$2.12 billion
Overseas Production Locations & Year Established	Malaysia (1966) China Hong Kong Sri Lanka (1993) Cambodia (1988) Myanmar (1997) + other locations	Indonesia (1992) Malaysia (late 1980s) China(1987) Hong Kong (1980) Sri Lanka (1990) Vietnam (1998) + other associates' locations	Sri Lanka (1977) China (1985) Indonesia (1970–sold 1982)	Extensive global network in >80 countries (mainly distribution; production in 5 countries) USA first (1988)	Extensive locations Marine(P'pines, UAE) Eng.(Asia, America, Europe) Property (Asia, America, Europe, Aust) Others (Asia, 1st 1975)
Entry Strategy	JVs (21–86%)	JVs (49– > 90%) Acquisitions	BOT JVs (20–40%)	WOS & acquisitions JVs	JVs WOS & Acquisitions
Key Motives	Low cost bases Quota	Market expansion Low cost	Market expansion Low cost	Market expansion Technology	Market expansion Regionalisation drive
Strategic Advantages & Traits	Cost-based Regional expertise Diversification Early movers in overseas mfg. (1966)	Product line-up Cost-based mfg Organic approach to overseas development (since 1980s)	Related diversification downstream Early movers in overseas mfg (1970s)	Technology leadership Distribution network Brand recognitionProduct line-up	GLC Diversification Beachhead approach in overseas expansion (P'pines in 1975)
Networks & Alliances	JVs (ethnic network) Regional grouping Licensing	JVs Regional grouping Licensing	JVs	Alliances Licensing JVs (ethnic networks)	GLC links JVs Strategic alliances
Future Plans	Consolidate as a regional company	Diversify into new market segments & products, value adding	Strengthen downstream diversifications (e.g. franchising)	Technology & product development Internet based business	Restructuring & cost reduction More regional (ASEAN) focus

Abbrev.: mfg = manufacturing; JV = joint venture; WOS = wholly owned subsidiary.

Table 2. Summary of Malaysian Case Studies

Characteristics	Textile Firm	Electrical Firm	Food Products	Electronics	Diversified (Lion Group)
Product	Textile, Garments, & Property	Diversified electrical & industrial products	Flour, edible oils, foods	Industrial electronics products	Conglomerate (steel, motor vehicles, retailing, foods, property, plantations)
Size (1998 sales)	US$88 million	US$144 million	US$1.16 billion	US$26 million	US$1.80 billion
Overseas Production Locations & Year Established	Sri Lanka (1993)	P'pines (1990) Indonesia (1992) China (1996) Australia (1996)	Myanmar, Singapore Vietnam (1998/99) Affiliates in Asia	China (1995) Australia (1995– closed 1997)	Indonesia (1972) Taiwan (1992) China (1993) USA, Germany (1990–sold) & other locations
Entry Strategy	WOS	JVs (35–80%), WOS Buy over JV stakes	JVs Technical support to affiliates	WOS Acquisition	JVs, WOS
Key Motives	Low cost Quota	Market expansion	Cost Market expansion	Market expansion R&D	Market expansion Diversification
Strategic Advantages & Traits	Cost-based Diversification to property, etc. Reputation & quality	Engineering expertise Product reputation & niches (adaptation)	Organic growth Related diversification Branding initiated	Technical expertise Competitive pricing Related diversification	Market knowledge & network Localization & staff development Long-term view
Networks & Alliances	Member of regional grouping JVs & established customers links	JVs Licensing Principals	Member of regional group & network JV partners Overseas principals	R&D partners Product Principals	Networks (Chinese) JVs
Future Plans	Another factory in Sri Lanka; bases in Mexico & Middle East; high value segments; consolidate property business	Expansion in China & another ASEAN co. Divestment to 3 core businesses	Expand capacity in Myanmar Increase regional operations Build up own brands	Looking for partners in China; aim for 50% overseas business Related diversification	Restructuring & rationalisation China focus on retailing, brewing & motorcycle

Abbrev.: mfg = manufacturing; P'pines = Philippines; WOS = wholly owned subsidiary; JV = Joint Venture.

Human Resources, Labour Markets and Unemployment: The Impact of the SARS Epidemic on the Service Sector in Singapore

GRACE O. M. LEE* & MALCOLM WARNER**
*Department of Public and Social Administration, City University of Hong Kong, China,
**Wolfson College and Judge Business School, University of Cambridge, UK

Introduction

On 12 March 2003, the World Health Organization (WHO) issued a 'global alert' on Severe Acute Respiratory Syndrome (SARS), a newly emerging respiratory illness associated with potentially significant morbidity and mortality (World Health Organization, 2003). International travel appeared to be responsible for the rapid intercontinental spread of this disease, and by 31 May 2003, SARS had affected 32 countries with a total number of 8,360 cases (916 proving fatal overall, with 33 dying in Singapore, we shall shortly see) (World Health Organization, 2003).

The outbreaks beyond the mainland People's Republic of China (PRC), namely in the Hong Kong Special Administrative Region, Singapore and Vietnam, as well as in Toronto and elsewhere, were initiated by cases that were mostly imported from *Guangdong,* the southernmost Chinese province, before the virus had been identified and before appropriate measures had been put in place to prevent its transmission (Hsu *et al.*, 2003; Lee *et al.*, 2003; Poutanen *et al.*, 2003). Singapore, like Hong Kong, has one of the busiest airports in South East Asia, and has numerous arrivals each day from countries in the region affected by health dysfunctions. The city-state was, and still is, therefore potentially vulnerable to the importation of SARS that could in turn initiate new cases.

This study begins with a brief background account of the imported cases of SARS to Singapore and then goes on to analyse the impact on the Singapore economy, its labour-market and one particularly vulnerable sub-sector of its now pre-eminent service industries (Khatri, 2004: 221–222), namely hotels (and hospitality). Thus, as will be apparent in our analysis, epidemics, mortality and urbanization are now arguably increasingly interlinked and mass air-travel has become a potentially critical transmission-belt in the contemporary, globalized world (see Morens *et al.*, 2003).

For some time, studies have attempted to estimate the economic burden of an epidemic based on the private and non-private medical costs associated with the disease (see, for example, Lee & McKibbin, 2003). The costs include private, as well as public, expenditures on diagnosing and treating the disease. The costs may be magnified by the need to maintain sterile environments, implement prevention measures, and carry out basic research. The epidemic costs can be substantial for major epidemics, such as AIDS. According to the UNAIDS (the Joint United Nations Programme on HIV/AIDS), at present 42 million people globally live with HIV/AIDS. The medical costs of various treatments of HIV patients, including highly active antiretroviral therapies (HAARTS) are estimated to be more than US$2,000 per patient per year. In the Southern African regions, the total HIV-related health service costs, based on assumed coverage rate of 10 per cent, ranges from 0.3 to 4.3 per cent of gross domestic product (GDP) (Haacker, 2002).

The costs of disease also include incomes foregone as a result of the disease-related morbidity and mortality. Malaria, for example, kills more than 1 million people a year. The HIV/AIDS disease, for instance, was estimated to have claimed 3.1 million lives in 2002. Foregone income is normally estimated by the value of lost workdays due to the illness. In the case of mortality, foregone income is estimated by the capitalized value of future lifetime earnings by the disease-related death, based on projected incomes for different age groups and age-specific survival rates. This cost can be substantial for large-scale epidemics (Lee & McKibbin, 2003). Given its ultimately relatively low morbidity and mortality, why then had the economic impact of SARS appeared to be so threatening? Much of the potential economic impact appeared to stem from the high degree of uncertainty and fear generated by SARS, as we shall shortly see.

The few Singapore residents who left the country, whether in panic or for other reasons, found that an airport official inserted a small brown card into their passports warning immigration officials at the destination that they 'may have been exposed to SARS'. At the airport in Manila, passengers disembarking from

Singapore Airlines flights were met by a Philippine nurse, who collected 'accomplished health', forms swearing that they were not suffering from a high fever, breathing difficulty, or other SARS symptoms (ibid.). Philippine officials manning the immigration counters wore surgical masks to protect themselves from inhaling the virus. In Thailand, travellers from stricken areas were also required to wear masks and stay in their hotels, or undergo a medical check every three days of their stay. Offenders could be punished by up to six months in jail or a maximum fine of US$235 and 'SARS-control officers' were said to be 'operating undercover' to ensure compliance (*TTG Daily News*, 2003).

International cooperation was judged to be crucial and bilateral meetings were arranged between the Association of South East Asian Nations (ASEAN) health ministers and their counterparts from China, Japan and South Korea. There was a united front on steps such as pre-departure screening of travellers and the exchange of information to assist in tracing and quarantining contacts of SARS patients (Henderson, 2003). Another forum standardized health declaration cards for departing passengers and implemented mandatory temperature tests at international airports (Henderson, 2003). People across Asia opted to stay at home to reduce the probability of infection. Service exports, in particular tourism-related exports, were to be particularly hard hit.

Hypotheses

In order to take our research one step further, we have formulated a set of appropriate hypotheses (see Lee & Warner, 2005) modified from those we had earlier used to date in our studies of the effects of the epidemic in China and Hong Kong, respectively:-

 (i) *The greater the adverse impact of SARS on the Singapore economy, the greater will be the negative impact on the service sector and specifically on the hotel industry.*
 (ii) *The greater the adverse impact of SARS on consumer demand in the Singapore hotel industry, the greater will be the negative impact on the related demand for labour in terms of hotel employees in specific hotel groups in the industry.*
 (iii) *The greater the adverse impact on the demand for labour in the Singapore hotel industry, the greater will be the negative impact on the labour-market in terms of the HRM implications such as lay-offs and redundancy among hotel employees in specific hotel groups in the industry.*

Methodology

In attempting to study the impact of SARS on the Singapore economy and specifically on hotel industry employment, *we adopted a two-pronged methodology*. First, we generated a database of information about the SARS epidemic, its economic as well as its HRM implications, by using the Internet, library resources and literature searches, taking into full account the limitations of official statistical sources, where used. Second, we carried out on-site empirical field research, involving interviewing over twenty key decision makers in the Singapore economy and its hotel industry, such as government officials, senior managers and union officials over the period of the epidemic and its aftermath.

The Importation of SARS in Singapore

The first fatal cases of 'atypical pneumonia', as it was first called, probably occurred in Guangdong province in southern China in November 2002 (Lee & Warner, 2005). The term SARS (Severe Acute Respiratory Syndrome) appears to have been first used for a patient in Hanoi who was visiting Vietnam, became ill on 26 February 2003, and was evacuated to Hong Kong, where he died on 12 March. This first case in Hanoi had stayed at a hotel, in Kowloon, Hong Kong, at the same time as a 64-year-old doctor who had been earlier treating pneumonia cases in southern China. This doctor stayed at the Metropole Hotel and was admitted to hospital on 22 February. He died from 'respiratory failure' soon afterwards (Tomlinson & Cockram, 2003). His was the first known case of SARS in Hong Kong and appears to have been the source of infection for most, if not all cases in Hong Kong, as well as possibly for the cohorts in Singapore, Taiwan, Thailand, Vietnam, as well as in Canada, a number of European countries, such as Germany and Ireland and the USA.

Of the six persons who imported SARS to Singapore, all were residents of Singapore and had visited Hong Kong (plus Guangdong province in two cases and Beijing in one case). Cases A and B travelled together to Hong Kong at the end of February 2003, and stayed on the 9th floor of the Metropole Hotel (Wilder-Smith *et al.*, 2003). They were likely to have been infected by the Chinese doctor from Guangdong, a SARS patient who had stayed on the same floor of the Metropole Hotel on 21 and 22 February, most probably in passing contact in the elevator. Upon their return to Singapore on 25 February, they developed a fever, and a few days later a dry cough, being subsequently admitted on 1 March to two different hospitals in Singapore and isolated six days later. The first case in Singapore admitted to Tan Tock Seng Hospital infected 20 close contacts (11 healthcare workers, and nine relatives or friends). These, in their turn, passed it on to 71 people (all healthcare workers, patients and relatives), who then contributed to the current epidemic in Singapore. Few infectious diseases are so selective for healthcare workers. Most of the 'nosocomial' SARS infections have occurred in individuals looking after undiagnosed patients before the widespread use of complete respiratory and contact precautions (Tambyah, 2002). Isolation and infection control for these patients was instituted on 6 March, hospital-wide infection control was enforced on 14 March, and Tan Tock Seng Hospital became the SARS-designated hospital on 22 March.

Case C was unrelated to the first cases but had been a guest at the Metropole Hotel in Hong Kong during the same period, and returned on 25 February. She developed a fever on 27 February, was admitted to Tan Tock Seng Hospital on 5 March, and was isolated the next day. Cases D and E were a mother (42 years old) and son (18 years old) who had returned on 23 March from visiting relatives in Guangdong province and Hong Kong. They developed symptoms within two days after arrival in Singapore, and were admitted and placed in isolation on 25

Table 1. Imported cases of SARS to Singapore, 25 February–31 May 2003

Duration of SARS symptoms in the community (days)	Interval between admission and isolation (days)	Imported cases (age, gender, ethnicity)	Imported from	Secondary cases	Outcome
4	6	23, female, Chinese	Hong Kong, the Metropole Hotel	20	Recovered
4	6	22, female, Chinese	Hong Kong, the Metropole Hotel	0	Recovered
7	1	33, female, Chinese	Hong Kong, the Metropole Hotel	0	Recovered
1	0	42, female, Chinese Indonesian (resident in Singapore)	Guangdong, Hong Kong	0	Recovered
2	0	18, male, Indonesian (resident in Singapore)	Guangdong, Hong Kong	0	Recovered
0	0	29, female, Chinese	Hong Kong, Beijing	0	Died

Source: Wilder-Smith *et al.* (2003)

and 27 March respectively. The father and other son who had travelled with them were not infected.

Case F was a 29-year-old designer who had been on a business trip to Hong Kong and Beijing and developed a high fever and a cough while in the latter city. She consulted two doctors in Beijing, but the diagnosis of SARS was not made at that time. She became very unwell and breathless on her return flight from the capital to Singapore on 26 March, but no precautions were taken on the aeroplane, as her diagnosis was not known. Immediately after arrival, her mother took her in a taxi to Tan Tock Seng Hospital, where she was isolated in the Intensive Care Unit. She developed acute respiratory distress syndrome and multi-organ failure, and died ten days later. Both the mother and the taxi driver were quarantined, but neither developed SARS. The Ministry of Health was able to contact 46 of the 47 passengers, as well as all the nine crew members, and they were put under home quarantine order and active surveillance for ten days; none of these became SARS patients.

Three of the six imported cases developed symptoms of SARS only after arrival in Singapore, whereas three had symptoms on the return flight to Singapore (cases A and B had fever only, case F had fever, cough and shortness of breath). The first two were admitted to a hospital at a mean of four days after the onset of symptoms, and placed in isolation six days later. Cases C to F had symptoms of SARS in Singapore for a mean of 2.5 days, and all were immediately placed in isolation after hospital admission (except case C: after one day). Cases A and B were therefore without infection-control measures for ten days, and cases C to F for a mean of 3.6 days. Only case A resulted in secondary transmission. No healthcare workers and no other contacts were infected by cases B to F (see Table 1).

The Economic Impact of SARS

We first present the available background of macroeconomic evidence from authoritative sources from our database, we then, second, set out microeconomic and HRM data collected at first hand by ourselves, followed by a discussion of their implications and last, our conclusions.

The Chief Economist for World Bank East Asia estimated that a direct impact effect of SARS would be to reduce East Asian growth by 0.4 to 0.5 per cent of

Table 2. Gross domestic product (GDP) forecast: before and after SARS

Country	Previous GDP forecast (%)	New GDP forecast (%)
China	7.5	7.5
Hong Kong	2.5	1.5
Indonesia	4.0	3.7
Malaysia	5.0	4.0
Singapore	3.5	2.0
Taiwan	3.5	3.3
Thailand	4.5	4.3

Source: Asia Pacific Business Network (2003) Vol. 7, No. 9.

GDP, bringing the estimated cost of SARS in the range of US$20 to 25 billion, a sizeable amount by any calculation (World Bank, 2003). The Asian Development Bank (ADB) calculated the likely effect of the disease under different epidemic scenarios, and forecast losses totalling up to US$20 billion in the four most vulnerable economies, namely China, Hong Kong, South Korea and Taiwan. ING Financial Markets cut its GDP forecasts for 2003 for Hong Kong, Singapore, Malaysia and Taiwan (see Table 2).

Singapore's rate of growth in the service sector, turned sharply negative in the second quarter of 2003, falling to − 4.2 per cent from positive growth of 1.7 per cent in the first quarter of 2003 (Ministry of Trade and Industry, 2004). Uncertainties associated with the war in Iraq, notwithstanding the SARS outbreak, also caused the growth momentum (on an annualized quarter-on-quarter basis) to dip sharply by 11 per cent, after an increase of 1.4 per cent in the previous quarter (see Table 3).

Since the service sector accounts for about 65.7 per cent of Singapore's gross domestic product (see Table 4) and the SARS crisis had a hugely damaging impact, it led to a 3.9 per cent fall in GDP in the second quarter of 2003 (see Figure 1).

There were a number of key ways by which the SARS outbreak could affect a given economy. We have simplified the *causal* links in our labour-market model to exemplify the main variables we have chosen to highlight, in order to present the human resources consequences (see Figure 2). One link may be seen as operating through 'supply-shocks'. If the outbreak could not be effectively contained (see Gerberding, 2003), the workforce would be reduced because of illness or precautionary measures to prevent the spread of SARS, thereby disrupting business operations and production (Asian Development Bank, 2003). There was also the risk of a demand 'shock', as people just stopped shopping and became paralysed into economic indecision, as appeared to be the case in Hong Kong (Field interviews, 1 August 2003).

Why had the economic threat arising from SARS appeared to be so prima facie serious? While SARS did pose significant medical risks, it also exercised a disproportionately sharp *psychological* impact on people. In the short run, its potential economic consequences arose in good measure from public perception and fear of the disease, harking back to accounts of medieval Asia or Europe. An understanding of 'fear epidemiology' is therefore important because early warning-systems, monitoring data from a large number of people, may not be able

Table 3. GDP of services producing industries, 2003 (unit: million S$)

	First quarter	Second quarter	Third quarter	Fourth quarter
Total	25,019.0	23,699.3	25,331.3	26,016.4
Wholesale & Retail Trade	4,849.0	5,052.1	5,100.9	5,684.0
Hotels & Restaurants	832.9	613.6	740.2	811.5
Transport & Communications	4,378.0	3,705.0	4,611.0	4,877.3
Financial Services	4,355.2	4,797.8	4,950.2	4,254.5
Business Services	5,322.5	5,181.7	5,246.4	5,274.9
Other Services Industries	5,281.4	4,349.1	4,682.6	5,114.2

Source: *Economic Survey of Singapore 2003*, Singapore Department of Statistics website.

Table 4. Gross domestic product by industry, 1999-2003 (unit: million S$)

Industry	1999	2000	2001	2002	2003
Goods Producing Industries	46,165	54,573	49,137	52,470	52,221
Manufacturing	32,521	42,078	36,548	41,080	41,601
Construction	11,125	9,966	9,444	8,530	7,834
Utilities	2,319	2,339	2,967	2,694	2,622
Other Goods Industries	200	189	178	166	164
Services Producing Industries	89,594	97,364	99,563	101,079	100,066
Wholesale & Retail Trade	18,008	20,003	19,079	19,511	20,686
Hotels & Restaurants	3,272	3,545	3,628	3,503	2,998
Transport & Communications	16,634	18,236	17,403	18,223	17,571
Financial Services	17,503	17,755	19,075	18,921	18,358
Business Services	19,637	21,518	22,214	21,641	21,026
Other Services Industries	14,540	16,307	18,164	19,280	19,427

Source: *Economic Survey of Singapore First Quarter 2004*, Singapore Department of Statistics website.

to discriminate between a 'biological epidemic' and an 'epidemic of fear' (Eysenbach, 2003).

Epidemics have clearly often had a major impact on world history, as is well documented, often with wide economic consequences (Cipolla, 1976). The medieval 'Black Death' spread across the Middle East and Europe from the fourteenth century onwards, allegedly involving bubonic plague, (but which may possibly have been closer to the more recently diagnosed Ebola virus) and it was one of the best-known examples, devastating both economies and societies. Some say it originally came from East Asia, carried by fleas on the backs of rats but the latter appear not to be mentioned in medieval historical accounts. It allegedly killed as many as one-third of the total population of Europe between the years 1346 to 1350, some say even up to a half in many towns.

Hunger and famine have been long seen as going hand in hand with the decline in medieval trade. Rising mortality rates adversely affected both the demand for and supply of goods, services and the labour-inputs that went into them, then as now.

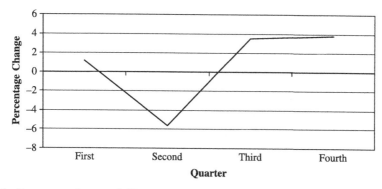

Figure 1. Percentage change of GDP over corresponding period of previous year, 2003 (unit: percentage). *Source*: *Economic Survey of Singapore 2003*, Singapore Department of Statistics website.

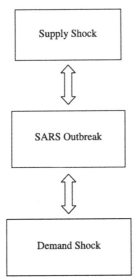

Figure 2. The economic impact of SARS

The English classical economist Malthus (1766–1834) had studied the major impact of plagues on populations and economies, as checks on demographic growth (Pressman, 1999: 29*ff.*). 'Crises' such as plagues led to peaks of mortality that linked population changes and labour supply with key economic variables (Floud & McCloskey, 1981). However, Malthusian gloom was challenged on a number of counts; some economists saw technology, rather than demographic shifts, as the 'engine of growth' in both agriculture and industry (Cipolla, 1976:136).

Plagues also led, according to many accounts, to mass hysteria, the burning of witches and the persecution of local Jewish communities, who were soon blamed for spreading the disease by their Christian neighbours (see, for example, Singer, 1998). One of the 'lessons of history' from past epidemics, like that of outbreaks of cholera and the numerous plagues that blighted medieval Europe (Watts, 1997), was the frequent pattern of 'victimizing and stigmatizing of helpless members of minority groups and the indifference of public officials callous to human suffering' (Briggs, 1961). 'Demonization', as a phenomenon, took root in most parts of Europe around this time, as simplistic explanations were sought by the afflicted. Zealous campaigns against witchcraft, in turn, continued long after.

Closer to the present day, the officially-outlawed Falun Gong cult was condemned by the Chinese government for allegedly 'hindering the prevention and control of SARS in China'. The cult members were accused of travelling to places to distribute printed material promoting the group; getting close to hospitals to contract the SARS virus for the purpose of spreading the disease; and linking it to 'doomsday' prophecies, claiming that those who practise Falun Gong could avoid catching it (ibid.). They were also accused of obliging their adherents to refuse treatment, as contamination was a 'sign' of 'being chosen'.

The most recent 'catastrophic' health disaster, early in the last century, was the global influenza epidemic just after the First World War ended in 1918, the so-called 'Spanish Flu'; it allegedly killed more people than all those who died in armed combat. Such epidemics, we argue, represent *exogenous*, as well as *endogenous*, 'shocks' that can have far-reaching impacts on economic activity, as well as inflicting human tragedy.

The pronounced psychological impact of SARS may arguably be attributed to the combination of two accompanying characteristics of the illness: the inexpensive and rapid transmission of information due to the development of modern media and communication technologies in MacLuhan's 'global village'; and perhaps more importantly the lack of sufficient medical information on SARS (Fan, 2003). This stimulus may be conceptualized as inducing a 'demand-shock', particularly impacting on consumption. In specific locations with a high incidence of SARS, physical movement of people was restricted, either voluntarily or involuntarily, thus potentially reducing consumer spending.

A 24-hour vegetable wholesale market in Singapore, for example, was ordered to shut down for ten days, as three workers there were diagnosed with SARS and where one of these had died. The Singapore government closed all schools temporarily on 26 March 2003, to prevent the spread of SARS, and the vast majority of Singapore's inhabitants – about one-quarter of whom are foreigners – had confined themselves to their homes for fear of catching the disease (*Business Week Online*, 2003). People had opted to stay at home to reduce the probability of infection. With schools closed, their offspring were at home all day, yet the parents were afraid to take them out for fear of exposing them to SARS. Playgrounds and swimming pools in many private housing estates were deserted – and at some complexes, the companies that manage them had even declared the areas off-limits (ibid.). Attendance at Singapore's exotic animal parks soon plummeted. The playground at Singapore's zoological garden was closed for 'renovations'. The Roman Catholic church in Singapore even suspended confessions, allowing priests to forgive all churchgoers for their sins instead (Crampton, 2003). Even the hospitals were nearly deserted; outpatients were missing appointments with their physicians for fear they would catch SARS by entering the facility. All this marked a major lifestyle-shift for Singapore residents.

SARS, we may thus surmise, initially affects the economy by mainly reducing demand. Consumer confidence did in fact dramatically decline in a number of economies, leading to a significant reduction in private consumption spending. Much of the impact stemmed from the great degree of uncertainty and fear generated by SARS. Three foreign chief executive officers (CEOs) returned from a conference in Hong Kong, where SARS was spreading even more rapidly than in Singapore, only to be told by their local colleagues to work from home in case they had come in contact with the virus (ibid.). Companies that manage office complexes all over Singapore studied contingency plans to shut down if SARS was detected in their buildings. They had warned tenants to procure personal computers for their employees at home to ensure that they were productive (ibid.).

Service exports, in particular those that were tourism-related, as noted earlier, were to be most hard hit. Investment was affected by reduced overall demand, heightened uncertainties, and increased risks. An executive of a US multinational with its regional headquarters in Singapore noted that 'between the [Iraq] war and SARS, every buyer in the world has an excuse not to make a commitment, especially for big projects' (*Business Week*, 2003). The possible fall in the demand for labour related to goods and services that people would not be buying would, from the specific focus of our study, therefore to be taken into account.

Although SARS had affected every component of aggregate demand, private consumption had particularly borne the brunt of the impact. Services involving face-to-face contact had been dealt a severe blow by the widespread fear of infection through such interactions. Tourism, transportation (particularly airlines), and retailing had been the hardest-hit sectors, as consumers shunned entertainment venues, restaurants, shops and so on, with many tourists cancelling trips. Singapore-based business people were especially unnerved by a 10 April government decree that all expatriates who left Singapore and re-entered from a SARS-afflicted country, including Canada, must be quarantined for ten days. That made frequent business travel impractical. The service sector shrank by 3.1 per cent, mainly reflecting the impact of the SARS outbreak on tourism and transport related industries (Ministry of Trade and Industry, 2004). It was thus very likely that there would be closely linked implications in terms of human resources and labour-markets.

Asian economies, as we have noted earlier, are heavily dependent on tourism, which accounts for at least 10 per cent of GDP in most of the affected countries. Destinations such as Hong Kong and Singapore are heavily dependent on the sort of service industries that demand regular and varied human contact – something many in the region were eager to avoid during the alert: these sectors are very labour intensive (see Table 5).

According to an analysis of the International Labour Organization (ILO), reduced travel due to new concerns over SARS, combined with the ongoing economic downturn, was set to cut up to 8 million jobs in the Asian tourism sector in 2003 (Belau, 2003). Airline passenger loads to Asia dropped by up to 70 per cent, and overall reservations in Asia were down 30 to 40 per cent in 2003, according to the World Tourism Organization. According to official statistics in April 2003, passenger rates had fallen by 60 per cent in Hong Kong, as compared to 40 per cent in Singapore and South Korea; 37 per cent in Bangkok and 36 per cent in Kuala Lumpur. The decline in tourist arrivals shocked Singapore – the figures were 61.6 per cent lower over the previous year in April 2003, contracted by 70.7 per cent in May (Singapore Tourism Board, 2003). Passenger traffic at

Table 5. Number of Employees by Industry, 1998–2002 (Unit: thousand persons)

Industry	1998	1999	2000	2001	2002
Manufacturing	404.4	395.6	434.9	384.0	367.6
Construction	131.3	130.7	274.0	124.9	119.1
Wholesale & Retail Trade	281.2	278.9	286.8	303.6	304.4
Hotels & Restaurants	118.9	121.2	114.5	128.3	125.3
Transport, Storage & Communications	206.4	203.7	196.5	228.2	218.8
Financial Intermediation	108.5	104.6	96.3	108.7	107.9
Real Estate, Renting & Business Activities	184.3	196.8	226.2	243.1	237.4
Community, Social & Personal Services	418.0	436.3	452.7	506.2	518.7
Others	16.8	18.0	12.9	19.7	18.4

Source: Department of Statistics, *Yearbook of Statistics Singapore 2003*, Singapore: Department of Statistics, 2003, p.45

Changi Airport was halved in April. Dragged down by the dismal performance of the air transport and the communications segments, the sector shrank by 10 per cent in the second quarter of 2003, compared with 1 per cent growth in the first three months of the year (Ministry of Trade and Industry, 2003). Air passengers and cargo handled fell by 50 per cent and 6.7 per cent respectively in the second quarter (ibid.).

As visitor arrivals had dropped, hotel occupancy rates had slumped significantly in China and Hong Kong, as well as in Singapore. The hotels and restaurants sector in the last of these shrank sharply in the second quarter by 33 per cent, after sliding 5.1 per cent in the first quarter of 2003 (Ministry of Trade and Industry, 2003). Visitor arrivals plunged by 62 per cent in the second quarter, while hotel occupancy rates fell to an average of 20 to 30 per cent, compared to normal levels of 70 per cent or above (ibid.). Revenues at some restaurants had halved. Attendance at main attractions was at least 50 per cent down and retail sales dropped by 10 to 50 per cent (Henderson, 2003). The future of many travel agents, most of which are small scale, was threatened and the industry overall was estimated to be sustaining weekly losses of S$23 million (US$13.1 million) (*Straits Times*, 2003a).

Unemployment in Singapore rose to a 17-year high of 4.7 per cent in 2003 (see Table 6). The resident unemployment rate jumped to 6.0 per cent in the second quarter although this was less than the Hong Kong jobless total over the period.

According to the Ministry of Manpower (MOM) of Singapore, overall employment diminished by 25,963 in the second quarter of 2003 – not only higher than the total number of jobs lost in 2002 – but also the largest quarterly decline since the mid-1980s recession (*Xinhua*, 2003). The Ministry attributed the heavy losses in jobs – 47 per cent in the service sector, 28 per cent in construction, and 25 per cent in manufacturing – to the weak economic conditions and the adverse impact of SARS, in particular. Another estimated job loss total was 33,160 posts, directly or indirectly (World, Travel and Tourism Council, 2003). In order to cut

Table 6. Number of unemployed residents and unemployment rate, 1993–2003

Year	Unemployed residents (thousand persons)	Resident unemployment rate (%)	Unemployment rate (%)
1993	29	2.1	1.9
1994	31	2.2	2.0
1995	32	2.2	2.0
1996	33	2.2	2.0
1997	30	2.0	1.8
1998	54	3.5	3.2
1999	61	3.8	3.5
2000	60	3.7	3.1
2001	63	3.8	3.3
2002	82	4.9	4.4
2003	92	5.3	4.7

Source: Manpower Research and Statistics, Singapore Ministry of Manpower website, http://www.mom. gov.sg/MOM/CDA_PopUp/1,1135,4023----5119--,00.html

costs and sharpen competitiveness, big corporations like Singapore Airlines (SIA) and PSA Corporation (one of the world's leading port operators) where retrenchment had never been heard for more than two decades, started to lay off employees (ibid.). SIA's subsidiary, SilkAir (flying mainly regional routes), suspended 35 weekly flights, about 25 per cent of its capacity, and terminated the contracts of eight expatriate pilots (Henderson, 2003). The restructuring and privatization of the Housing Development Board (HDB) brought on the deletion of another 2,600 jobs. About 9,500 workers were laid off in the first six months of 2003 (*Xinhua*, 2003). Unlike previous retrenchments that only affected blue-collar workers, white-collar employees were also affected by the SARS crisis. The resident unemployment rate increased to 5.3 per cent, mostly reflecting the adverse impact of the spread of SARS since mid-March 2003, compounded by structural unemployment as high value-added investments are capital intensive, not labour intensive, and as factory jobs continued to relocate to China and other cheaper manufacturing destinations (*The Asian Wall Street Journal*, 3 November 2003). Disentangling these multiple economic factors, is of course, very difficult but it is clear that SARS seriously aggravated both cyclical and structural factors already operative.

Discussion and Evaluation

We now turn to a discussion and evaluation of the economic and HRM impact of SARS on Singapore, specifically focusing on its hotel sector.

We will discuss the evidence we have collected in terms of the set of hypotheses we adumbrated earlier. Taking each hypothesis in turn, to recapitulate, we posited that:

> (i) *The greater the adverse impact of SARS on the Singapore economy, the greater will be the negative impact on the service sector and specifically on the hotel industry.*

Figure 3 shows the impact of SARS on the output of services in Singapore. The imported cases of SARS in Singapore started in late February and March 2003, and the WHO global alert was issued on 12 March 3003. These led to a fall in the percentage change of the GDP in the service sector over the corresponding period in 2002 (see Figure 3).

As seen in Figure 4, the number of tourist arrivals drastically declined after the travel advice was issued by the World Health Organization (WHO press release, 12 March 2003). The number of visitor arrivals, from the first quarter of 2003 to the second quarter dropped significantly from 1,815,100 to 698,000 (see Table 7). Hong Kong also experienced a broadly comparable decline in tourist numbers.

There had already been a marked slowdown in the growth rate of international tourism by the 1990s, affected by the Asian financial crisis at the end of the decade and the 11 September 2001 terrorist attacks in the USA. Despite the bombings on the Indonesian island of Bali in 2002, which raised questions about security throughout South East Asia, recovery seemed under way as there were more than 7.5 million visitors. The uncertainties relating both to Middle East tensions and

SARS, dominated expectations and over time these were made worse by the onset of the epidemic being totally unexpected (see Table 8).

The average hotel occupancy rates, average room rates, hotel room revenue and food and beverage revenue recorded dramatic falls, when compared to 2002 (see Figure 5). The hotel occupancy rate plummeted from 72 per cent to 42 per cent within a quarter (see Table 9). The *volatility*, as well as *vulnerability*, of such indices speaks for itself.

The second hypothesis which was posited was as follows:

(ii) *The greater the adverse impact of SARS on consumer demand in the Singapore hotel industry, the greater will be the negative impact on the related demand for labour in terms of hotel employees in specific hotel groups in the industry.*

To survive in such turbulent environments, hotels in Singapore resorted to various HRM measures to cut costs. This step led to a falling demand for labour. Figure 6 shows the steep plunge in the number of those employed in the service sector, in the second quarter in particular.

Table 10 shows a fall in the number of employees working in the industry. There was a decline of 12,100 of those in employment, with hotels and restaurants suffering the biggest cut of 5,800 employees (see Table 10).

The third hypothesis which was posited was as follows:

(iii) *The greater the adverse impact on the demand for labour in the Singapore hotel industry, the greater will be the negative impact on the labour-market in terms of the HRM implications such as lay-offs and redundancy among hotel employees in specific hotel groups in the industry.*

Between March and June 2003, many business sectors in Singapore had been adversely affected. Starting from the outbreak of SARS and the issue of the global advisory warning by the World Health Organization on Singapore, businesses related to tourism – including airlines, hotels, retail and restaurants – had seen a fall in demand. With regard to air transport, Singapore Airlines (SIA) cancelled approximately 30 per cent of its weekly timetable (Henderson, 2003). Tourists from all over the world had postponed or cut out their visits to Singapore.

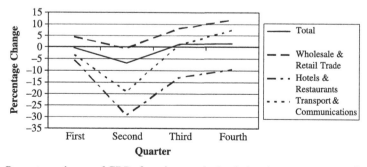

Figure 3. Percentage change of GDP of services producing industries over corresponding period of previous year, 2003 (unit: percentage). *Source*: *Economic Survey of Singapore 2003*, Singapore Department of Statistics website.

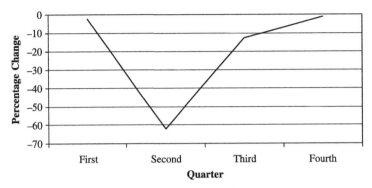

Figure 4. Percentage change of total visitor arrivals over corresponding period of previous year, 2003 (unit: percentage). Source: Research and Statistical Information, Singapore Tourism Board website, http://app.stb.com.sg/asp/tou/tou02.asp#VS.

We now go on to discuss the Human Resource Management (HRM) implications of the changing labour demand and labour supply consequences noted above (see Figure 7).

In order to cut costs and sharpen competitiveness, the HRM departments of big corporations like those of Singapore Airlines (SIA) and PSA Corporation, one of the world's leading port operators, where retrenchment had never been heard of for more than two decades, started to lay off employees. Notably, SIA suffered from a deficit of over US$200 million as at June 2003, and decided to lay off 414 employees, of which 129 were ground-staff. The Housing Development Board (HDB) cut another 2,600 jobs. About 9,500 workers were laid off in the first six months of 2003, bringing the total number of jobless to some 102,000 (*China Daily*, 2003). Among them, around 25,000 had remained unemployed for at least six months. Unlike previous retrenchments, not only blue-collar workers' jobs had been affected, but also those of white-collar employees. The Singapore government embarked on a series of initiatives to help laid-off workers, including retraining. The government launched the new Workforce Development Agency (WDA) and gave a second phase of cash injection of S$280 million (US$160 million) to a Skills Redevelopment Programme to help co-fund the retraining of workers (ibid.).

At the organizational level, the HRM consequences were severe, as our on-site interviews revealed. Hotels froze recruitment and overtime, dismissed casual workers and cut pay at every level (Henderson, 2003). An HR manager from

Table 7. Visitor arrivals, 2003 (unit: thousand persons)

Quarter	Total	Asia	Oceania	Europe	America	Africa	Others
First	1,815.1	1,264.6	130.3	300.7	102.1	17.3	0.2
Second	698.0	494.4	58.4	106.7	32.2	6.1	0.2
Third	1,700.0	1,243.7	143.1	212.0	84.3	16.8	0.1
Fourth	1,913.5	1,397.8	143.8	257.6	96.1	18.1	0.1

Source: Research and Statistical Information, Singapore Tourism Board website, http://app.stb.com.sg/asp/tou/tou02.asp#VS

Table 8. Visitor arrivals, 1998-2003 (unit: thousand persons)

Year	Total	Asia	Oceania	Europe	America	Africa	Others
1998	6,242.2	4,223.8	519.8	982.7	425.4	79.1	11.3
1999	6,958.2	4,797.3	564.5	1,050.0	444.3	90.2	12.0
2000	7,691.4	5,320.8	616.6	1,127.9	483.0	99.5	43.7
2001	7,522.2	5,224.1	656.5	1,114.6	433.6	88.0	5.4
2002	7,567.1	5,326.7	644.1	1,101.9	416.4	72.8	5.2
2003	6,126.6	4,400.5	475.5	877.3	314.7	58.3	0.2

Source: Research and Statistical Information, Singapore Tourism Board website, http://app.stb.com.sg/asp/tou/tou02.asp#VS

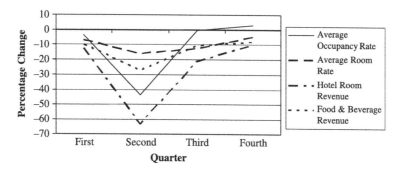

Figure 5. Percentage change of hotel statistics over corresponding period of previous year, 2003 (unit: percentage). *Source*: *Economic Survey of Singapore 2003*, Singapore Department of Statistics website.

a logistics firm, who declined to be named, said that the sectors likely to face wage-cuts were likely to be hotels, as well as recreation and travel. The cuts were expected to range from 2 to 15 per cent. According to a survey of 272 companies polled in May 2003 by the Singapore Human Resource Institute and Remuneration Data Specialists, variable bonuses, excluding the annual wage supplement, would

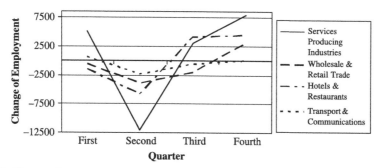

Figure 6. Change of employment in services producing industries over the previous period, 2003 (unit: persons). *Source*: *Economic Survey of Singapore 2003*, Singapore Department of Statistics website.

Table 9. Hotel statistics, first–fourth quarter 2003

Quarter	Average occupancy rate (%)	Average room rate (S$)	Hotel room revenue (million S$)	Food & beverage revenue (million S$)
First	72.0	121.5	221.7	374.3
Second	42.1	106.7	92.6	284.8
Third	73.6	107.3	191.8	357.7
Fourth	76.9	117.4	220.2	399.6

Source: *Economic Survey of Singapore 2003*, Singapore Department of Statistics website.

Table 10. Changes of employment over the previous period, 2003 (unit: persons)

Industry	First quarter	Second quarter	Third quarter	Fourth quarter
Total	−4,100	−26,000	900	16,200
Goods producing industries	−9,200	−13,800	−2,100	4,300
Manufacturing	−2,600	−6,400	0	4,100
Construction	−6,500	−7,100	−1,900	−2,000
Others	−200	−200	−200	2,100
Services producing industries	5,100	−12,100	3,000	12,000
Wholesale & retail trade	−600	−3,900	−2,000	4,200
Hotels & restaurants	−1,400	−5,800	4,100	5,100
Transport & communications	600	−2,300	−600	900
Financial services	800	700	−100	900
Business services	0	1,400	700	−1,600
Other services industries	5,700	−2,100	1,000	2,500

Source: *Economic Survey of Singapore First Quarter 2004*, Singapore Department of Statistics website

dip from 1.4 months a year ago to 1.3 months (ibid.). The survey also found that eight in ten firms supported the National Wages Council guidelines that SARS-hit companies cut wages, and urged wage reforms to more flexible pay systems. With regard to air transport, SIA's cabin crew employees were instructed to take several days' unpaid leave every two months until 2004 and over 200 trainees were released. A similar arrangement for cockpit crew became an issue for negotiation, after resistance from the pilots' union (ibid.). Senior management took salary cuts of 22.2 per cent to 27.5 per cent.

Even government ministers, whose monthly pay was reduced by 10 per cent in November 2001, had their wages frozen further for another year until December 2003 (*Business Times*, 2003). The then Deputy Prime Minister and Finance Minister, Lee Hsien Long, told the Parliament in his May Day Rally speech that 'when all have to take bitter medicine, we must start at the top' (ibid.).

The implications for training were also evident, as our interviewing made clear. Staff were asked to go on unpaid leave, retrained and redeployed where appropriate. The SARS Relief Tourism Training Assistance grant scheme, which was part of the government's S$230 million relief package, trained nearly 1,000 workers in the tourism sector in just three weeks in May 2003 (*Straits Times*, 2003d). There were 104 approved courses for the scheme, ranging from making

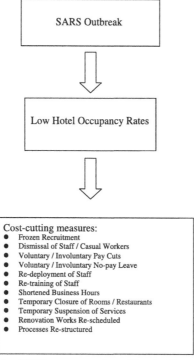

Figure 7. Cost-cutting HRM measures adopted by the Singapore hotel industry

sauces to hotel law and security. Most of the retrainees were rank and file workers like chambermaids, tour guides and event organizers; most of these were schooled up to the secondary school level and had limited skills at best. According to the deputy director of the Manpower Ministry's (MOM) labour market development division, resistance to training had been a 'big issue' in the tourism sector for many years. A café hostess, aged 48 who had worked at the Grand Hyatt Hotel for 31 years, remarked after taking a two-week refresher course on the food and beverage industry that 'this is the first time I've been able to train for two weeks at a stretch, because we now have so few guests' (ibid.). A restaurant manager of the Raffles Hotel was trained for a totally different job – as a concierge, but he said that 'it will help me a lot as I have patrons who ask me for recommendations on entertainment or places of interest here'. Under the new grant scheme, the government paid an employer S$6.90 an hour for every worker aged 40 or older sent for training; it also paid the course fees. For a younger worker, the government would pay his employer S$6.50 an hour and 90 per cent of the course fees. Such arrangements resulted from negotiations among the MOM, the Singapore Tourism Board, the National Trades Union Congress and other stakeholders in April 2003. The chairman of the Association of Singapore Attractions informed that they had 'set aside S$30,000 to pay the remaining ten per cent of course fees not subsidized by the grant' as their members' main problem was cash-flow.

At the height of the outbreak, the Shangri-La Rasa Sentosa resort had its sales staff double as banquet waiters, so as to cut down on its part-time labour costs (*Wall Street Journal*, 2003). To boost the morale of staff who sat idle for much of the day, the hotel organized inter-departmental volleyball games every afternoon on the beach (ibid.).

A few hotels offered steep discounts to encourage consumer spending (and boost employment) when SARS was at its worst. Raffles International offered two nights for the price of one at its Singapore properties – the Plaza, Swissotel and Merchant Court – in April and May to Singaporeans. Other packages included lessons in dancing, financial management and cookery in the hotel kitchens (*Straits Times*, 2003b). In order to stimulate interest, one hotel opened all its rooms for a free night's stay to locals prepared to queue for 24 hours (*Straits Times*, 2003c).

Some hotels offered low rates through packages put together with airlines. For example, SIA passengers got 50 per cent discounts at a number of Raffles Group hotels in Singapore; and SIA offered a US$579 'Singapore Plus' package that included airfare to Singapore from New York, San Francisco or Los Angeles and three nights at a five-star lodging with transfers, breakfast and some tours.

Concluding Remarks

It is clear that the impact of SARS on the Singapore economy and specifically the hotel industry may be seen as relatively negative in the time-period in question. Both the quantitative, as well as the qualitative, data we have gathered, points in this direction, although we must be cautious to over-generalize. The HRM implications, as set out in our hypotheses, were confirmed, both in a conceptual as well as in an empirical framework, as both immediate and direct, as can be seen from our findings.

As the economy revived by mid-2003, it was thought that recovery in service-sector jobs above all, in industries like hotels, both in low- as well as high-valued added products and services would compensate for earlier job losses. The SARS epidemic of early and mid-2003 has no doubt been a sharp reminder to both Hong Kong and Singapore, both Nanyang city-state economies, of their economic vulnerability. The Chinese mainland case was somewhat different, given the lower weighting of the service-sector in that economy. Today, there is less of a major 'crisis of confidence' but spirits remain low as the economy slowly recovers and the labour-market still remains fragile.

The Singapore economy, given its market-oriented flexibility (see Hampden-Turner, 2003: 173–176) fortunately recovered fairly quickly. The stock-market index jumped to around half as much again as it had been at the beginning of the year.

The Singapore economy grew by 12.5 per cent in the second quarter of 2004. During the quarter, growth of external demand rose by 26.3 per cent – exports of both goods and services rose significantly – reflecting the impact of increased visitor arrivals on receipts from travel and transportation services (Ministry of Trade and Industry, 2004). Tourism helped the economy to recover in the second half of 2003. The hotel sector ultimately recovered as the year unfolded.

The hotels and restaurants sector registered a 37.6 per cent gain in output during the second quarter of 2004, compared to 3.1 per cent in the first quarter of 2004 (Ministry of Trade and Industry, 2004). This boost mainly reflected the impact of SARS on activity in 2003. However a number of concerns remained, among them *structural* problems. Compared to the second quarter of 2002, the sector showed a decline of 3.0 per cent. Although the average hotel occupancy rate remained well supported by strong visitor arrivals, which grew by 9.2 per cent when compared to the second quarter of 2002, lower room rates depressed hotel room revenue in the quarter (ibid.). Even though total employment rose by 10,400 in the second quarter of 2004, it was a smaller number than the 13,700 gained in the previous quarter. The decline reflected the lower increase of 6,700 jobs in the service sector, compared with 11,400 in the first quarter of 2004. During the quarter, a smaller number of retrenchments of 1,900, compared with 2,962 in the first quarter of 2004 contributed to higher total employment. Despite the increase in total employment, the seasonally adjusted unemployment rate remained stable at 4.5 per cent, unchanged since December 2003 (ibid.).

We can nonetheless posit that the SARS effect had a relatively negative impact on the economy and human resources, with both employment and psychological consequences that may have medium, even long-term implications, as in the case of Hong Kong. If it was thought that the expansion of service employment, such as in the hotel sector or any other, would create a positive and stable employment equilibrium and compensate for the earlier loss of manufacturing jobs, the Singapore, like the Hong Kong, authorities may have to reconsider their long-term economic strategy and continually be on their guard against unforeseen circumstances. In today's globalized economy (see Warner, 2002), *exogenous* shocks may affect labour demand within weeks, and the HRM implications may be felt almost as rapidly and no one can accurately predict the coefficient of vulnerability.

References

Asian Development Bank Action Plan to Address Outbreak of Severe Acute Respiratory Syndrome (SARS) in Asia and the Pacific, May. (2003)

Belau, D. (2003) New Threats to Employment in the Travel and Tourism Industry – 2003, *ILO Report* (Geneva: ILO).

Briggs, A. (1961) Cholera and society in the nineteenth century, *Past and Present: Journal of Historical Studies*, 19, pp. 76–96.

Business Times (2003) 2 May.

Business Week (2003) 28 April.

China Daily (2003) 24 September.

Cipolla, C. M. (1976) *Before the Industrial Revolution; European Society and Economy 1000–1700* (London: Routledge, reprinted 1997).

Crampton, T. (2003) Asian isolation grows in response to SARS. *International Herald Tribune*, 10 April.

Eysenbach, G. (2003) SARS and population health technology, *Journal of Medical Internet Research*, 5(2), pp. e14.

Fan, E. X. (2003) SARS: economic impacts and implications. ERD Policy Brief, series no. 15, Asian Development Bank.

Floud, R. & McCloskey, D. (1981) *The Economic History of Britain since 1700*, 1, pp. 1700–1860 (2nd edn., reprinted 2000) (Cambridge: Cambridge University Press).

Gerberding, J. L. (2003) Faster... but fast enough? Responding to the epidemic of Severe Acute Respiratory Syndrome, *New England Journal of Medicine*. 348(20), pp. 2030–2031.

Haacker, M. (2002) The economic consequences of HIV/AIDS in South Africa, IMF Working Paper, WP/02/38.

Hampden-Turner, C. (2003) Culture and management in Singapore, in: M. Warner (Ed.) *Culture and Management in Asia*, pp. 171–186 (London: RoutledgeCurzon).

Henderson, J. (2003) Managing a health-related crisis: SARS in Singapore, *Journal of Vacation Marketing*, 10(1), pp. 67–77.

Hsu, L. Y. L. C., Green, J. A. & Ang, B. (2003) Severe Acute Respiratory Syndrome (SARS) in Singapore: clinical features of index patient and initial contacts, *Emerging Infectious Disease*, 9(6), pp. 713–717.

Khatri, N. (2004) HRM in Singapore, in: PawanS. Budhwar (Ed.) *Managing Human Resources in Asia-Pacific*, pp. 221–238 (London, New York: Routledge Resource).

Lee, G. O. M. & Warner, M. (2005) The impact of SARS on China's economy, labour market and level of employment, Epidemics, labour-markets and unemployment: the impact of SARS on human resources management in the Hong Kong hotel industry. *International Journal of Human Resource Management*, 17(5), pp. 860–880.

Lee, J.-W. & McKibbin, W. J. (2003) Globalization and disease: the case of SARS. Paper presented to the Asian Economic Panel Meeting, Tokyo, May.

Lee, N., Hui, D. & Wu, A. (2003) A major outbreak of Severe Acute Respiratory Syndrome in Hong Kong, *New England Journal of Medicine*, 348(20), pp. 1986–1994.

Ministry of Trade and Industry (2003) *Performance of the Singapore Economy in Second Quarter 2003 and Outlook for 2003*.

Ministry of Trade and Industry (2004) *Performance of the Singapore Economy in Second Quarter 2004 and Outlook for 2004 and 2005*.

Morens, D. M., Folkers, G. K. & Fauci, A. S. (2004) The challenge of emerging and re-emerging infectious diseases, *Nature*, 430, pp. 242–249.

Poutanen, S. M., Low, D. E. & Henry, B. (2003) Identification of Severe Acute Respiratory Syndrome in Canada, *New England Journal of Medicine*, 348(20), pp. 1995–2005.

Pressman, S. (1999) *Fifty Major Economists* (London: Routledge).

Singapore Tourism Board (2003) Weekly fact sheets, April to May.

Singer, M. (1998) Forging a Political Economy of AIDS, in: M. Singer (Ed.) *The Political Economy of AIDS* (New York: Baywood Publishing Company).

Straits Times (2003a) Singapore loses at least $23m a week, 5 April.

Straits Times (2003b) Get inn-spired Here, 10 June.

Straits Times (2003c) Calling for Singaporeans, 14 May.

Straits Times (2003d) Tourism workers flock to retrain under new scheme, 25 May.

Tambyah, P. A. (2002) The SARS outbreak: how many reminders do we need?, *Journal of the Singapore Medical Association*, 44(4), pp. 165–204.

Tomlinson, B. & Cockram, C. (2003) SARS: experience at prince of Wales hospital, Hong Kong, *The Lancet*, 361(3), pp. 1486–1487.

TTG Daily News (2003) Taking extra precautions, 7 May.

Wall Street Journal (2003) 5 June.

Watts, S. (1997) *Epidemics and History: Disease, Power and Imperialism* (New Haven, CT and London: Yale University Press).

Wilder-Smith, A., Goh, K. T. & Paton, N. I. (2003) Experience of severe Acute Respiratory syndrome in Singapore: importation of cases, and defense strategies at the airport, *Journal of Travel Medicine*, 10(5), pp. 259–262.

World Health Organization (2003) *Summary Table of SARS Cases by Country, 1 November 2002 – 7 August 2003* (Geneva: WHO).

World Travel and Tourism Council (2003) *Singapore: Special SARS Analysis – Impact on Travel and Tourism* (London: WTTC).

Xinhua (2003) 24 September.

Multinational NGOs and Expatriation: A Case Study of a NGO in Vietnam

YING ZHU* & DAVID PURNELL**

Department of Management, University of Melbourne, Australia

Introduction

Globalization has led to the emergence of organizations that span national borders and cultures (Adler, 1986). Multinational organizations (MOs) need to create a balance between local responsiveness and global integration (Prahalad & Doz, 1987; Bartlett & Ghoshal, 1990; Dowling *et al.*, 1994). It is important for MOs to leverage their worldwide knowledge and resources through global integration for efficiency. Meanwhile, MOs need to be responsive to their local operating environment so that they are relevant and effective to the different contexts they operate within. The balance between global integration and local responsiveness is unique to each organizational circumstance.

In the process of establishing and managing MOs, headquarters (HQs) and subsidiaries may have incongruent goals due to the conflict between global integration and local responsiveness (global-local conflict) (Egelhoff, 1984; O'Donnell, 2000). HQ has goals that take advantage of global efficiencies (Black & Gregersen, 1992). Subsidiaries pursue local responsiveness as they gather information on the local environment and perceive opportunities unique to the local context (Black & Gregersen, 1992). These different goals cause conflict, thus HQs will seek mechanisms of organizational control to influence subsidiary behaviour (Ouchi, 1977; Egelhoff, 1984; O'Donnell, 2000).

HQ can control subsidiaries through expatriate management (Egelhoff, 1984; Boyacigiller, 1990; O'Donnell, 2000). Expatriates control subsidiary operations and strategy formulation and maintain the MO's identity in the subsidiaries (Boyacigiller, 1990). Expatriates are also a reliable source of information flow between HQ and subsidiaries (Keegan, 1974; Tung, 1982; Kobrin, 1988; Boyacigiller, 1990). However, expatriation may not be so successful and the failure causes high costs associated with expatriate relocation and replacement (Holmes & Piker, 1980; Tung, 1982; Swaak, 1995). The tension of managing the global-local conflict and enduring cross-cultural difficulties contribute to expatriate failure (Tung, 1982; Harris & Holden, 2001).

NGOs tend to be driven by value-based ideological purposes (Sills, 1957). NGOs predominantly pursue development in local communities (Ha, 2001). Hence, NGOs must understand and be responsive to the local context of the local community to implement effective development.

This work examines multinational NGOs' management of the global-local conflict through expatriation management. These issues are rarely addressed in the international human resource management literature, despite being extensively covered in the profit-driven organization literature (Bonache *et al.*, 2001).

A pilot case study of a NGO subsidiary operating in Vietnam is undertaken to analyse organizational strategy and structure. This is because subsidiary strategy formulation processes influence the subsidiary's management of the global-local conflict. Organizational control is investigated because it reflects how HQ can influence subsidiary decision making to pursue global integration policies in conjunction with local responsiveness. The role of expatriates is examined due to the significant effect of the expatriate on subsidiary strategic decision making (O'Donnell, 2000; Harris & Holden, 2001; Gregersen & Black, 1992). Finally, the relationships between expatriates, organizational entities, and the Vietnamese government, employees, and communities are studied. These interrelationships affect how the expatriate manages the influences from both HQ for global integration as well as the subsidiary's Vietnamese stakeholders for local responsiveness.

This work comprises five sections. Section 2 reviews the theoretical and empirical literatures pertaining to structure, strategy and organizational control in MOs as well as expatriation management. Then, a framework for fieldwork design is presented in Section 3. Section 4 outlines the research findings. Section 5 concludes the work by identifying the theoretical and empirical implications for NGOs' expatriation management.

Literature Review

There is a lack of research which examines NGOs in regard to organizational strategy, structure, control and expatriation (Bonache *et al.*, 2001). For this reason, the majority of the literature whichc is reviewed pertains to profit-driven multinational corporations (MNCs). The review will provide a framework for the application of theory in the MNCs sector to the NGO sector. In fact, Suutari and Brewster (2001) claim that the research on multinational organizations and expatriation is influenced by large variances in contextual variables.

The multinational NGO context may produce unique results that may have similar as well as different facets as other profit-driven MNCs.

Theory

Strategy and structure.   An important aspect of managing the global-local conflict is the formation and implementation of strategy and structure within a subsidiary. If HQ can establish control of subsidiary strategy and structure, then HQ can ensure that the subsidiary pursues HQ mandated goals. If HQ control is minimal, or the subsidiary has a high degree of autonomy in strategic decision making, then the subsidiary can pursue goals motivated by local responsiveness at the expense of HQ mandated goals.

The literature surrounding strategy of MNCs is strongly related to the global-local conflict that MNCs face. The global strategy aims to maximise integration of activities without concern for local responsiveness (Bartlett & Ghoshal, 1990). The multinational/multi-domestic strategy focuses on local responsiveness rather than global integration (Bartlett & Ghoshal, 1990).

While Bartlett and Ghoshal's (1990) generic strategy options are useful at a broad level of analysis, it is important to identify strategy formulation techniques used by MNCs. Mintzberg and Waters (1985) identify ideological control as one means of HQ influencing subsidiary strategy formulations. HQ establishes ideological control by inserting subsidiary leaders who subscribe to the beliefs, values, and ideology of the HQ (Mintzberg & Waters, 1985). HQ can have confidence that strategy formulation by the HQ-inserted leaders will fulfil HQ goals based on HQ ideological beliefs (Mintzberg & Waters, 1985).

Mintzberg and Waters (1985) identify the 'umbrella' approach to strategy formulation which is relevant for emergent subsidiary strategy formulation. Within the 'umbrella' approach, HQ allows subsidiaries to make strategy choices, but sets boundaries and guides for decision making (Mintzberg & Waters, 1985). This approach attempts to overcome the limited knowledge HQ has of the local context by decentralizing strategy decisions to subsidiary managers. However, HQ still maintains a degree of control by setting broad strategies and goals as guides for subsidiaries.

Another approach to strategy formulation is strategic decision making through organizational politics (Pettigrew, 1977). This is more prominent in organizational change literature. Drory and Romm (1990: 1133-34) have described organizational politics as 'concealed and self-serving'. However, Pettigrew (1977) and Huff (1988) have identified organizational politics as a forum where the debate of ideas and negotiation of decisions can lead to compromise. Managers' perspectives are broadened, and more information is shared between intra-organizational entities (Huff, 1988). With the understanding of the rationale of a decision, there is reduced resistance to strategies (Huff, 1988). Buchanan and Badham (1999) state that organizational politics can lead to positive outcomes for strategy formulation, but potential negative outcomes must be managed.

The interrelations between different organizational entities affect strategy formulation. The MNC's structure determines how different organizational entities are inter-related. The MNC's structure is affected by the global-local conflict. Global strategies are focused around product division, seeking to create economies of scale in homogenous products for all countries (Bartlett & Ghoshal, 1990; Cullen, 2002). The locally responsive strategies lead to geographical divisions where the MNC seeks to customize its operations to certain locations (Bartlett & Ghoshal, 1990; Cullen, 2002).

Hence, these literatures lead us to consider the relevance to the NGO and one of the key research questions of this work is how the NGO context affects approaches to strategy formulation and implementation as well as organizational structure and relationships.

Organizational control. Organizational control is an important factor in determining the degree that HQ can influence the subsidiary's management of the global-local conflict. Martinez and Ricks (1989) take a multidimensional approach to organizational control, claiming that many forms can exist simultaneously. In addition, Pfeffer and Salancik's (1978) resource dependence perspective argues that HQ can establish control of the subsidiary through resource control. The subsidiary is not self-sufficient and is therefore forced to pursue HQ goals otherwise the resources from HQ may be withheld. Through increasing interdependence between the subsidiary and HQ, the control weakens as HQ becomes dependent on resources the subsidiary accrues (Pfeffer & Salancik, 1978).

O'Donnell (2000) presents an analysis of agency theory that provides insight into the issue of the MNC's control of subsidiaries. Agency theory states that subsidiaries can act in self-interest by pursuing organizational goals not mandated by HQ (Eisenhardt, 1989). Monitoring is necessary to decrease information asymmetry between HQ and subsidiaries (Eisenhardt, 1989). With improved information through monitoring, HQ can implement policies to ensure that subsidiary behaviour is in accordance with HQ goals and mandates (Eisenhardt, 1989). The expatriate is one means of HQ control over subsidiaries through the reduction of information asymmetry (Egelhoff, 1984).

Jaeger (1983) suggests that HQ can establish control of subsidiaries through the transplant of HQ's culture. Organizational culture is a set of shared values and beliefs between organizational members (Ouchi, 1981). Social pressure controls behaviour as employees conform to the organizational values and culture (Jaeger, 1983). Intense use of expatriates, socialization programmes and frequent HQ-subsidiary contact allows the HQ culture to be transplanted to the subsidiary (Jaeger, 1983). This leads to the potential for long-term HQ control of subsidiary behaviour and decision making (Jaeger, 1983).

Jaeger (1983) claims that subsidiaries that are controlled via a transplant of HQ's culture have limited flexibility in adjusting behaviour to avoid conflict with the host government's regulation. HQ is unwilling to allow the subsidiary to change behaviour that affects organizational culture (Jaeger, 1983). Therefore, the subsidiary must expend resources when justifying reasons for changing behaviour to meet government regulation to HQ (Jaeger, 1983).

The literatures of organizational control give us a sense of direction for investigating the types of control used in the NGO context that allows its HQ to influence subsidiary management of the global-local conflict.

The role of expatriates. Expatriates are important for implementing direct and indirect HQ control in subsidiaries. Therefore expatriates have an effect on the management of the global-local conflict.

Harris and Holden (2001) examine the tension between expatriate autonomy and HQ control. Autonomy refers to the degree of freedom expatriates have in strategy formulation and decision making. The expatriate desires autonomy in order to manage the conflict between global integration and local responsiveness (Harris & Holden, 2001).

Another pressure for expatriates is to judge what HQ's policies mean, and how these policies fit in the local context (Harris & Holden, 2001). Many times these policies are developed at HQ level without the subsidiary's context in mind (Harris & Holden, 2001). This means that, sometimes, policies need to be adjusted in order to fit in the local context. However, some case studies show that expatriates are frustrated about not enough autonomy being given by HQ (Bhuian *et al.*, 1996; Harris & Holden, 2001).

The Vietnam context

Since 1986, Vietnam has embarked on economic reform (*Doi Moi*). The reform transferred economic control from a central planning system to a market oriented economy (Duiker, 1989; George, 1995). GDP has grown 7 per cent annually and Vietnam's exports have increased 20 per cent since *Doi Moi* (World Bank, 2004). While the reform has increased national wealth and has reduced poverty, the focus of gains has been on urban areas (Ha, 2001). There is still significant poverty in remote areas of Vietnam (Ha, 2001).

The programme of foreign aid by multinational NGOs in Vietnam is characterized by providing basic support to people who live in remote areas and need the most assistance (George, 1995; Ha, 2001). However, due to ideological differences that occur between the Vietnamese government and multinational NGOs, the Vietnamese government seeks to regulate through legislative measures (Wischermann, 2003). The *Handbook of Foreign Non-Governmental Organizations in Vietnam* (PACCOM, 2003) outlines Vietnamese government regulations which include registration, staffing restrictions, and visa limitations on expatriates. It is important for expatriates to be sensitive regarding local regulations and ensure ongoing cooperative relationships with local governments for effective NGO operation there.

Dunning (1998) states that there has been a progression from hostile relationships between multinational NGOs and host governments to an increasingly cooperative relationship. Luo (2001) identifies four 'building blocks' for improving cooperative relationships between governments and multinational NGO – resource commitment, personal relations, political accommodation and organizational credibility.

Propositions

HQ-subsidiary relationship. The literature identifies MNC strategy formulation techniques that transfer the locus of decision making from HQ to the subsidiary.

These approaches are possible because HQ can trust the subsidiary because of either ideological control, and/or an expatriate manager. In addition, organizational politics has been established as a method of strategy formulation. Furthermore, structure is a focus in determining how the NGO's context influences the HQ-subsidiary relationship. Therefore:

> **Proposition 1**. Organizational ideology, politics, strategy and structure have significant impacts on the NGO's subsidiary strategy formulation and implementation.

The role of expatriates. Expatriates will experience a high degree of cross-cultural conflict. However, due to the ideological motivation of the expatriate, the negative cultural-conflict experiences will be rationalized against the positive experiences of fulfilling personal, social and community development goals. Therefore:

> **Proposition 2**. Expatriates working for the NGO will have intrinsic ideological motivations that will lead to expatriate work satisfaction despite cross-cultural difficulties.

Expatriate relationships with the key stakeholders. Alignment of ideology and values between the expatriate and HQ will allow HQ to trust the expatriate with minimal monitoring. In addition, due to the NGO bringing aid and expertise to the development in Vietnam, cooperation between the NGO and the local governments, employees and communities is crucial for the realization of the goal of development. Therefore:

> **Proposition 3**. Expatriates working for the NGO will have a distant relationship with HQ and cooperative relationships with local governments, employees and communities.

Data Analysis

This research project is a pilot case study of a multinational NGO with the religious background of Christianity. Its HQ is located in Melbourne, Australia with subsidiaries operating in Vietnam. The NGO was chosen for this case study because it has the unique values and ideology of Christianity that help to illustrate the proposition regarding ideology and value issues. It is also the major NGO operating in South East Asia and it has been in Vietnam since the late 1980s. It was one of the earliest NGOs to enter Vietnam under the management of expatriates. Globally, the NGO was established in the 1950s, operates in numerous countries with many expatriates, and has a total global budget exceeding US$1 billion annually. Due to its size, extensive project network, and experience, it is an important member of the NGO sector in Vietnam, and internationally. In addition, the NGO works with government bodies are departmentally structured, and exist at four main levels; national, provincial, district and commune. One unique factor is the presence of the support office (SO) in the NGO structure. SO is responsible for the allocation of funding to NGO subsidiaries.

Table 1. The profile of interviewees

	P1	P2	P3	P4	P5
Position	Expatriate director	Expatriate non-director	SO employee	Government official	Director of NGO support organization
Purpose of interview	Establish subsidiary and expatriate perspective	Establish subsidiary and expatriate perspective	Establish HQ perspective of interactions with subsidiary and expatriates	Establish Vietnam government Perspective	Create context of the Vietnam development environment
Gender	Male	Male	Male	Male	Male
Nationality	Australian	Australian	Australian	Vietnamese	Australian
Previous posting overseas	Yes	Yes	Yes	NA	No
Roles	Director of subsidiary	Manager of HR and organizational development	Monitor projects funded by Australia in Vietnam	Maintain relationship between Vietnamese government and NGO in Vietnam	Provide support services for NGOs in Vietnam

The semi-structured interview was chosen. An advantage of the semi-structured interview for this case study is that it gives the researcher the flexibility to pursue clarification and elaboration when greater understanding of the interviewee's views and perceptions are needed, while still defining the topic areas and boundaries (May, 1997). A second advantage is that the subjective aspects of 'autonomy', 'control', and 'relationship' can be explored, to ensure that a clear understanding is established (May, 1997) and overcome the subjective nature of such terms (Otterbeck, 1981). In addition, semi-structured interviews are effective for clarifying and gathering information on the many issues that were unforeseeable, or were context specific to this case study.

Five interviews were held, including interviews with two expatriates working for the organization (P1 and P2), an SO employee (P3), a Vietnamese government official (P4), and one expatriate supporting officer for NGOs in Vietnam (P5) (see Table 1). All interviews were conducted in Vietnam except one interview with the SO employee which was held in Melbourne, Australia.

Case Study

The case studies cover the NGO's strategy and structure, organizational control, the role of the expatriate, and the expatriate's relationships with the key stakeholders. Figure 1 highlights the expatriate's relationships with the HQ, the Support Office, and the local governments and communities (see Figure 1).

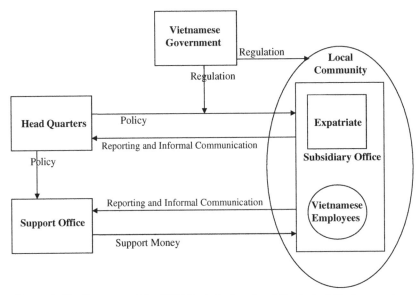

Figure 1. The Structure of the NGO Organisational and Contextual Environments

The NGO's strategy formulation and implementation. HQ has control over the introduction of global strategies that promote global integration throughout the NGO. An example of this is the Area Development Program (ADP) model which is the standard approach to community development of the NGO's subsidiaries. HQ recognized the ADP model as important knowledge for all subsidiaries and mandated its adoption throughout the organization.

While HQ has ultimate control of subsidiary strategy, the subsidiary has a high degree of autonomy to make adjustments to the strategy so that it matches the needs of Vietnamese communities. The ADP strategy is an example of where subsidiary offices decide which aspects of health, education, and other dimensions of development should be included in an ADP project depending on local needs. When discussing the freedom the subsidiary has in adjusting policies to be locally responsive, P1 stated:

> 'we are modifying the policy; we are fulfilling the spirit of the policy, but maybe not all the detail because it is just not feasible in our situation'.

The NGO's strategy formulation and implementation extensively uses organizational politics. The subsidiary is expected to report any changes to strategy or policy to HQ through informal communication. HQ can challenge these changes if it does not agree. The subsidiary can debate and justify its reasons for changing a policy. There are no apparent time constraints; debate can continue for years after a strategy has been adjusted and implemented. While it was stated that HQ has the final authority, there were no reported examples where HQ overruled an implementation decision.

Structure of the NGO. The structure of the NGO includes three main organizational entities (see Figure 1). The subsidiary is the representative of the NGO in Vietnam. The subsidiary is responsible for the implementation of locally responsive projects and the management of the NGO's Vietnam development programme.

HQ is responsible for policy development at the global level. HQ coordinates and mandates broad level development policies for the other organizational entities. While a subsidiary or Support Office may be set up under the framework of HQ, it is considered to be a separate organization with a high degree of autonomy.

Within the subsidiary, the structure is expatriate leadership, with Vietnamese employees generally responsible for operations and project management. P2 reported responsibility for a project as part of his role, because his expertise was complementary with the project.

NGO organizational control. The NGO subsidiary has a limited source of current or potential income and is dependent on funding from the Support Office. This resource dependency gives a degree of power to the Support Office. An example of this was the organization-wide introduction of the ADP model, outlined in the following statement by P1: 'in some individual countries, they didn't want to go down the ADP route, but it soon became apparent that they would be struggling to get funding through child sponsorship if they did not adopt this approach to development'.

While the Support Office has a degree of power through resource dependency, the power is dispersed through many Support Offices. In addition, the NGO subsidiary has autonomy that allows it to choose who it receives funding from. These two factors mediate the amount of power the Support Offices have through resource dependency. A reported example is that one Support Office donor has unusually high formal reporting standards, low use of informal communication methods, and shows little concern for the effect the Vietnamese context has on the subsidiary. P1 and P2 have decided to reject future funding offered by the Support Office donor. This decision was made without any evident guidance from HQ.

Expatriate management. Expatriate management is a form of HQ control of the subsidiary in the NGO. One area of control was in reporting. The expatriates develop subsidiary reports regularly for HQ, and assist Vietnamese employees in developing reports on projects for Support Offices. The expatriate's involvement in reporting ensures that HQ has a source of information regarding the subsidiary's activities and performance. Expatriates also informally communicate knowledge to HQ and Support Offices through relationships with HQ and Support Office employees established before and during their foreign assignment.

HQ and Support Office employee visitation also enforces HQ and Support Office control of the subsidiary. Support Office employees are more likely to make regular visits to Vietnam and inspect progress of projects. HQ employees make infrequent and irregular visits.

Expatriates establish HQ's culture in the subsidiary. This is a direct form of culture control for HQ. The expatriates' decision making reflects the values and beliefs of HQ's culture.

Organizational culture. As stated, the expatriate establishes HQ control of the subsidiary through the transfer of HQ's culture to the subsidiary. The most implicit, but influential form of control is the transplanting of culture and values from HQ to the subsidiary. The NGO is based on religious values, established by the founder of the NGO. The NGO's core values stated by P1 are: 'We are Christian, we are partners, we value people, we are committed to the poor, we are good stewards with the resources that are given to us, and we are responsive.'

P1, P2 and P3 showed strong support for these values. P1 and P2 stated that they were unwilling to change HQ policies to be locally responsive if they did not support the enforcement of organizational values in the subsidiary. P1 stated:

'It [organizational values] is something that we can't compromise on, and something that we don't want to compromise on.'

Furthermore, P1 expressed the need to reinforce the values in the Vietnam subsidiary through socialization programmes: 'we spend a lot of time in Vietnam promoting the key value areas of [NGO name removed]... we try to have all of the values in all of our training and orientation, and they are unified with the partnership'.

P1 and P2 expressed a responsibility to other entities within the NGO to be effective stewards of resources, follow the guidance from HQ, and report frequently and promptly to SOs. P1 stated: 'we are accountable to them as another member of the [NGO name removed] partnership'.

Interpretation and implementation of HQ strategy and policy. P1 and P2 stated that they experience little or no frustration through the process of interpreting and implementing HQ strategy and policy in the local context due to their autonomy. P1 stated: 'What I do feel I am about to control in certain ways is to be able to negotiate some of the policies and the way that they are applied in Vietnam.' He also said:

'In many ways every single country has to take the policy and say "what does this mean to us in our context?".'

While interpretation and implementation could occur freely, the expatriates engage the political process to justify any changes to HQ. This process allows the expatriates to state their point of view for changing a strategy or policy.

Support Offices and HQ recognize the need for the subsidiary to be locally responsive. P3 stated that 'local, on the ground knowledge' is best for decision making. This general attitude throughout the organization reinforces the expatriates' perception of their autonomy, and the right to adjust policy to be locally responsive.

Expatriate ideology and cross-cultural difficulties. At an individual level, the expatriates believe in the alleviation of poverty, and improving the livelihoods of

Vietnamese people through community responsive development. A priority of the expatriates is to ensure that development occurred effectively in Vietnam.

P1 and P2 stated that personal difficulties involved with living in Vietnam were based on language barriers, cross-cultural conflict, and separation from family members. These personal difficulties led to feelings of frustration and sadness.

P1 and P2 reported enjoying their work for the NGO. Both expatriates see first-hand results and fulfilment of their personal goals of poverty alleviation and community development. P2 stated: 'when a woman wants to thank me and show me, with tears in her eyes, what difference [NGO name removed] biogas project has made to her life then I do see, have seen what the projects are doing, have done, for the lives of people'. He also said: 'I love being here.'

Expatriate ethnocentric vs. geocentric behaviours. An already identified role of the expatriates is to uphold the identity and core values of the organization in a country where it is difficult to recruit Vietnamese leadership according to the religious values of the NGO. The expatriates are also expected to embed the HQ values and culture into the subsidiary. The HQ culture and policies, however, is based on the western values and culture of the founders of the NGO. Therefore the expatriate's function in this regard can be viewed as ethnocentric.

A main role of the expatriate, which was recognized by all interviewees, was to impart development and management techniques to the Vietnamese employees who often lack experience and knowledge about community development and management. As a part of this role, developing leadership and capacity building in the Vietnamese employees are seen as a priority. This role was described by P2 as 'working myself out of a job'. P1 and P2 focus on 'partnerships' with the Vietnamese government and local communities. These objectives are fully supported by the HQ and the SO. Teamwork was used to describe the relationship with the Vietnamese employees. P1 stated: 'we have a senior management team that comprises of 8 reps [5 expatriates and 3 Vietnamese employees]... and when it comes to changing partnership level policy it is on the agenda for the senior management team'.

This shows that the attitudes and behaviours are generally geocentric-oriented.

Expatriate relationships with the HQ. The relationship between HQ and the expatriates is quite distant. The relationship is best represented through the findings regarding organizational communication.

There is minimal formal communication between HQ and the expatriates. The expatriate director was expected to report monthly to his supervisor about the operations and activities within the subsidiary. While this reporting is quite frequent, its importance in the relationship is minimal. P1 stated: 'I am required to prepare monthly reports to the regional office, to my boss. To a certain extent they may be read.'

If formal reports are not being read or discussed, then they are a minimal form of communication between the expatriate and HQ.

Informal communication was much more prevalent in the relationship, but it relies on expatriate initiation. P1 stated: 'I... go out of my way to contact my superior informally to work through certain issues and be accountable for what I think is important for Vietnam, and in some ways to keep us upon the map.'

There is a perception that HQ is likely to overlook a subsidiary in the short term if some degree of informal communication is not occurring. The evidence indicates that informal communication is the only way that P1 would communicate local-specific changes to HQ policies, and are not mandated or required.

Expatriate relationships with the support office.   The relationships between the Support Offices and the expatriate were not foreseen in the case study; however, the results are relevant and important.

The expatriates must manage many relationships with different Support Offices as there are many Support Offices that give funding to Vietnam. Once again the relationship is characterized by the communication between Support Offices and the expatriates.

There is a limited formal communication between Support Offices and the expatriates. Support Offices receive formal reports directly from project managers, who tend to be Vietnamese employees. The majority of communication is project-specific. Expatriates are only required to provide information to a Support Office if there is a major conflict or concern. P3 stated: 'If... we [P3 and Vietnamese employees] weren't getting anywhere, I'd take it to the next level which would be the national director.'

Expatriates are involved in the subsidiary-Support Office communication through the training of Vietnamese employees in how to fulfil reporting requirements for Support Offices. This is an ongoing task as all Support Offices have different and changing reporting standards.

There are informal relationships between the expatriates and Support Offices that are a means of communication. Through informal relationships, the expatriates communicate intentions of projects and reports to Support Offices. Due to the fact that information passes through informal relationships, P3 reported: 'It's up to me to make sure that the relationship [with P1] was good enough to have those types [informal] of conversations.'

Expatriate relationships with the local governments.   Generally speaking, the relationships between the expatriates and the local governments were described by P1, P2, and P4 as a 'partnership'. The expatriates saw it as a goal to establish and maintain a good working relationship with the government for the subsidiary.

Development approaches and objectives are similar between the subsidiary and the Vietnamese government. P1 stated 'we have the same approach [to community development]. Government programs and [organization name removed] projects. Even in Government programs we have people centred development, so the philosophy is the same.'

The relationship characteristics vary depending on the level of government. At the national level, there was the most conflict between national government and foreign NGOs. The national government implemented restrictions over the subsidiary through regulations such as limits on the number of Vietnamese employees and NGO registration. The subsidiary was in breach of regulatory limits on Vietnamese employees. The expatriates were in ongoing negotiations with the government on this issue. P4 stated:

> We [the NGO subsidiary and the government] have been talking for years about reducing the number of Vietnamese staff. We [the Vietnamese government office] understand that they [NGO subsidiary] need staff to operate the program, but we have been talking about building the capacity of the local people.'

At the provincial, district, and commune levels, it was found that the relationship involved less explicit conflict. While there was partnership, the expatriates reported that the government's role as a community representative at this level could be a source of conflict. The expatriates were focused on community development, and disagreed with the idea that the government represented the community, as opposed to the actual people who would receive the benefit.

Another characteristic of the relationship between the government and the expatriates is the need for the expatriates to interpret the interactions with the government. One example was reported by P2. A meeting was called by a high-ranking official who reprimanded the expatriate and the NGO for a minor breach in regulation. After the formality of the meeting had ended, the same government official began to express his excitement in the project's potential and how happy he was that the project was going ahead. This polarization in interactions means the expatriates must interpret what is the 'official' point of view, and what is the government official's personal point of view. Incorrect interpretations can lead to a breach of official regulation, or offending a government official.

Despite the concerns and issues raised by the expatriates and government official, generally the relationship was expressed as cooperative and effective.

Expatriates' relationships with local employees and communities. The relationships with the Vietnamese employees were developed through managing local employees and team-based work. The expatriates reported one aspect of their role to be the empowerment and development of Vietnamese employees in subsidiary management and community development. There was teamwork between the expatriates and senior Vietnamese employees in strategic decision making, and as to how HQ policies and strategies would be made locally responsive to the Vietnamese context.

The relationships between the expatriates and local communities were characterized by cooperation and partnership. The expatriates saw partnership with local communities as the key to effective development. Knowledge sharing, open discussion, and community formed solutions were all described as important indicators of a successful relationship between the subsidiary and local communities. These initiatives were facilitated by the expatriates.

Discussion

This topic on multinational NGOs and expatriation in developing economies has not been widely researched. The findings of the case study demonstrate that a unique NGO approach to strategy formulation, implementation and organizational structure determine the outcome of NGOs' management of the global-local conflict. Regarding the three propositions raised earlier, we now offer the following responses.

> **Proposition 1**. Organizational ideology, politics, strategy and structure have significant impacts on the NGO's subsidiary strategy formulation and implementation.

This proposition is supported. There is a strong use of organizational ideology, politics, values and policies in the strategic decision making of the subsidiary. HQ's ideology and values are transplanted to the subsidiary through expatriates and socialisation programmes. The values are fundamentally based on the religious beliefs that guide the philosophical reason as to why the NGO operates. The case study shows that the expatriates directly control strategic and operational decision making by following the ideology and values of the HQ. The expatriates also improve information flow between the HQ, the Support Offices, and the subsidiary through reporting and informal communication. However, in terms of HQ control through resource dependency, the evidence shows that HQ does not have very much control over resources, but Support Offices have more influence on this aspect due to the NGO's specific organizational structure which enables the Support Offices to control the financial resources in the NGO.

> **Proposition 2**. Expatriates working for the NGO will have intrinsic ideological motivations that will lead to expatriate work satisfaction despite cross-cultural difficulties.

This proposition is also fully supported. The results show that the expatriates experience cross-cultural stress. However, despite the cross-cultural stress, the expatriates do not consider early departure. On the contrary, the expatriates experience great satisfaction working for the NGO in Vietnam. The key reason for this is that the expatriates intrinsic motivations for working abroad met. Any negative experiences or hardships that the expatriates may endure are rationalized against the fulfilment of personal goals and intrinsic motivations.

> **Proposition 3**. Expatriates working for the NGO will have a distant relationship with HQ and cooperative relationships with local governments, employees and communities.

This proposition is partially supported. The relationship between the expatriates and HQ is characterized by minimal formal communication and little monitoring. The relationship is distant because the ideological alignment allows HQ to trust the expatriate with a high degree of autonomy. Informal relationships partially replace the lack of close HQ-expatriate contact. Informal communication is normally initiated by the expatriate.

However, cooperation is evident in the relationship between the expatriate and local governments but with a certain degree of conflict due to ideological differences. In addition, the expatriates' relationships with Vietnamese employees are cooperative and team based. There is cooperation between expatriates and Vietnamese employees because the expatriates have long-term goals, mandated and supported by HQ, of empowerment and leadership for the Vietnamese employees. Inclusion of Vietnamese employees in important decision making not only allows the subsidiary to be locally relevant, but it also develops the ability of Vietnamese employees to lead the NGO's Vietnam subsidiary in the future. This form of relationship with the Vietnamese employees is a product of a geocentric mindset within the expatriates, and in the wider organization. The expatriates and NGOs believe that the Vietnamese employees have the capacity to effectively manage the subsidiary in the future.

Furthermore, the relationships between the expatriates and local communities are in the form of cooperation and partnership. This is because the expatriates have a geocentric approach to interaction with the local people. The expatriates see the relationship with the local people as a learning opportunity about development approaches in Vietnam.

Implications

There are implications for readers, theoretical literature and NGO's business and management practices in the area of multinational NGOs and expatriation. Generally speaking, the results reinforce the fact that the research on multinational organizations and expatriation is influenced by large variances in contextual variables (Suutari & Brewster, 2001). The NGO context has produced unique results in many facets of multinational NGO management and expatriation. For instance, the ideological alignment can be a mechanism for organization to empower expatriates but still ensure the strategic decision making at subsidiary level is aligned with the goals of the multinational organization. Organizational politics is also a tool to reduce the tension among expatriates. Informal communications between HQ and expatriate and between SO and expatriate are important for strategy formation as well as a crucial part of organizational politics.

The findings also show the cooperative relationships between NGO and the local governments are a crucial aspect for success. This is attributed to the resource commitment, political accommodation, organizational credibility and personal relationships. However, a degree of conflict exists because of different ideologies and development priorities between the NGO and the local governments. Hence, careful discussion and negotiation as well as compromise between each other are the necessary steps for maintaining a good relationship as well as achieving a win-win outcome.

In addition, there are implications for the wider theoretical literature on multinational organization and expatriation. There is strong support for Mintzberg and Waters's (1985) ideological and 'umbrella' theories regarding strategy development. The findings show that an adequate ideology enables HQ to set broad strategic policies for global integration and meanwhile allows subsidiaries with a high degree of autonomy to be locally responsive. There is also support for theories of organizational politics as a positive approach to strategy formulation (Pettigrew, 1977; Huff, 1988). The findings show that the shared values and beliefs between HQ and expatriates ensure the expatriates do not act in a self-serving way and abuse the political system by withholding key information.

Bartlett and Ghoshal's (1990) multi-domestic structure is also evident in the NGO. HQ, SO and different subsidiaries are treated as separate organizations operating in their individual contexts. However, the division of HQ from sources of financial resource in the NGO has not been widely discussed in MNC literature. This is a unique organizational structure among multinational NGOs. In addition, the findings support Jaeger's (1983) approach about social pressure existing in cultural control circumstances within a multinational organization. Shared culture amongst the organizational entities of the NGO creates a self-governing subsidiary that will fulfil its role dutifully without the need to be regularly monitored. The results show that there are strong, embedded, and sustainable sources of control available at the HQ level and that helps HQ to establish cultural control over subsidiaries.

As for the implications for the NGO's business and management practices, several key aspects are highlighted here:

(1) The NGO structure does not encourage any inter-subsidiary communication or knowledge sharing. The results show that the subsidiary is able to operate by only interacting with HQ and SOs.
(2) the success of the expatriates is directly linked to their intrinsic motivations and personal belief in the NGO's values. The personal belief in the goals of the wider NGO has led to ongoing commitment to the subsidiary despite organizational and cross-cultural hardships. To maintain expatriate success, the NGO must ensure expatriates share the motivations and beliefs through recruitment and selection.
(3) Cooperation between expatriates and local employees through team-work is a major way to assist of foreign NGOs local responsiveness. Inclusion of Vietnamese employees in decision making allows for information sourced from local communities to flow 'upwards' to the expatriates.

Conclusion

This pilot study creates a starting point for future research into management of the global-local conflict in NGOs, and the role of expatriates in NGOs. It has revealed a unique approach to management of the global-local conflict that exists in one particular NGO. The power of ideology in subsidiary strategy formulation is evident. The global-local conflict can be well managed by expatriates who realize the importance of the local context, but subscribes to the organization's ideology in strategy formulation. Organizational structure and politics provide a forum for which HQs can listen to reasons for subsidiary-specific changes to strategy and policy. HQ control of subsidiaries can be established through organizational culture. Eventually, expatriate failure can be reduced through intrinsic ideological motivation and autonomy.

The limitation of the research is the difficulty in generalizing from the case study to the wider NGO and MNC sectors (Bryman, 2000). However, in response to this limitation, a quote from P1:

> There are very few situations where a policy comes down and 100 countries adopt it, and only one office has to change it. In many ways every single country has to take the policy and say 'what does this mean to us in our context'?

Management of the global-local conflict and expatriation is always context dependent. Survey or quantitative research on many subsidiaries will not reveal the complexities of each individual context or interpersonal relationship. Therefore the contribution of the case study approach to discovering the contextual complexities and building a deeper understanding of the role of the expatriate is valuable.

Future research lies in studying how prominent the unique structure found in this analysis is across the NGO sector. If there is a prevalence of this structure in NGOs, there may be implications for management of multinational organizations in general. In light of this first pilot study, a more specific area of future research is to examine the HQ-SO relationship. This will give greater insight and a deeper understanding of the reasons for the division of strategic decision-making and financial resources between different organizational entities.

References

Adler, N. J. (1986) *International Dimensions of Organizational Behavior* (Belmont: Kent).

Bartlett, C. & Ghoshal, S. (1990) *Managing Across Borders* (London: Hutchinson Business Books).

Bhuian, S. N., Al Shammari, E. S. & Jefri, O. A. (1996) Organizational commitment, job satisfaction, and job characteristics: an empirical study of expatriates in Saudi Arabia, *International Journal of Commerce and Management*, 6(3), pp. 57–80.

Black, J. S. & Gregersen, H. B. (1992) Serving two masters: managing the dual allegiance of expatriate employees, *Sloan Management Review*, 33(4), pp. 61–71.

Bonache, J., Brewster, C. & Suutari, V. (2001) Expatriation: a developing research agenda, *Thunderbird International Business Review*, 43(1), pp. 3–20.

Boyacigiller, N. (1990) The role of expatriates in the management of interdependence, complexity, and risk in multinational corporations, *Journal of International Business Studies*, 21(3), pp. 357–381.

Bryman, A. (2000) *Research Methods and Organisation Studies* (London: Routledge).

Buchanan, D. & Badham, R. (1999) Politics and organizational change: the lived experience, *Human Relations*, 53(5), pp. 609–629.

Cullen, J. B. (2002) *Multinational Management: A Strategic Approach*, 2nd edn (Cincinnati, Ohio: South-Western Thomson Learning).

Dowling, P. J., Schuler, R. S. & Welch, D. (1994) *International Dimensions of Human Resource Management*, 2nd edn (Boston, MA: PWS-Kent).

Drory, A. & Romm, C. T. (1990) The definition of organizational politics: a review, *Human Relations*, 43(1), pp. 1133–1154.

Duiker, W. J. (1989) Vietnam: the challenge of reform, *Current History*, 88, pp. 177–196.

Dunning, J. H. (1998) An overview of relations with national governments, *New Political Economy*, 3(2), pp. 280–284.

Egelhoff, W. G. (1984) Patterns of control in U.S., UK, and European multinational corporations, *Journal of International Business Studies*, 15(2), pp. 73–81.

Eisenhardt, K. M. (1989) Agency theory: an assessment and review, *Academy of Management Review*, 14(1), pp. 57–74.

George, I. (1995) Vietnam: assessing the achievements of *Doi Moi*, *The Journal of Development Studies*, 31(5), pp. 725–750.

Gregersen, H. B. & Black, J. S. (1992) Antecedents to commitment to a parent company and a foreign operation, *Academy of Management Journal*, 35(1), pp. 65–90.

Ha, N. K. (2001) *Lessons Learned from a Decade of Experience. Hanoi: A Report on International Non-Government Organization Operations and Effectiveness from 1991–2001* (Hanoi: NGO Resource Centre of Vietnam).

Harris, H. & Holden, L. (2001) between autonomy and control: expatriate managers and strategic IHRM in SMEs, *Thunderbird International Business Review*, 43(1), pp. 77–100.

Holmes, W. & Piker, F. K. (1980) Expatriate failure: prevention rather than cure, *Personnel Management*, 12, pp. 30–32.

Huff, A. S. (1988) Politics and arguments as a means of coping with ambiguity and change, in: L. R. Pondy, R. J. Boland & J. Thomas (Eds) *Managing Ambiguity and Change*, pp. 79–90 (Chichester: John Wiley).

Jaeger, A. M. (1983) The transfer of organizational culture overseas: an approach to control in the multinational corporation, *Journal of International Business Studies*, 14(2), pp. 91–114.

Keegan, W. J. (1974) Multinational scanning: a study of the information sources utilized by headquarters executives in multinational corporations, *Administrative Science Quarterly*, 19, pp. 411–412.

Kobrin, S. J. (1988) Expatriate reduction and strategic control in American multinational corporations, *Human Resource Management*, 27(1), pp. 63–75.

Luo, Y. (2001) Towards a Cooperative View of MNC-Host Government Relations: Building Blocks and Performance Implications, *Journal of International Business Studies*, 32(3), pp. 401–419.

Martinez, Z. L. & Ricks, D. A. (1989) Multinational parent companies' influence over human resource decisions of affiliates: U.S firms in Mexico, *Journal of International Business Studies*, 20(3), pp. 465–488.

May, T. (1997) *Social Research: Issues, Method and Process* (London: Open University Press).

Mintzberg, H. & Waters, J. A. (1985) Of strategies, deliberate and emergent, *Strategic Management Journal*, 6, pp. 257–272.

O'Donnell, S. W. (2000) Managing foreign subsidiaries: agents of headquarters, or an interdependent network?, *Strategic Management Journal*, 21, pp. 525–548.

Otterbeck, L. (1981) *The Management of Headquarters-Subsidiary Relationships in Multinational Corporations* (Aldershot: Gower).

Ouchi, W. G. (1977) The relationship between organizational structure and organizational control, *Administrate Science Quarterly*, March, pp. 95–113.

Ouchi, W. G. (1981) *Theory Z* (Reading: Addison-Wesley).

PACCOM (2003) *Handbook of Foreign Non-Governmental Organizations in Vietnam* (Hanoi: Vietnam's Union of Friendship Organizations People's Aid Coordinating Committee and National Political Publisher).

Pettigrew, A. M. (1977) Strategy formulation as a political process, *International Studies of Management and Organization*, 7(2), pp. 78–87.

Pfeffer, J. & Salancik, G. (1978) *The External Control of Organizations: A Resource Dependence Perspective* (New York: Harper & Row).

Prahalad, C. K. & Doz, Y. (1987) *The Multinational Mission: Balancing Local Demands and Global Vision* (New York: Free Press).

Sills, D. L. (1957) *The Volunteers* (New York: Free Press).

Suutari, V. & Brewster, C. (2001) Expatriate management practices and perceived relevance: evidence from Finnish expatriates, *Personnel Review*, 30(5), pp. 554–577.

Swaak, R. A. (1995) Expatriate failures: too many, too much cost, too little planning, *Compensation and Benefits Review*, 27, pp. 47–73.

Tung, R. L. (1982) Selection and training procedures of US, European, and Japanese multinationals, *California Management Review*, 25(1), pp. 57–71.

Wischermann, J. (2003) Vietnam in the era of *Doi Moi*: issue-orientated organizations and their relationship to the government, *Asian Survey*, 43(6), pp. 867–889.

World Bank (2004) Vietnam at a Glance. Available at http: //www.worldbank.org/data/countrydata/aag/vn-m_aag.pdf (accessed 18 October 2004).

Trust and Uncertainty: A Study of Bank Lending to Private SMEs in Vietnam

THANG V. NGUYEN*, NGOC T. B. LE** & NICK J. FREEMAN[†]
*National Economics University, Vietnam and Faculty of Business Administration, University of Macau, China, **NEU Business School, Hanoi, Vietnam, [†]Institute of Southeast Asian Studies, Singapore

Introduction

The burgeoning private sector is playing an increasingly important role in developing and transitional economies. Access to bank financing is critical for this sector to develop. However, lending to private small and medium-sized enterprises (SMEs) in the transitional economies is a challenging task for all banks. Previous empirical studies concur that private SMEs tend to be high-risk borrowers, with an inadequate basis for calculating risk when lending to private firms in transitional economies. The countries' market and financial institutions and legislative frameworks are often underdeveloped; property rights are not well defined, and private sector legitimacy is not always well protected (Boisot & Child, 1996; Peng & Heath, 1996; Nguyen, 2005). Data on private firms and the general business environment in which they function tends to be unavailable or unreliable. Further, most banks and private firms are newly established, and they have little history of working with each other. Thus, conventional risk management techniques, such as credit scoring or pricing for risk, are of limited use in such contexts. This raises a very basic question: how – in the absence of more robust market institutions and business data – can banks lend to private businesses?

This study addresses the question of how banks lend to private sector SMEs within the context of uncertainty (not risk), and whether different types of banks employ differing strategies. Specifically, this study attempts to answer four questions: 1) How do bankers in Vietnam perceive risks and uncertainty involved in lending to private SMEs?; 2) What are their strategies to cope with uncertainty?; 3) What trust-building strategies do they adopt with new business partners?; and 4) Do bankers from state-owned commercial banks differ from their counterparts in joint stock banks in their uncertainty-coping and trust-building strategies? We explore these issues using a qualitative, interview-based research survey of bankers in Vietnam. Vietnam offers a relatively unique natural laboratory, where bank lending to private firms is conducted in the absence of a well-established legal infrastructure, contracting and property norms, as well as the associated market-oriented ideological underpinnings. Both banks and private sector SMEs in Vietnam have to cope with considerable uncertainties, and provide us with critical insights into how banks cope with these uncertainties, beyond more conventional risks.

Our analysis proceeds as follows. The next section briefly reviews the current literature and theory on risk, uncertainty, trust and commercial bank lending to private SMEs. In this section we argue that banks in transitional economies face high uncertainty, rather than conventional risk, in lending to SMEs. Thus, Knight's (1957) distinction of risk and uncertainty, and insights from literature on trust, is useful in studying how banks in these countries lend to SMEs. We then present an overview of bank lending to private sector SMEs in Vietnam, highlighting the general underdevelopment of banking sector institutions, as well as the dynamic growth of the private sector in Vietnam. Next, we describe the research methodology, and then report the key findings. Finally, we conclude with our analysis and discussion of the results.

Theoretical Background

Risk, Uncertainty and Market Institutions

Mainstream economic theory does not distinguish risk and uncertainty (Guseva & Rona-Tas, 2001). Neither do studies of business management in transitional economies (Boisot & Child, 1996; Peng & Heath, 1996; O'Connor, 2000; Child & Tse, 2001). In Knight's (1957, originally published in 1921) seminal work, risk comprises objective probabilities of future events that the decision maker can calculate, based on a known distribution of outcomes across a group of past events. Uncertainty, on the other hand, is a situation where these probabilities cannot be assigned in a meaningful way (Langlois & Cosgel, 1993). According to Knight, 'when there is *no valid basis of any kind* for classifying instance' (Knight, 1957: 225, emphasis in original); when past events cannot be classified into homogeneous groups, an actor must resort to 'estimates'. These correspond to uncertainties.

Thus, the key distinction between risk and uncertainty lies in two possibilities. First, risk and uncertainty differ in the possibility of classifying and homogenizing instances (Langlois & Cosgel, 1993; Guseva & Rona-Tas, 2001). In the situation of uncertainty, we simply do not know which alternatives are possible. Second, risk and uncertainty differs in the possibility of assigning objective probability of future events. Objective probabilities, according to Knight (1957), are those that everyone would agree to, or those that could be publicly verifiable. In the context of bank lending to SMEs, statistical probabilities of past successful loans – as used by credit scoring companies, for example – indicate the practical level of risks banks must face.

Three conditions are needed to reduce uncertainties to risk. First, there needs to be a reasonable similarity across cases. In the specific case of lending to private SMEs, this means that previous borrowers must be classified, so that current applicants can be seen as highly comparable with a previous subset. This requires a high level of standardization, and the existence of credit information institutions that can gather, collate and verify such data, and thereby develop such classifications.

Secondly, there needs to be a reasonable similarity over time, which requires stability. In the context of bank lending to private SMEs, this means that past experiences of SMEs' business behaviour are not much different from present (or future) experiences. Thirdly, there needs to be a substantial number of past observations to ensure the reliability of the probability calculation.

In bank lending, the first two conditions can be provided by appropriate institutions. For example, in virtually all developed countries, commercial banks can rely on other banks, auditing companies or relevant governmental agencies to collect, standardize and verify information on potential customers. A large number of private businesses that operate over time allow banks to develop a reliable calculation of probability of the applicants' behaviour. Banks are then able to calculate the chances they take when they lend to new SMEs; and they can factor these chances into their loan pricing.

Unfortunately, such institutions have not yet begun to operate effectively in some transitional economies, including Vietnam. It is extremely difficult for banks in such countries to reduce such uncertainties into more quantifiable risks (O'Connor, 2000). In this context, guidance provided by western textbooks and consultants on risk management techniques is of limited utility. Private SMEs are a relatively new phenomenon in these countries, and bank lending to them is even more recent, so the requirements of i) stability, ii) comparability, and iii) an adequately large database of past loans (conditions two and three, above) are hard to attain. Yet banks in transitional economies still have to make loan decisions. How exactly do they do this is a question that remains largely unanswered in the current body of research literature. We turned to the literature of trust for possible directions.

Trust in the Interfirm Relationships

It has been recognized that trust is an effective strategy to cope with uncertainty (Lewis & Weigert, 1985; Guseva & Rona-Tas, 2001). In this study, we adapt the definition of Mayer *et al.* (1995), and define trust as the willingness of one party (the trustor) to be vulnerable to the actions of another party (the trustee), based on the expectation that the trustee will perform a particular action important to the trustor, irrespective of the ability to monitor and control that other party. Trust is a psychological state characterized by confidence that the partner will perform certain actions. It includes confidence in the partner's capability and integrity, and faith in the partner's benevolent intentions.

Trust is a complex concept. First, it is a multilevel construct, in that trust at the individual level is thought to relate to trust at the firm level (Zaheer *et al.*, 1998; Jeffries & Reed, 2000). Second, trust is multidimensional, in that partners can trust in each other's capabilities and benevolent intentions (Mayer *et al.*, 1995). Third, trust can play multiple causal roles, as outcome, antecedent and mediator (Rousseau *et al.*, 1998). For example, trust can be the outcome of partners' past collaboration, and the antecedent of their future collaboration.

Activities or mechanisms to build trust have not been explicitly discussed in the literature, although two basic mechanisms can be deduced. First, trust can emerge naturally (*emerging trust*) as a result of repeated deals (Zucker, 1986; Ring & Van de Ven, 1992). In this view, trust emerges as a consequence of repeated market transactions between the parties. Trust is seen as a fragile relationship that takes time to develop, and that is layered on top of ongoing market mechanisms. At some point, trust becomes sufficiently robust to begin serving as an alternative organizing principle, opening up new options for organizing, namely trust-based transactions. This mechanism requires the passage of considerable time and extensive experience for the partners to learn about and trust each other. Second, trust can be inherited (*inherited trust*) from the parties' past relationships and/or third parties' referrals. In other words, managers prefer collaborating with partners they already know or those who have been endorsed by trusted third parties (Granovetter, 1985; Coleman, 1988; Redding, 1990).

In East Asian countries, the development of trust has been widely recognized as a critical ingredient for doing business (for example, Hofstede & Bond, 1988; Redding, 1990; Boisot & Child, 1996; Xin & Pearce, 1996; Nguyen, 2005). A notable example of this are the ethnic Chinese, who have displayed a high level of entrepreneurial skill and success throughout Pacific Asia, partly through networking (Redding, 1990). This tendency may be ascribed to a combination of cultural pre-determinants and as a response to certain kinds of business environment. The Chinese cultural heritage, which is essentially Confucian, places an especially high value on core family membership as a source of identity, support and loyalty. It also legitimizes a paternalistic authority structure which accords great influence to the father-figure role, and supports benevolent autocracy with ethical underpinnings (Hofstede & Bond, 1988; Redding, 1990). Trust in this society is a matter of forging bonds of interpersonal obligation, enough to cement specific relationships between family units, and to use such networks to offset a high level of mistrust generally in society (Redding, 1990; Xin & Pearce, 1996).

These legacies of East Asian social history are strongly supportive of small-scale business with wide networks. The networking tradition is especially valuable in coping with environments of high uncertainty, where information is scarce and where change in the political sphere may cause high uncertainty in business. The co-opting of political support is crucial in such contexts, not just for alleviating threats, but for revealing opportunities in such disorderly and imperfect markets (Redding, 1990; Xin & Pearce, 1996).

To date, scholarly research on Vietnamese businesses has been quite sparse. Recognizing the country's Confucian cultural heritage and the underdevelopment of market institutions, several studies have pointed to the important role of trust in doing business in this country (McMillan & Woodruff, 1999; Nguyen, 2005; Nguyen *et al.*, 2005). In these studies, trust is found as a substitute for developed market institutions and legal infrastructure necessary to facilitate business transactions, and networks are used to sanction defaulting partners. Vietnamese managers were found to be skilful in deliberately developing trust with new business partners, so as to cope with uncertainty.

Bank Lending to SMEs

The existing literature has documented the great importance of bank credit to SMEs in developed countries (Ulrich & Casel, 1975; Blackwell & Winters, 2000). The literature has also documented the challenges banks face in lending to SMEs. These challenges include high failure rates of SMEs (Hannan & Freeman, 1984), the existence of significant information asymmetry between SME borrowers and banks (Berger & Udell, 1995; Binks & Ennew, 1997; Frame *et al.*, 2001), and the complicated mix between the owner's personal and their company's finances and assets (Levin & Travis, 1987).

To mitigate these problems, banks have to approach SMEs somewhat differently than they do larger clients. Some well-known techniques that banks use to cope with problems of lending to SMEs have been documented. These include taking ample collateral, developing long-term relationships with borrowers, credit scoring, and pricing for risk (namely, adjusting the interest rate on the loan to a level commensurate with the perceived degree of risk). Adequate collateral long-term relationships between lenders and borrowers are said to help mitigate problems of information asymmetry (Binks & Ennew, 1997; Frame *et al.*, 2001). A close relationship between banks and borrowers generates trust, which in turn provides the bank with a degree of confidence that the firm will use the loan in the right way. Research has shown that building close ties with the bank increases credit availability and reduces the interest rate for firms (Petersen & Rajan, 1994; Binks & Ennew, 1997).

In recent years, banks have implemented another solution for making loan decisions to SMEs: automated underwriting systems, based on credit scoring. Credit scoring is a process of assigning a single quantitative score to a potential borrower, representing an estimate of the borrower's future loan performance (Frame *et al.*, 2001). The scoring models often use an applicant's personal information, and sophisticated models can even utilize data on personal spending habits, social pursuits and family commitments. Such a personal credit history is said to be highly predictive of a loan repayment. When applicable, credit scoring does help banks to reduce the time and transaction cost of one-on-one interaction with borrowers, thereby reducing the price of small business loans, and increasing credit availability for SMEs (Frame *et al.*, 2001).

Notwithstanding all of the above, the current literature has not sufficiently distinguished between risk and uncertainties in lending to SMEs, particularly in more unstable business environments. This becomes a serious shortcoming when we examine the issue in the context of transitional economies like Vietnam. In such countries, banks face greater uncertainties, as well as heightened risks, stemming in part from the more volatile and immature business environment, the lower level of regulatory oversight, and the sheer pace with which the economy is growing from a relatively low base point. The next section further discusses this issue with an overview of the private and banking sectors in Vietnam.

Overview of the Private and Banking Sectors in Vietnam

The private sector in Vietnam has been growing at a rapid rate since the mid-1990s, and particularly speedily since 2000. In the three-year period between 2000 and 2002, 55,793 new enterprises were formally established, compared to less than 45,000 in the nine-year period preceding 2000. Indeed, the private sector has become an important engine of macroeconomic growth, a major source of employment and an important generator of foreign exchange earnings, in Vietnam. The vast majority of private sector companies in Vietnam are small and medium-sized enterprises (Nguyen, 2005).

Although the enabling environment for private sector SMEs has improved markedly in recent years, a number of constraints continue to inhibit the development of this sector. These constraints include ongoing problems in accessing adequate and suitable sources of funding, both for short-term working capital and more long-term fixed capital needs. Notwithstanding a marked improvement in the spectrum and scale of funding sources, private sector SMEs still cite financing as one of the major challenges that they face, along with insufficient access to land.

Over the last 20 years, the banking sector in Vietnam has changed considerably, from a centrally-planned mono-banking system, to a relatively more complex and market-oriented financial sector, comprising multiple participants. The development of the banking sector remains an ongoing task, and the commercial banking sector as a whole is not yet able to provide Vietnam with an efficient financial intermediation service. To date, there are five state-owned commercial banks, 34 private (or joint stock) banks, four joint venture banks, and 28 branches of foreign banks operating in Vietnam.

While banks in Vietnam view private SMEs as a potential client base, they nevertheless face high uncertainty in lending to this sector. Our exploratory research addresses these questions of how banks perceive and cope with uncertainty in such a context, and if state-owned and private banks employ different strategies. We also explore if trust is one strategy, and then how banks develop trust with these nascent firms in the absence of market institutions.

Field Method

Research Design

A qualitative interview-based study is the most appropriate methodological approach for an exploratory research project of this kind. Vietnam is a relatively under-studied country, and this research is exploratory in nature. Moreover, there is little tradition of independent, confidential inquiry in Vietnam (Adair, 1995). In this context, good personal relationships between researchers and interviewees play a crucial role in gathering and securing relatively sensitive information that is not normally in the public domain.

Sample

The interviewees were credit officers and relevant senior managers of both state-owned and private banks currently operating in Vietnam, all of which are presently lending to private SMEs. We directly contacted senior managers of the banks (mostly the heads of credit departments or the equivalent), briefed them on the nature of the research, and requested interviews with those personnel directly involved in small business lending. Every manager we contacted agreed to participate in the interviews and/or set up interviews with relevant bank officials. These interviews were conducted in the period between December 2003 and February 2004. In total, 23 credit officers and managers from 11 different banks, located in both Hanoi and Ho Chi Minh City, were interviewed. This sample provides a relatively robust cross section of bank lending activity in Vietnam, at least as it pertains to private SME credit provision, and within the logistical constraints of conducting primary research in Vietnam (see the Appendix for the interviewees' profile).

Interview Structure

The interviews were semi-structured. The questions contained in the research tool were largely open-ended. The first section contained questions that sought to shed light on each bank's history of lending to private SMEs. The second section focused on the main challenges banks faced in lending to private SMEs. Interviewees were encouraged to give specific examples of loan applications that were both approved and declined, and the factors behind the decision, in order to better 'flesh out' the answers given. The third section of the interview tool focused on the specific methods used by the bank to glean and analyse sufficient information to make a loan decision. The fourth section focused on how banks interact with their private SME borrowers, and how they supervise the loans.

Data Analysis

All interview data was transcribed and stored verbatim. We categorized and compared the data according to the typical process a bank undertakes in evaluating, lending to, and monitoring a private SME borrower. In each category, we detected the challenges (uncertainties) banks faced. We identified two strategies to cope with uncertainties (namely uncertainty avoidance and relying on trust) and developed coding schemes for each strategy (see Tables 1 and 2). Similarly, we identified two basic mechanisms to develop trust, and developed coding schemes for each mechanism.

Then, based on a content analysis of the interview data, we identified the presence of those criteria (strategies and trust mechanisms) in each interview. Two authors conducted this content analysis independently of each other. We then

Table 1. Coding schemes for strategies to cope with uncertainties

Strategies	Descriptions
Uncertainty avoidance	Loan decisions are based primarily on the following criteria: • *Sufficient collateral*: all legal requirements are met (for example, pink book for land); prices are set conservatively (about 50% of the estimated market price), and the loan is only up to 70% of the collateral value. • *Highly certain business plans*: Owners must put considerable capital in the project; the plans must show some certain customers (for example, tentative and/or signed contracts) of the products or services. • *Close monitoring*: Close and expensive monitoring procedures are applied (for example, frequent visits, regular reports, closely monitoring clients' inventories). • *Legally reported document*: The loan decisions are made primarily based on formal and legally reported documents.
Reliance on trust	Loan decisions are based on the trustworthiness of the applicants (the firms and the owners) together with the fulfilment of legal requirements of the applications (legal document, legal collateral). Specific criteria (evidence) are: • *Trustworthiness*: Both the firm and the [real] owners show their capability and integrity (See Table 3 for detailed criteria). • *Collateral*: the price can be closer to the estimated market prices; the loans can be more than 70% of the collateral values. • *Business plans*: The certainty of the business plans can be relaxed. • *Monitoring*: It is rather supporting interactions than monitoring or supervision of the loans. • *Documents*: The loan decisions are made based on both formal documents and other informal data.

compared the results and any inconsistency was discussed until there was agreement.

Results

Bankers' Perceptions of Uncertainties

The interviews reveal that banks in Vietnam face numerous uncertainties in lending to private SMEs. These uncertainties confront bank officers at each and every step of the lending process (for example, developing the client database, learning about and assessing new applicants' capability, assessing collateral, assessing business plans and monitoring the loans). The main sources of these uncertainties appear to be the country's ineffective legal system, unavailable and unreliable business data and inefficient professional agencies. The interview data

Table 2. Coding scheme for trust mechanisms

Mechanisms	Descriptions
Inherited trust	Banks trust private business clients primarily because: • The clients are previous successful borrowers. • The clients have used some other services from the banks (for example, open accounts, money transfer). • The clients are referred and guaranteed by respected third parties (individuals or organizations). • The clients have a reputation in the market (for example, they have got the Vietnamese high quality product award or Red Star award)
Constructed trust	Banks trust clients by doing (some of) the following: • Actively approaching new potential clients and exploring opportunities to cooperate. • Developing informational network with other individuals and organizations to learn about new clients. • Actively interacting with potential clients' managers (for example, interview, visit, social gathering). • Providing some coaching and supporting service to the firms' owners/managers

confirms our expectation that there is no solid basis for bankers to calculate risks in lending to the nascent private sector in Vietnam. This observation holds for both private and state-owned commercial banks. We identify and depict these challenges by briefly working through the various sources of the uncertainties, and Table 3 summarizes our findings.

The lack of business information. In developing a client database, the data from all sources tends to be highly fragmented, out of date, prone to errors and omissions, and generally unreliable. For example, the company registration department at the provincial or city level should theoretically have a database of registered companies within its area. The database, however, contains registration information and rarely updates on firm changes or even bankruptcy. Another possible source of information is industry directories. According to the interviewees, this source is unreliable because the industries' statistical systems are not up to date, and also because most private firms tend to be new (less than ten years old) and frequently changing. Some other sources of information tend to be more reliable (customs and tax agencies, Ministry of Trade or Chamber of Commerce and Industry), but access to these sources is said to be limited.

There is also a serious lack of market price data when banks want to assess an applicant's collateral. The most common type of collateral is land and property. As the real estate market in Vietnam is underdeveloped, housing prices tend to be highly case specific and change very quickly. As several interviewees stated, the government price could be ten times lower than the market price for a single piece

Table 3. Sources of uncertainties

	Legal system	Professional agency	Information
Developing client database	Registered fields of businesses may not match the firm's real businesses	Lack of agencies (for example, market research) that have good database on private firms	Availability and quality of information
Learning about/ assessing new clients	Lack of effective corporate governance and transparency (for example, a firm can have different accounting books)	Some auditors' lack of credibility Lack of certification agencies (for example, product quality, consumer protection)	Availability and quality of macro information Lack of firm documents (for example, strategies, policies)
Collateral	Lack of clear property right (land) Cumbersome law enforcement	Lack of efficient real state market and agencies	Lack of market price information of land (as collateral)
Assessing business plans	Changes in the government regulations		Lack of quality business data
Monitoring loans	Weak law enforcement		

of land, and there is confusion over how to get a house valued for collateral. One manager of a private bank in Hanoi summarized this problem:

> How to get the market price is not an easy task. The real estate offices and companies can be one reference. Sometimes they do not cooperate, because we do not buy their goods and services. We have to go to the neighbourhood, look at the newspaper, consult real state offices, etc., and still feel insecure about our estimates.

The lack of quality business data, as recognized by the interviewees, has a profound impact on developing (for applicants) and assessing (for bankers) business plans. As three bank managers articulated it, assessing business plans was largely a 'theoretical' or 'cosmetic' task. Market information on customers, competitors, and suppliers is very sparse and unreliable for most industries, as banks themselves testify. It is very hard to get reliable information on market competition in each industry. The following comments evidence this clearly:

> We had to verify information given in the business plans, such as the state of the market, competition and input prices. This was a very hard job because the information is fragmented. Assessing business plans, especially middle and long term plans, is largely subjective.

We examine market prices and projections in business plans. In fact, this is a theoretical exercise because both firms and banks do not have solid information to form the basis for the calculations.

I often turn to our trusted clients in the same business areas and ask them for relevant information contained in a business plan. They provide what they know, which is better than nothing.

The lack of effective market institutions.   The weakness of Vietnam's legal system stems from both a lack of laws and ineffective enforcement of them. Firstly, upon their establishment, private firms are required by law to register with the Department of Company Registration in their relevant town or district. However, the officially registered ownership of the firm, and the business it conducts, can be quite different in practice. This lack of law enforcement makes the company database of limited use, and even misleading. The following quotes from our interviews should be considered:

> By law, it is very easy for people to register a company. They only need several hundred thousand Dong [equivalent to US$20–30] and as few as two people to establish a company. Thus, newly registered companies are everywhere. Many of them are fake companies, but nobody knows how many.

> The data from Company Registration provides the legal status of a firm, and nothing else! Even the owner of the firm in the registered document may not be real. Some people are working in military or government organizations. They are not allowed to establish their own companies. They therefore ask someone else to be the 'owner' in the paper. We have to find out in every case who the real owners of the firms are.

> Our bank focuses on export-oriented firms. The registration data can be very misleading because many firms register as exporters, but in practice they do not export at all. The opposite can also be true.

Secondly, there is a lack of corporate governance and transparency for private SMEs. This is evidenced when a banker wants to review a firm's financial books. Besides the lack of financial skills, private SMEs often are motivated to have different accounting books. With a great deal of effort, bank officers may get firms' real financial data. However, should the banks decide to use such real data, bank officers do not have the legal document on the client's financial status to support their lending decision. This creates a dilemma. If banks rely on the clients' formal financial documents, they may not have a sufficiently strong economic justification to give loans. But if banks rely on their clients' so-called 'real' financial data, they may have strong economic justification to lend, but they would not have the legally more robust formal data to back up their lending decisions.

The lack of transparency and good corporate governance system also make it hard to be certain which firms are successful and which are not. As one banker of a private bank told us: 'If a firm appears to be very successful, it often invites government investigation. Tomorrow, that firm may be in trouble.' This also reflects the low level of managerial knowledge and skills of most Vietnamese entrepreneurs in the start-up and growth phases of their firms. Consequently, bankers need to conduct some coaching or consulting activities in helping firms to develop convincing and valid fund requests. That is a part of the trust building strategy presented in a later section of the report.

Thirdly, the weakness of the legal system strongly influences the assessment of collateral. Property rights are not clear on the most common type of collateral: land and housing. To be used as collateral, the house (and accompanying piece of land) must have a 'pink book' granted by the government (as a recognition of the right to use and transfer the land). However, the process of granting the 'pink book' has only recently been started and is progressing very slowly, as the following quote from one of the interviewees illustrates: 'The only way is to wait for a "pink book", if you want to use your land as collateral. When will you get it? Nobody knows!'

Finally, the weakness of the legal system strongly influences the resolution of non-performing loans. On the one hand, banks may not want to report non-performing loans. This is because a report showing the aggregate size of non-performing loans over an acceptable limit may result in a visit by inspectors from the State Bank of Vietnam. On the other hand, liquidating collateral provided as security on a delinquent loan can be particularly time-consuming.

Strategies to Cope with Uncertainties

Avoiding Uncertainties and Relying on Trust

As presented in the previous section, lending to private business in Vietnam is case and time specific. Conventional risk management remains a somewhat 'theoretical' and artificial exercise, in the eyes of many bank officers, and not applicable to the situation in Vietnam. As a result, banks in Vietnam try to cope more directly with uncertainty. There are basically two key strategies adopted in coping with uncertainty: avoiding it and placing greater emphasis on trust.

The first alternative is an attempt to avoid uncertainties. Banks pursue this strategy through a combination of limiting themselves to only short-term loans and applying a careful lending procedure. Both state and private banks granted short and medium-term loans (of up to one year) to private businesses in most cases. These loans are often for simple business transactions which can be easily verified, such as export credit or trade financing. The other major element of this strategy is the application of a conservative and careful lending procedure. Legal documents are checked carefully and collateral is valued conservatively (see Table 1). The business plans need to show a high level of owners' commitment to the project (owners' capital) and certainty (for example, they already have some customers' orders). Bankers often follow a close and expensive monitoring process. Just take an example of a close and expensive monitoring process that one bank applies for some of its private clients.

> We have now developed a two key system. The firm has one key for their inventory, and we have another. If they sell the goods in the inventory, they will need both keys. Thus, we follow their business closely.

The strategy of avoiding uncertainty, by itself, has limitations. Short-term loans entail higher transaction costs. Banks could hold collateral, but they do not wish to become virtual 'pawnshops'. Neither do they have adequate resources to become too involved in lenders' day-to-day businesses by applying close monitoring processes. Thus, applying this strategy means seriously limiting the number of loans to be granted to private firms.

The second strategy is to rely on trust with clients. Consistent with the literature on inter-firm trust, two objects of trust and two levels of trust emerge from the data. Banks trust their applicants at both levels: 1) the personal level (trust in an individual owner and/or contact managers); and 2) the organizational level (trust in the firm itself). At both levels, banks trust both their partner's capability (such as resources and expertise) and their integrity (intentions, motivation, and benevolence). Table 4 summarizes the different signals or indicators of trust that banks often look for in prospective lenders. At least one type of trust needs to be deemed high for the loan to be granted.

The avoiding uncertainty strategy emphasizes the *ex ante* commitment of the borrowers, and assumes low *ex post* flexibility of the loans (that is, close monitoring). By contrast, relying on trust emphasizes the *ex post* commitment from both sides. Both sides are assumed to work together in any circumstances to make the loan a success. Note that the trust-based strategy cannot totally replace strategies of uncertainty avoidance. Pure trust-based decisions are largely subjective and can lead to serious systemic errors. In fact, several disclosed cases of fraud and corruption concerning large loans in recent years in Vietnam were rooted in purely personal, trust-based considerations. However, with trusted borrowers, banks can lessen some of the uncertainty avoidance tactics (for example, close monitoring), and thus facilitate the expansion of the market.

Types of Banks and Adopted Strategies

How do different banks cope with uncertainties? Table 5 indicates that bankers from state-owned banks tend to use the uncertainty avoidance strategy more frequently than those from private banks. In contrast, bankers from private banks adopt trust-based strategies more extensively than those from state-owned banks. A closer look at Table 5 shows that in each cell, the observed frequencies are clearly quite different from the expected frequencies. Specifically, bankers from private banks are more frequently associated with trust-based strategies than would be expected, and bankers from state-owned banks are more associated with uncertainty avoidance strategy. This finding suggests the presence of a strong relationship between types of banks and strategies (Chi-square p < .001).

Table 4. Signals of trust in the Bank-SME Relationship

	Trust in a person	Trust in the firm
Capability *(have enough resources and expertise to manage the loan)*	• Relevant background and education • Experience in the field of business • Strong personal network • Positive referral on expertise • Positive impression with bankers – demonstrate business knowledge and skills • Positive learning in working with banks' procedure	• Resources (office, plant, car, managers, etc.) • Management system (strategy, structure, culture, formalized policies) • Clear, professional accounting system and reports • Promising businesses (products and markets) • Good performance • Positive referral or reputation
Integrity *(strong intentions, motivation to use the loan effectively and properly, and to cooperate with banks)*	• Positive referral on integrity • Positive impression with bankers – demonstrate cooperative attitude • Willingness to share sensitive and real information with the banks • Positive experience in working with banks	• Number of services the firm used from the bank (the more the better) • Number of banks the firm has a relationship with

How and why do different banks cope with uncertainties differently? The answer to this question is revealed by the interview data. A simple explanation is based on the availability of a bank's choices of clients. State banks, with longer histories, better support from the government and more reliable, traditional state-owned clients are less motivated to take on the uncertainties. For state-owned banks, private SMEs are viewed as an add-on type of client, that helps the banks look better 'politically'. Private SMEs may become important in the future for the state-owned banks, but not at the moment. The following quotes from two state banks' managers should be considered:

1)   Since 2001 we have started to lend to private businesses as a way to diversify our clients.
2)   Lending to private firms fits with the government's new policies.

In contrast, private banks have a shorter history, less resources and weaker support from the government. These banks have no choice but to focus on the more uncertain and new private sector. In most cases, neither private banks nor

Table 5. Cross-site display table of the types of banks to strategies

Strategies	State banks # of bankers (15) responses	Private banks # of bankers (8) responses
Avoiding uncertainties		
• Conservative pricing collateral	8	0
• Loans are only up to 70% of the collateral	12	2
• Owner must put in considerable capital	4	0
• Certain customers	6	1
• Close monitoring procedure	10	3
• Relying primarily on formal documents	12	0
Total	*52 (37.7)*	*6 (20.2)*
Relying on trust		
• Clients' trustworthiness	8	8
• Collateral price can be closer to the market price (more than 50% of the market price)	1	5
• Loans can be more than 70% of collateral value	2	3
• The certainty of the business plans can be relaxed	4	4
• Considering other data besides formal document	2	6
Total	*17 (28)*	*26 (15)*

* *Note*: $X^2 = 27.7$, $p < .001$ (expected frequencies in parentheses)

their private business clients have built a strong reputation. They, however, are forced to work with each other, largely on trust. As several bankers put it: 'we have to live with the 'flood' [*dangerous situations – namely, uncertain clients*]', or 'the most important factor for us to develop business is relationship with clients, both organizationally and personally'. Here we observed a situation where both banks and their private business clients have not developed reputation in the market. They cannot rely on market institutions for some first transactions. Yet, they need to work with each other somehow. Trust-based strategies appear to be the most realistic alternative for them to approach each other. Thus, the trust-based strategy is not only an add-on alternative for conventional market transactions. Nor does it emerge from ongoing market transactions. Instead, relying extensively on the trust-based strategy appears to be the only choice for these private banks, even in a very early stage of the business relationships.

Mechanisms of Trust

Inherited and constructed trust. How, in the absence of market institutions, do banks and firms develop trust with each other? The data reveals two common mechanisms in which trust is unfolded: 1) trust can be inherited from past organizational and/or individual relationships; and 2) trust can be actively constructed from the beginning of the business relationship.

Consistent with the current literature (for example, Granovetter, 1985; Coleman, 1988; Guseva & Rona-Tas, 2001), trust can be inherited from past relationships. In our study, this type of trust stems from three sources. First, banks trust their previous clients. Firms that have a well-managed account in the bank, or have frequently used the bank's services before, are deemed more trustworthy. As several interviewees stated, a bank will trust a firm more if the firm has used more services from the bank. Four interviewees referred to this type of clients as 'blood-relation clients' [*equivalent to loyal clients*]. In contrast, a firm may lose trust from a bank if the firm has relationships with other banks. Second, banks can trust a client if there is some personal relationship between bankers and managers of the firm. In fact, bankers often trust firms that are owned or managed by their relatives or close friends, or by people known to the bankers. However, some interviewees noted that personal trust cannot totally replace organizational capability. Personal relationships only help starting the relationship. Finally, trust can also be transitive from third parties. Five interviewees acknowledged that some of their private business clients were introduced and recommended by reputed organizations or by respectable individuals (for example, high positioned government officials). The banks trust these clients because 'these clients were trusted by the recommenders, and we trust the recommenders'.

The second alternative to develop trust is for the banks to actively construct trust with their private SMEs clients (*constructed trust*). That is actually a process of learning to trust. Banks often have two ways to learn about new clients: 1) developing an information network; and 2) direct interaction with the clients. Most interviewees recognized that their banks have wide information networks with other organizations and individuals. Inter-organizational information networks include networks with other banks, government authorities, long-term clients and business associations. Officers from both state-owned and private banks acknowledged that they often try to get information from these organizations.

To get more refined and sensitive information, bank officers have to turn to their interpersonal networks. Bankers' interpersonal networks include their colleagues in other banks, government officials at various levels, business people and managers, and their friends and relatives. Almost all interviewees suggested that using their interpersonal networks is an efficient way to get more up-to-date and sensitive information. Sometimes bankers have to pay fees (under different names) for the information they receive. The downside of this information is that it is informal. Bankers can rely on it to make decisions, but they cannot use it to formally support their lending decisions.

The most important source of information, however, is direct interaction between bankers and firms' owners/managers. This was acknowledged by most interviewees. With all new applicants, credit officers or bank managers must communicate directly with the owners/key managers of firms. These bankers often go to visit the firms' premises, observe the firms' operations, and interview pertinent people. Sometimes bankers have to find appropriate ways to ask for the real financial data, in addition to the formal financial documents. As several interviewees suggested, the firms need to trust credit officers before they can provide their real financial data. These credit officers often have to promise to keep this real data confidential, and use them only for the loan application assessment. Credit officers, in many cases, have to also work closely with firms' managers in preparing the application package.

During such interactions, bankers continuously analyse and make judgements on the firm's capability and integrity. While judgement on the status of firms' financial resources and their other resources can be more objective, an assessment on management capability and integrity is largely subjective. Most interviewees used words like 'intuition', 'feelings', and 'impressions' to describe how they assessed their potential clients. And these subjective and qualitative assessments often get more weight than the financial quantitative data. Some loan applications subsequently get approved. For these clients, banks actually learn to trust them. This trust is neither inherited nor transitive; it is constructed organically by the bankers and firm managers. The bankers' role is critical in this process. Their emotions, skills, intuitions, and tacit knowledge all play a part in how they assess a new client.

Types of banks and mechanisms of trust. We examined if different banks employed different mechanisms to develop trust. Table 6 suggests that state-owned banks rely on inherited trust more frequently than do private banks. In contrast, private banks constructed trust more extensively and actively than state-owned banks. This finding suggests the presence of strong relationships between types of banks and mechanisms of trust (Chi-square $p < .001$).

Table 6. Analysis of types of banks and mechanisms of trust

Mechanisms	State banks # of bankers (15) responses	Private banks # of bankers (8) responses
Inherited trust		
• Previous successful borrowers	6	1
• Previous clients of other services	4	2
• Guaranteed by trusted parties	4	2
• Selected quality clients	10	0
Total	*(24)*	*(4)*
Constructed trust		
• Approach new potential clients	6	6
• Develop information network with other organizations	10	6
• Develop information network with individuals	6	4
• Direct business interactions with clients (interview, visit, reading clients' reports, etc.)	10	8
• Direct personal interactions with clients (visit, social gathering, common friends, etc.)	0	8
• Coaching and supporting activities	10	6
Total	*(42)*	*(38)*

Note: $X^2 = 10.89$, $p < .001$ (expected frequencies in parentheses)

We came back to the status of the banks for explanations. Inherited trust requires sufficient past contacts between the partners. In addition, banks need to have a reasonable reputation to attract and keep quality clients. In that respect, state-owned banks are in a better position to accumulate inherited trust with private business clients. In contrast, most private banks have reputation than state-owned banks, and provide fewer services than state banks. As a result, young private banks need to join with their prospective trading partners to actively construct trust.

Based on our findings, we propose:

> **Proposition 1**. In transitional economies, bankers use a combination of uncertainty avoidance and trust-based strategies to lend to the private businesses. Bankers from state-owned banks use uncertainty avoidance strategies more extensively than those from private banks. Conversely, bankers from private banks rely on trust-based strategies more extensively than those from state-owned banks.

> **Proposition 2**: In developing trust with private business clients, bankers use a combination of inherited and constructed trust. Bankers from state-owned banks use inherited trust more extensively than those from private banks. In contrast, bankers from private banks use constructed trust more extensively than those from state-owned banks.

It should be noted that our classification of private and state-owned banks is possibly confounded with some other possible variables (size, age and history of the banks). Further research is needed to extract the influence of these variables from that of ownership on trust mechanisms.

Discussion

This study addressed the question of how – in the absence of institutions that legitimate markets, contracts, and private property, and the lack of business data – banks make loan decisions to the private sector. Our result suggests that, facing considerable uncertainties (rather than risks), Vietnamese banks employ a combination of uncertainty avoidance and reliance on trust in lending to their private business clients. Trust between banks and their private business clients is primarily inherited from past contacts and/or actively constructed at the beginning of the relationships. We also found a strong association between types of banks and uncertainty coping strategies, as well as strong relationships between types of banks and trust development mechanisms.

Our essay contributes to current literature in several areas. First, our data suggests that personal trust can be used to cope with uncertainty. The extensive literature on bank lending to small business has focused on risk management techniques. The general belief is that under uncertainty, banks need to apply risk management techniques. This study demonstrates that reducing uncertainty to risk requires the development of market institutions and business data. Therefore, calculating risk is a social capacity that takes time to develop, and until such social capacity develops, banks have to cope with uncertainties.

Our study suggests that relying on trust can be an effective strategy to cope with uncertainty. In the absence of market institutions and reliable business data, such techniques as credit scoring and pricing for risk are of limited use in this context. It becomes essential for banks to find partners who appear to be capable of managing the loan and serious in paying the money back. In other words, techniques that try to mitigate the risks of the deals become of secondary importance. Of primary importance is the strategy that reduces the uncertainty of the partner's benevolence.

Secondly, we also uncovered several mechanisms of trust building. The current literature suggests two ways that trust between firms can be developed. Trust can be inherited from past interpersonal and/or inter-organizational relationships (Granovetter, 1985; Coleman, 1988; Redding, 1990), or has emerged from ongoing market transactions (Ring & Van de Ven, 1992). Both of these mechanisms exclude the possibility that business partners construct trust with each other at an early stage of their relationships.

Our findings indicate that trust between partners can also be actively constructed at the beginning of business relationships. The process of learning to trust their new partners is distinctive. In our study, bankers cannot rely on available data sources, as their counterparts in developed countries would do. Rather, they learn about potential private firm clients by developing their own information network and by directly interacting with firms' managers. They have to accept the fact that most data are problematic, and then work with these problems. They cannot interpret data independently from their relationships with the sources, and their relationships with the sources provide insights into how to interpret the data. The bankers' willingness to trust, and their relationship building and coaching skills, are essential for this constructed trust.

Implications

Theoretical Implications

Our study suggests several directions for future research. First, future research could examine the effectiveness of risk calculation versus uncertainty avoidance strategies under different contexts. It is reasonable to hypothesize that the effectiveness of these strategies are contingent on the levels of institutional development. Second, given that banks in transitional economies have to rely on uncertainty avoidance and trust-based strategies, bankers' required competencies could be different from those in developed countries. Such questions as 'What are the key required competencies?' 'How do these competencies influence bankers' performance?' need to be examined. Finally, future research could explore how best to construct trust with business partners at the inception of relationships.

Managerial Implications

This study suggests that a reliance on western risk management techniques is not adequate for credit officers in Vietnamese banks at present, particularly when lending to private SMEs. Bank officers need to be trained in uncertainty management techniques, in addition to more conventional risk management techniques. Besides financial analysis, business planning, and credit scoring, bankers need to be competent in developing interpersonal networks, gathering and analysing what is often incomplete or conflicting information, in order to appraise a lender's business and creditworthiness. Some data collection skills, such as interviewing and detailed observation can also be of benefit in this regard.

For owners of young private firms, banks' trust in the benevolence of the owners of firms is critical for firms to get bank loans. Networking appears to be the most effective channels for young start-up firms to be known, endorsed and trusted. The more people know about them, their quality and their firms, the better the chances these firms have of getting bank loans.

Conclusion

This study has demonstrated the uncertainty Vietnamese banks face in lending to private SMEs, and strategies they employ to cope with that uncertainty. In time, stronger market institutions in Vietnam should develop, and commercial banks should be able to reduce gradually the current spectrum of uncertainties into more calculable risks. Until then, however, banks in Vietnam will need to continue to find ways of coping with these uncertainties. Vietnam is not unique in this respect, and these issues – and the strategies employed to surmount them – are probably apparent in numerous other developing and transitional economies. If so, there may be scope for banks in different countries to learn from their peers, and not just struggle to absorb and adapt the standard 'international best practice' textbooks and consultancy guidebooks that often seem to dominate.

Acknowledgements

The authors wish to thank the Asian Institute of Management's Gov. Jose B. Fernandez, Jr. Center for Banking and Finance for financial support in conducting this research project.

References

Adair, J. (1995) The research environment in developing countries, *International Journal of Psychology*, 30(6), pp. 643–662.

Berger, A. N. & Udell, G. F. (1995) Relationship lending and lines of credit in small firm finance, *The Journal of Business*, 68(3), pp. 351–381.

Binks, M. R. & Ennew, C. T. (1997) Smaller business and relationship banking: the impact of participative behaviour, *Entrepreneurship Theory and Practice*, 21(4), pp. 83–92.

Blackwell, D. & Winters, D. (2000) Local lending markets: what a small business owner/manager needs to know, *Quarterly Journal of Business and Economics*, 39(2), pp. 62–79.

Boisot, M. & Child, J. (1996) From fiefs to clans and network capitalism: explaining China's emerging economic order, *Administrative Science Quarterly*, 41, pp. 600–628.

Child, J. & Tse, D. (2001) China's transition and its implications for international business, *Journal of International Business Studies*, 32(1), pp. 5–21.

Coleman, J. S. (1988) Social capital in the creation of human capital, *American Journal of Sociology*, 94, pp. S95–S120.

Frame, S., Srinivasna, A. & Woosley, L. (2001) The effect of credit scoring on small-business lending, *Journal of Money, Credit, and Banking*, 33(3), pp. 813–825.

Granovetter, M. (1985) Economic action and social structure: the problem of embeddedness, *American Journal of Sociology*, 91(3), pp. 481–510.

Guseva, A. & Rona-Tas, A. (2001) Uncertainty, risk, and trust: Russian and American credit card markets compared, *American Sociological Review*, 66, pp. 623–646.

Hannan, M. & Freeman, J. (1984) Structural inertia and organizational change, *American Sociological Review*, 49, pp. 149–164.

Hofstede, G. & Bond, M. H. (1988) The Confucius connection: from cultural roots to economic growth, *Organizational Dynamics*, 16(4), pp. 4–21.

Jeffries, F. L. & Reed, R. (2000) Trust and adaptation in relational contracting, *Academy of Management Review*, 25(4), pp. 873–882.

Knight, F. (1957) *Risk, Uncertainty and Profit* (New York: Kelley and Millman).

Langlois, R. N. & Cosgel, M. M. (1993) Frank Knight on risk, uncertainty, and the firm: a new interpretation, *Economic Inquiry*, 31, pp. 456–465.

Levin, R. I. & Travis, V. R. (1987) Small company finance: what the books don't say, *Harvard Business Review*, 65(6), pp. 30–32.

Lewis, D. J. & Weigert, A. (1985) Trust as a social reality, *Social Forces*, 63(4), pp. 967–985.

Mayer, R. C., Davis, J. H. & Schoorman, F. D. (1995) An integrative model of organizational trust, *Academy of Management Review*, 20(3), pp. 709–734.

McMillan, J. & Woodruff, C. (1999) Interfirm relationships and informal credit in Vietnam, *The Quarterly Journal of Economics*, 114(4), pp. 1285–1320.

Nguyen, V. T. (2005) Learning to trust: a study of interfirm trust dynamics in Vietnam, *Journal of World Business*, 40(2), pp. 203–221.

Nguyen, V. T., Weinstein, M. & Meyer, A. D. (2005) Development of trust: a study of interfirm relationships in Vietnam, *Asia Pacific Journal of Management*, 22(3), pp. 211–235.

O'Connor, D. (2000) Financial sector reform in China and Vietnam: a comparative perspective, *Comparative Economic Studies*, 42(4), pp. 45–66.

Peng, M. & Heath, P. (1996) The growth of the firm in planned economies in transition: institutions, organizations, and strategic choice, *Academy of Management Review*, 21(2), pp. 492–528.

Petersen, M. & Rajan, R. G. (1994) The benefit of lending relationships: evidence from small business data, *The Journal of Finance*, 19(1), pp. 3–37.

Redding, G. (1990) *The Spirit of the Chinese Capitalism* (New York: de Gruyter).

Ring, P. S. & Van de Ven, A. H. (1992) Structuring cooperative relationships between organizations, *Strategic Management Journal*, 13, pp. 483–498.

Rousseau, D. M., Sitkin, S. B., Burt, R. S. & Camerer, C. (1998) Not different after all: a cross-discipline view of trust, *Academy of Management Review*, 23(3), pp. 393–404.

Ulrich, T. A. & Cassel, H. S. (1975) Factors influencing the extension of bank credit to small businesses, *Journal of Small Business Management*, 13(1), pp. 28–34.

Xin, K. R. & Pearce, J. L. (1996) *Guanxi*: Good connections as substitutes for institutional support, *Academy of Management Journal*, 39, pp. 1641–1658.

Zaheer, A., McEvily, B. & Perrone, V. (1998) Does trust matter? Exploring the effects of interorganizational and interpersonal trust on performance, *Organization Science*, 9(2), pp. 141–159.

Zucker, L. G. (1986) Production of trust: institutional sources of economic structure, 1840-1920, in: B. M. Staw & L. L. Cumming (Eds) *Research in Organizational Behavior*, 8, pp. 53–111 (Greenwich, CT: JAI Press).

Appendix: Field sample

	Interviewee	Bank	Location	Ownership
1.	Head of Business Department	Agriculture Bank	Hanoi	State
2.	Credit Officer	Agriculture Bank	Hanoi	State
3.	Head of Credit Department	Asia Commercial Bank	Hanoi	Private
4.	Credit Officer	Bank for Investment and Development	Hanoi	State
5.	Credit Officer	Bank of Investment and Development	Ho Chi Minh City (HCMC)	State
6.	Head of Credit Department	Bank of Investment and Development	Hanoi	State
7.	Credit Officers	Hanoi Commercial Joint Stock Bank	Hanoi	Private
8.	Deputy Head of SME Department	Bank of Industry and Commerce (Incombank)	Hanoi	State
9.	Credit Officer	Incombank	Hanoi	State
10.	Credit Officer	Incombank	Hanoi	State
11.	Deputy Director	Incombank	Hanoi	State
12.	Credit Officer	Incombank	Hanoi	State
13.	Credit Officer	Incombank	HCMC	State
14.	Credit Officer	Incombank	HCMC	State
15.	Credit Officer	Indovina Bank	Hanoi	Private
16.	Credit Officer	Military Joint Stock Bank	Hanoi	Private
17.	Credit Officer	Sacombank	HCMC	Private
18.	Head of Credit Department	Saigon Industrial and Commercial Bank	Hanoi	Private
19.	Deputy General Director	Vietnam International Commercial Joint Stock Bank (VIB)	Hanoi	Private
20.	Deputy Head of Marketing Department	VIB	Hanoi	Private
21.	Head of Credit Department	Bank of Foreign Trade of Vietnam (Vietcombank)	Hanoi	State
22.	Deputy Head of Investment Department	Vietcombank	Hanoi	State
23.	Credit Officer	Vietcombank	Hanoi	State

Conclusion: Whither Business and Management in South East Asia?

MALCOLM WARNER* & CHRIS ROWLEY**
*Faculty of Management Cass Business School, City University, London, UK, **Wolfson College
and Judge Business School, University of Cambridge, UK

Introduction

Analysing what is specific about business and management in a particular part of
the world economy is a serious scholarly challenge. There are several levels of
analysis in the study of comparative management: *global*, *regional*, *sub-regional*,
national and so on. Clearly, each level is interrelated with the others and a
complex interplay of factors may be envisaged.

In the summary of the eight contributions in this collection of essays, we have
presented the thrust of each under the headings of *country* and within each a *theme*
(for example, culture), *basis* (for example, macro-) and *author* (see Table 1). Most
studies are in a single national setting but two are based upon a two-country
comparison. They cover a wide range of themes (from culture to accounting). Most
authors are based (teach/research) in the region, but others are located elsewhere.

Business and management in South East Asia have, for example, a great deal in
common with similar phenomena around the world. Globalization has brought a
degree of 'convergence'; multinational enterprises (MNEs) diffuse management
practices across the planet (Dunning, 1993). Whether called 'development'or
'modernization', the process of change has featured heavily in the last few decades.
This is as true of South East, as in East and North East, Asia. But 'divergence' and
'diversity' are still strong factors. Business and management in East and North East
Asia have, of course, common features with South East Asia. Nevertheless, we find
specific characteristics that relate to specifically the latter and the countries
concerned (*Thailand*, *Malaysia*, *Singapore*, *Vietnam*). The specific region has its

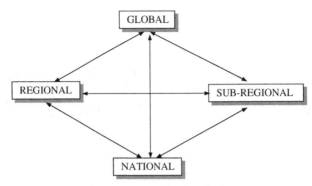

Figure 1. Levels of analysis

Table 1. Content by country, themes, basis and author

Country	Themes	Basis	Authors
Thailand	Culture Comparison Cultural imperatives	Macro	Niffenegger *et al.*
Malaysia, UK	Accruals accounting Development Comparison	Government accountants Questionnaire	Saleh & Pendlebury
Malaysia	Customer expectations Quality Performance, satisfaction and retention	Telecommunications Interviews Questionnaire	Kassim
Malaysia	HRM HR practices E-HRM readiness	SMEs Manufacturing industry Observation, Interviews, Questionnaire	Hooi
Malaysia, Singapore	MNEs Internationalization strategies Comparison	MNEs Case Studies Interviews	Sim
Singapore	HR Labour markets Employment	Service sector Hotels Interviews	Lee & Warner
Vietnam	Organizational strategy and structure Control of subsidiaries Expatriation	Non-profit organizations, NGOs Case Study Interviews	Zhu
Vietnam	Risk and uncertainty Trust Bank lending to SMEs	SMEs State and private owned banks Interviews	Nguyen *et al.*

own strategic geographical location. Each of the specific countries has its own historical and cultural tradition, as well as its socio-economic setting, and so on. All are still 'growth economies' and have grown at a rate above 5 per cent in the last year alone, although Hong Kong has also grown above 8 percent and China above 9 percent (see *Economist*, 2005b).

'Convergence'

'Convergence' has been a topical concept in social science and particularly in comparative management since the 1950s.[1] It has in its worst manifestations a rather *simpliste* perspective. Nevertheless, many have found it useful as a concept to understand common experiences across the board in business and management. It has been applied to management in the Asia Pacific region in a critical manner in recent times (Rowley, 1998; Rowley & Benson, 2002, 2004; Warner, 2002, 2003). Furthermore, Warner (2002) has used the term 'relative convergence' to take into account doubts about the literal nature of fusion and absorption of international practice. At the same time Rowley *et al.* (2004) used the ideas of 'levels' within a system to disaggregate developments, trends and convergence.

'Divergence'

The converse of 'convergence', 'divergence' has also been suggested as a counterweight to the ongoing debate. Some have even spoken of 'glocalization' (Ohmae, 1990). A *relative* version of both convergent and divergent trends has been conceptualized by Warner (2002, 2003). It is hard to see absolute examples of the categories and a degree of relativity is probably wiser. How far one takes this latitude is a moot point. Which set of influences must one take into account?

History is clearly a major factor, sometimes the major one, that distinguishes the experience of each of the countries in the region but one must not labour the obvious too much. It unites but it also divides nonetheless. The ghost of tradition hovers over the land and indeed stretches back thousands of years, as these countries derive from ancient civilizations, Chinese in the deep past and Islam more recently.

Each of the countries has a different *cultural* and *religious* tradition and in many we find a multicultural frame. The past weighs heavily on the region. Buddhism and Islam, amongst others, blend with Christianity. There are value-systems for each country that may be analysed (see Hofstede, 1980, 2002). *Culture* may be a common theme running through all the contributions, in that each has a cultural and institutional setting that acts as a *constraint* on the behaviour of the actors within the organizations (governments, firms, and so on). In this collection, Niffenegger *et al.*, for example, examined the conflicting cultural imperatives between Thailand and western cultures (specifically the US), as well as some potential avenues for future Thai economic growth and development as we have seen earlier. These authors argue that Thailand possesses its own *uniqueness* which rests on the essence of Thai Buddhism as expressed in the 'Four Noble Truths'.

Language is still a strong factor. Local parlance divides the common peoples of the region, even if English unites the elite. Malaysia has a diversity of tongues;

Singapore has English and Mandarin Chinese as official languages; Thai and Vietnamese are very distinct indeed.

Ethnicity is of fundamental importance in South East Asia (see Rowley & Bhopal, 2005, 2006a, 2006b, for example) and also features prominently and interrelates with faith. It is also closely linked to culture. Thais and Vietnamese are ethnically closer to the North; Malays to the South. Mixed with the indigenous groups are Overseas (*Nanyang*) Chinese, most numerous as a minority in Malaysia, but as a majority in Singapore. They are often more prosperous than the average of the indigenous population in which they find themselves.[2] The spread and operations of the firms (all Chinese owned) – noted in the contribution by Sim in this collection on the internationalization of Malaysian and Singaporean firms – were aided by the use of their extensive ethnic and social networks (as we noted earlier in the 'Introduction').

There is also a distinct *political* and derived *legal* background in each locale. Both Malaysia and Singapore inherited the British legacy. Thailand avoided colonial rule and even Japanese occupation, unlike the others. Vietnam experienced both as well as American involvement in the South; it saw partition, civil war and then reunification in a window of three decades. French colonialism had an influence still felt there today.

The economic, political and social system in Vietnam shares some characteristics with China – in that it professes a Communist origin.[3] Both countries have seen rapid economic growth in recent years (see Warner *et al.*, 2005). Both economies are now in 'transition' although this process is further behind in the former than in the latter. Market and financial institutions and legislative frameworks, as pointed out in our 'Introduction', vis-à-vis the contribution by Nguyen *et al.* on banking, are often underdeveloped, with '*property rights*' – essential for robust lending activity – not always clearly set out and guaranteed.

Indeed, 'equitization' is the term used for the cautious, partial privatization in Vietnam. One relevant example to our collection is in banking where the 'Big 4' state commercial banks account for about 70 per cent of total lending and of that about 60 per cent of loans are to state enterprises (Kazmin, 2005a). For example, the state-owned Vietcombank was the first in the process with reforms to improve the credit analysis skills of staff and it has reduced state enterprise lending from 90 per cent (2000) to 50 per cent of its portfolio, albeit it still faces traditional political interference, namely, to hire scions of loyal party cadres and to be put under pressure for loans to state enterprises, regardless of creditworthiness as such lending is encouraged because of the fear of worker unrest if ailing companies lose financial lifelines, (ibid). Also, while many family small firms sprung up post-2001 when the government eased restrictions, problems remain as the biggest banks are state-owned and their operations are murky while foreign banks operate under severe restrictions and stock markets in their infancy, which all make it difficult for small firms to raise funds (*Economist*, 2005a).

Although each country experienced the '*developmental state*' as a common factor in their evolution as competitive economies, they all saw this emerge in a specific way. In Sim's contribution to this collection, the author argues that western theories have overlooked the active role played by the state and neglected the contextual perspective in the internationalization of Asian firms. Thus, he adds, there is a need to examine MNEs *within the context of their institutional and socio-cultural embeddedness.*

On a similar theme to the above is that in the 1990s, Vietnam gave exclusive rights to import and distribute foreign goods to state enterprises and favoured supporters of the regime (Kazmin, 2005b). Although now any Vietnamese can import products, many big wholesalers remain politically well connected (ibid). The country is an important trading area, for example, Vietnamese exports of garments, footwear, wood furniture and other products to the USA were US$800,000 in 2000 but US$6 billion by 2005 (Kazmin, 2005b).

Economic Implications of the Above

Each country has its own *economic* underpinnings. We set out in the 'Introduction' to this collection the key economic and other relevant statistics that guide business and management in the countries in the region. Geography determines its locational and resource coordinates. Demography determines the human resource base. Population size has been a major factor in permitting this but the largest nation by numbers is the poorest (Vietnam) and the smallest, the richest (Singapore).[4] We would not argue, however, that there was an obvious correlation between the variables in hand here. Singapore is in many ways *sui generis* as it was not a nation-state until quite recently and was a breakaway from one that was moulded by British hegemony as a single political entity. Its strategic position as an entrepôt, like Hong Kong, gave it a very strong point of departure, although built on the policies of the 'developmental state' – in ways the latter did not, as the nearest entity to the *laissez-faire* model to be found in Asia Pacific as a whole, some say in the entire world economy.

'Convergence' and 'divergence' shape both *demand* and *supply* sides of the equation. Demand factors are often rooted in traditional needs but are now more often influenced by contemporary tastes. Supply-side factors relate to both demographic as well as economic underpinnings. An abundance of human resources is available, with the cheapest labour to be found in Vietnam, with Thailand second in line here. Malaysia is now more developed in human capital, with Singapore top of the tree. Business and management in South East Asia see the interplay of both demand and supply influences in local economies – as well as vis-à-vis global markets.

'External Shocks'

'External shocks' are often a major factor in economic life that may disturb any given equilibrium between local and global linkages. A number of 'external shocks' have plagued the Asia Pacific region as a whole in the last decade. As well as the Asian financial crises of 1997, there was the backwash of '9/11', the SARS epidemic of 2003, the tsunami of 2004 and so on. A possible 'bird flu' pandemic adds to the scenarios on the horizon.[5] The Asian financial crisis affected all parts of the region; '9/11' had an impact on tourism in many of the states; SARS was a serious matter in both Vietnam and elsewhere but principally in Singapore; the tsunami heavily devastated parts of the Thai economy. Stock markets on each occasion were destabilized across the region. The devaluation of Thai Baht in July 1997, many observers believe, had triggered the Asian financial crises, from which several nations in the global economy are still recovering (see Rowley & Warner, 2004), as noted in our 'Introduction' to this collection. Asset values were greatly undermined: currencies were sold off in panic; a sequence of currency devaluations followed.

'Export-led Growth'

For decades, policy makers have encouraged 'export-led growth' and this has brought great developmental benefits. More recently, questions have been asked regarding the wisdom of such over-reliance on global markets and the degree of vulnerability such a linkage brings. South East Asia has been particularly reliant on this strategy. It has brought it a high degree of prosperity (GDP growth per capita) but it has also seen considerable reliance on export markets for both goods and services. Tourism is a good example of the latter and it has been an 'Achilles heel' (as described above) vis-à-vis the external shocks the region has experienced in the last decade. Lee and Warner's contribution in this collection shows how an epidemic that spreads from afar can bring tourism in the richest economy in the region to a standstill for weeks running into months, as it did in China, Hong Kong, Taiwan and elsewhere.[6] Much of the impact of the epidemiological crisis stemmed from the great degree of uncertainty and fear generated by SARS. Service exports, particularly those tourism-related, were to be most hard hit. This was also true of the all the four countries we have included here.

Conclusions

We can learn a great deal from the work contributed to this collection (see Table I). First, the concept of 'convergence' only partially fits the cases reviewed here, although a few examples make sense in this regard. While globalization and internationalization are ongoing in, for example, the Malaysian and Singaporean exemplifications, there remains some particularity of capital and business organization. Second, the concept of 'divergence' better fits the cases offered in this collection than 'convergence'. Third, and linked to the first two, the continuing importance of history and context – political, economic and social – remains clear. For instance, despite practices that may be seen as global (for example, accrual accounting, risk analysis, e-HRM), their introduction, implementation and practice remains local. The contribution by Zhu and Purnell in this collection is indicative of such phenomenon as the case study reveals the management of the global-local conflict that exists and the importance of the power of ideology in this. Fourth, emergent economies, especially 'late' developers, have less in common with earlier ones in Asia that have blossomed, such as Japan, South Korea, Taiwan and so on. This is a further warning to those who bestow the rubric 'Asia' or 'Asian bloc' all too readily without the necessary caveats and nuances. This is not just do with semantics, the lexicon is important as using the term 'Asia' can often hide as much diversity under it as any uniformity implied. Finally, the collection also indicates a range of possible research methods, with both their advantages and pitfalls, to be considered and utilized in future work on South East Asia.

Notes

[1] The notion suggested that economies that industrialize become similar in their characteristics to each other.

[2] The Overseas Chinese have often been accused of economic dominance in their communities and have been penalized for doing this, for example in Malaysia a policy of affirmative action was established to given the local Malays countervailing power.

[3] See Warner *et al.* (2005), for a comparison between China and Vietnam.

[4] Statistical data on all four countries is set out in Table II in the 'Introduction' to this collection.

[5] At the time of writing, Vietnam was the country the most afflicted by cases of bird flu.

[6] But most of the 'external shocks' in the region had also hit tourism detrimentally over the decade, not just health scares.

References

Dunning, J. H. (1993) *Multinational Enterprises and the Global Economy* (Workingham: Addison-Wesley).

Economist, The (2005a) Vietnam: changing gear, 26 November, p.71.

Economist, The (2005b) Statistical summaries, 24 December, p.150.

Hofstede, G. (1980) *Culture's Consequences: International Differences in Work Related Values* (Beverly Hills, CA: Sage).

Hofstede, G. (2002) *Culture's Consequences: Comparing Values, Behaviours, Institutions and Organizations Across Nations* (Beverly Hills, CA: Sage).

Kazmin, A. (2005a) Hanoi takes first step on road to reform, *Financial Times*, 9 August, p.26.

Kazmin, A. (2005b) Tariff reductions allow Vietnam to hit above its weight, *Financial Times*, 22 August, p.7.

Ohmae, K. (1990) *The Borderless World* (London: Collins).

Rowley, C (Ed.) (1998) *Human Resources in the Asia Pacific Region: Convergence Questioned* (London: Frank Cass).

Rowley, C. & Benson, J. (2002) Convergence and divergence in Asian HRM, *California Management Review*, 44(2), pp. 90–109.

Rowley, C. & Benson, J. (2004) (Eds) *The Management of Human Resources in the Asia Pacific Region: Convergence Reconsidered* (London: Frank Cass).

Rowley, C., Benson, J. & Warner, M. (2004) Towards an Asian model of HRM: a comparative analysis of China, Japan and Korea, *International Journal of HRM*, 15(3), pp. 236–253.

Rowley, C. & Bhopal, M. (2005) The role of ethnicity in employment relations, *Asia Pacific Journal of Human Resources*, 43(3).

Rowley, C. & Bhopal, M. (2006a) Ethnicity as a management issue and resource: examples from Malaysia, in: H. Dahles & W. Loh (Eds) *The Remaking of Boundaries in Asian Multicultural Organizations* (London: Routledge).

Rowley, C. & Bhopal, M. (2006b) The ethnic factor in state-labour relations: the case of Malaysia, *Capital and Class*, 88, pp. 87–116.

Rowley, C. & Warner, M. (2004) The Asian financial crisis: the impact on human resource management, *International Studies of Management and Organization*, 34(1), pp. 3–9.

Warner, M. (2002) Globalization, labour markets and human resources in Asia-Pacific economies: an overview, *International Journal of Human Resource Management*, 13(3), pp. 384–398.

Warner, M. (Ed.) (2003) *Culture and Management in Asia* (London: RoutledgeCurzon).

Warner, M., Edwards, V., Polonsky, G., Pucko, D. & Zhu, Y. (Eds) (2005) *Management in Transitional Economies: From the Berlin Wall to the Great Wall of China* (London: RoutledgeCurzon).

INDEX

accountability 6, 32–7, 144, 146
Accountant General's Department (AGD) 37, 40
accountants 7, 34, 40, 43
accounting 3, 22, 79, 163
    accruals 6–7, 32–45, 180
    standards 32, 37, 40
Acer 103
administration 33, 43, 54–5, 74–5, 81, 85
administrators 33, 36
advertising 8, 48, 66, 83
Africa 26
after sales service 83, 103
age 49–50, 54–6, 64, 66–7, 80, 115, 170
agency theory 138
aggregation 33
agri-business 24
agriculture 76, 122
agronomic engineering 24
AIDS 115
air travel 115
airlines 124, 127, 132
airports 115–16, 125
airtime prices 53
alliances 104–5, 107
AMOS software 55
anthropology 24, 27
Area Development Program (ADP) 142–3
Asia 3, 10, 16, 67, 76
    emerging MNEs 95–100
    epidemics 116, 124
    financial crises 20, 24, 27, 126, 179–80
    future trends 175
Asian Development Bank (ADB) 120
assets 32–3, 37, 75, 101–2, 105–6, 157
assistant accountants 40
Association of Singapore Attractions 131
Association of South East Asian Nations (ASEAN) 101–2, 116
attribution theory 48–9
Auditor General 37
audits 33, 43, 155

Australia 6, 32, 101, 103–4, 106, 140–1
Australian Wheat Authority 102
autocracy 17, 21, 25

B2B/C/E 83
Badham, R. 137
balance sheets 33, 76
Bali 126
banking 3, 11–12, 20, 24
    customer expectations 64, 67
    future trends 178
    internationalization 99, 103
    Vietnam SMEs 153–74
bankruptcy 20–1, 24, 161
Bartlett, C. 137, 150
benchmarking 35
benefits 74
best practice 80, 172
Bhumibol Adulyadej Maharaj, King 23
billing 52–3, 64–5, 67
biogas 145
bird flu 1, 179
Black Death 121
blood-relation clients 168
blue-collar employees 126, 128
borrower standardization 155
brands 48, 101, 103, 105–7
Brewster, C. 136
British Empire 178–9
bubonic plague 121
Buchanan, D. 137
Buddhadasa 24, 25
Buddhism 5–6, 15–19, 21, 23–7, 31, 177
budgets 35–6, 42, 44, 80, 140
Bumrungrad Hospital 2
bureaucracy 20, 24–5, 106
Burma/Myanmar 14, 102
Business Planning and Development Scheme 92
business plans 160, 162–4, 172
business reengineering 37

business relationships 19, 22, 26–7, 78, 105–8, 167–8
Buun Kuhn 19, 22, 27

Cambodia 14
Canada 16, 32, 117, 124
capacity building 145, 147, 171
capital 20, 35, 37, 78, 80
    epidemics 126
    flow 3, 14, 24–5
    future trends 180
    internationalization 95
    lending 158, 164
capital gains tax 2
capitalism 5–6, 15, 25–7, 99
car makers 2
case studies 95–109, 135–51
cash-flow 131
Caspian Sea 104
casual workers 10
cellular telephones 48–67
centralization 17
CGI Precision 75
Chambers of Commerce and Industry 161
Changi Airport 125
Chapter 11 proceedings 20
cheap labour 102, 179
Chen, T.J. 105
chi square statistic 55, 165, 169
chief executive officers (CEOs) 100, 103, 105, 123
child sponsorship 143
China 2, 25, 99, 101–6, 115–17
    exports 180
    history 177–8
    SARS 120, 122, 125–6, 132
cholera 122
Christianity 122, 140, 144, 177
Chulalongkorn, King 23
churches 123
CitiBank 20
civil service 34
class 49
CnetG 75
collaboration 25, 156
collateral 157, 160–2, 164–5
collectivism 4, 16–17, 19, 22, 27
colonialism 178
colonization 3, 14, 24
communication 8, 22, 74–5, 81
    epidemics 123, 125
    expatriation 142–3, 145–6, 148–50
    manufacturing 84–6, 90
Communism 178
company profiles 81–3
comparative fit index (CFI) 55–6

compensation 8, 74, 84–6
competition 80, 162
competitive advantage 9, 103, 105–6, 108
competitiveness 8, 24, 27, 35, 48
    epidemics 126, 128
    future trends 178
    internationalization 101–2, 104
    manufacturing 74, 78, 82
computers 36–7, 85, 103, 123
confidence 155, 157
confirmatory factor analysis (CFA) 7, 55–6
Confucianism 17, 20, 23, 27, 156
constraints 8, 49, 75, 80, 86–8
    banks 158–9
    expatriation 142
    history 177
    internationalization 101
    manufacturing 90–2
constructed trust 168, 170
consultants 155
consumers 23, 123–4, 127, 132
consumption 10, 50, 52, 123–4
context 9, 11, 98–9, 107, 109
    expatriation 135–9, 144, 149–51
    future trends 179–80
    lending 156–7, 171
contingency model 33–4
contracting 35, 107, 154
control 3, 6, 10–11, 23, 25
    accounting 32, 35–6, 44
    banks 155
    internationalization 97, 104, 106
    NGOs 135–44, 148, 150
    SARS 117, 119, 122
convergence 13, 175, 177, 179–80
cooperation 25–6
corporate cultures 79
corruption 165
cost-benefit analyses 43, 92
costs 35–7, 42–3, 54, 74–5, 78–9
    banks 157,165
    internationalization 96, 102–3, 105, 107–8
    manufacturing 86, 88, 90–2
    NGOs 136
    SARS 115, 120, 126–7, 132
coverage 52, 64–5, 67
Creative Technology 101–3, 105–6, 108
credit information 155
credit officers 168–9, 171–2
credit scoring 153, 155, 157, 171–2
Cronbach alpha scores 54
cultural imperatives 14–31
culture 3–5, 9, 11, 15, 98–9
    assets 33
    banks 156

definition 17
future trends 176–8
internationalization 101, 106–7
NGOs 138, 140, 144–5, 148, 150–1
currency 14, 16
customer expectations/satisfaction 3, 7, 47–73
customer service outlets 52–3, 56, 65, 67

databases 54, 109, 116, 119, 155, 160–1, 163
debt 15, 20
delinquent loans 164
Delta Air 21
demand 10, 27, 120–1, 123–4, 127–8, 132, 179
demographics 7–8, 47–73, 78, 80–1, 122, 179
demonization 122
Department of Company Registration, Vietnam 163
depreciation 33, 37
deputy directors 40
deregulation 48
devaluation 3, 180
developed countries 9, 34, 41
internationalization 96–8, 101–2, 104–6
lending 155, 157, 171
developing countries 11–12, 43
expatriation 148
internationalization 97–8, 101, 104
lending 153, 172
telecommunications 47–8
development 2, 6, 8–9, 23–7, 96–8
banks 158,171
expatriation 140, 142–3, 145–7, 149
exports 180
future trends 175
history 177
internationalization 107–8
monks 25
state 178
dial-up modems 83
dialects 106
diary products 3
differentiation 107
directors 40
divergence 13, 177–80
diversification 102–3, 105–6
diversity 1–13
Doi Moi 139
domestic workers 3
donors 143
dress codes 53
Drory, A. 137
Dunning, J.H. 95–6, 105, 107–8, 139
dynamism 1–13

e-commerce 8, 22, 83
e-communication 85
e-HRM *see* electronic human resource management
e-learning 83–4
East Asia 1, 119, 121, 156, 175
Ebola virus 121
Eclectic Paradigm 96–7
economics 1–4, 6, 10, 23–8
banks 163
crises 16, 20, 24, 126, 179–80
development 2, 6, 96–8, 108
efficiency 78
environment 101
future trends 178–80
indicators 15
performance 17
reform 139
SARS 115–16, 119–26, 132–3
theory 154
economies of scale 138
economists 19, 21, 23, 119, 122
education 2, 8, 21, 49, 54–6
expatriation 142
internationalization 98
manufacturing 78, 82–3
telecommunications 65–7
Eightfold Path 18, 23
electronic human resource management (e-HRM)
definitions 75
future trends 180
implementation 3, 8, 74–93
electronics 2, 8, 22, 77, 100–6, 108
elites 177
employees 8, 10–11, 19–21, 53
e-HRM 74–6, 79–85, 88–92
NGOs 136, 138, 140–1, 143, 145–50
SARS 116, 123, 126–8, 130
telecommunications 66
employers 3, 131
employment 10, 76, 78, 116, 125
epidemics 127, 132–3
lending 158
empowerment 79, 147, 149
enforcement 6, 10, 19
Engchanil, N. 14–31
English language 81, 177–8
enterprise resource planning (ERP) 87
entrepreneurship 20, 98–9, 156, 164
environment 10, 135, 156–8
epidemics 3, 10, 114–33, 179–80
equitization 178
Erramilli, M.K. 104
ethics 156
ethnicity 1–2, 7–9, 49–50, 54–6

e-HRM 80
future trends 178
internationalization 104–8
telecommunications 60, 65–6
ethnocentrism 145
Europe 23, 101, 103–4, 108, 117, 121–2
European Commission 76
Exim bank 99
expatriation 11, 24, 135–51
expenses 33
experts/expertise 35, 40, 52
e-HRM 87–9, 91–2
expatriation 143
internationalization 103
telecommunications 54–5
exports 2, 10, 21–2, 98, 116, 123, 139,
163–4, 180
external shocks 179–80

face-to-face contact 22
failure rate 157
Falun Gong 122
families 20–1, 49, 156, 178
famine 121
fashion 2
fear 10, 17, 115, 120–1, 123–4, 180
Federal Agencies 36
Federation of Malaysian Manufacturers
Directory 75
femininity 16, 19
Financial Management Initiative (FMI)
34–5, 42
Financial Package for Small- and Medium-scale
Industries 92
firm size 79
First World War 122
foregone income 115
foreign aid 139
foreign direct investment (FDI) 3, 9, 95,
97–100
foreign exchange 158
Four Noble Truths 5–6, 18–19, 23,
31, 177
Four Sublime States of Consciousness 6,
18–19, 21
France 178
franchising 102
fraud 165
Freeman, N.J. 153–74
Fulton Report 34, 42
funding 140, 143, 158, 164, 178
future trends 27–8, 175–81

GAAP 35
game-plans 10
garments 2

gender 7–8, 49–50, 54–6, 60, 65–6
General Services Administration 36
geocentrism 145, 149
geography 179
Germany 23, 101, 117
Ghoshal, S. 137, 150
global village 123
global-local conflict 11, 135–9, 148,
150–1, 180
globalization 8, 23–4, 28, 78
epidemics 115
expatriation 135
future trends 175, 180
strategies 101, 103, 105
'glocalization' 177
goals 135, 137–8, 140, 148–50
Godfrey, A.D. 33
goodness-of-fit indicators 55
government 2–3, 6–7, 9–10, 14–15
accounting 32–5
banks 155, 161, 163–4, 166, 168
culture 20, 24–5
e-HRM 92
epidemics 117
ethnicity 178
internationalization 98–9, 104–5,
107–8
NGOs 136, 138–41, 145–7
SARS 122–3, 128, 130–1
Government Financial Management
Accounting System (GFMAS) 37
government-linked corporations (GLCs) 98,
103–5
graduates 92
greed 23
gross domestic product (GDP)
accounting 34
epidemics 115, 120, 124, 126
expatriation 139
future trends 180
role 2, 4, 10
growth rate 4, 10, 14, 23, 25
culture 27
epidemics 119–20, 126
future trends 177, 180
lending 158
guanxi 105–7

hardware 87
Harris, H. 139
headquarters (HQs) 3, 11, 16, 135–50
hegemony 179
heritage 33
highly active antiretroviral therapies
(HAARTS) 115
HIV 115

Hofstede, G. 5, 16–18, 23, 26–7
Holden, L. 139
Hong Kong 116–17, 119–20, 123–5
　epidemics 132–3
　future trends 177, 179–80
　Special Administrative Region 115
Hooi, L.W. 8, 74–93
hospitality 115
hospitals 117, 119, 122–3
hotels 10, 115–17, 125–7, 129, 131–3
Housing Development Board (HDB) 126, 128
Huberman, A.M. 100
Huff, A.S. 137
Human Capital Development Division 75
human resource management (HRM)
　epidemics 116, 119, 126–8, 132–3
　expatriation 136
　implementation 74, 78–82, 84–6, 90–2
　role 3, 8, 10
Human Resource Service Centres 85
human resources (HR) 3, 8–10, 36
　e-HRM 74–5, 79–83, 85–6, 90, 92
　epidemics 114–33
　future trends 179
hunger 121

ideology 11, 27, 136–7, 139–40
　expatriation 144–5, 148–51
　future trends 180
　lending 154
imperialism 23
imports 23, 97, 179
incentives 43
income 7–8, 24–5, 49–50, 54–6, 64–7,
　115, 143
individualism 16–17, 19, 21, 27
Indonesia 27, 105, 126
Industrial Linkage Programme (ILP) 92
Industrial Technical Assistance Fund 92
industry 2, 4, 77, 92, 98–100
　epidemics 116, 122, 125, 127, 132
　internationalization 102–3, 105
　lending 162
inequality 17
inflation 2
influenza 122
information asymmetry 138, 157, 172
information and communication technology
　(ICT) 80
information flow 148
information technology (IT) 8, 23–4, 37, 40,
　82, 87
infrastructure 2, 8, 19, 33, 83
　e-HRM 86–8, 90–2
　lending 154, 157
ING Financial Markets 120

inherited trust 156, 170
innovation 36–7, 40, 97, 107
insolvencies 20, 22
inspectors 164
institutions 9, 12, 20–1, 98–9
　history 177–9
　internationalization 107–8
　lending 153–5, 157, 163–4, 167
integration 135–7, 139, 142, 150
interest rates 24, 157
interfirm relationships 155–7, 165
International Federation of Accountants
　(IFAC) 32
International Labour Organization (ILO) 124
International Monetary Fund (IMF) 24
International Public Sector Accounting
　Standards 40
internationalization 3, 8–9, 95–109, 178–80
Internet 22, 24, 74–5, 81–3, 100, 116
interviews 52, 116, 128, 141
　expatriation 145
　lending 154, 158–60, 162–4, 166,
　　168–9, 172
intranet 74, 81–5
inventory 22, 165
investment 2, 4, 14–15, 18–20
　accounting 33
　culture 22, 26
　e-HRM 74, 79–80, 83, 90
　epidemics 123, 126
　internationalization 95–9, 106
investment development path (IDP) thesis 3, 9,
　95–7, 99, 101, 103, 105–8
investors 19–20, 23, 105–6, 108
Iraq 120, 123
Ireland 117
ISDN 83
Islam 177

Jaeger, A.M. 138, 150
Japan 27, 105, 116, 178, 180
Jews 122
jit waang 25
jobs 2, 10, 20–1, 25, 125–6, 128, 132–3
joint stock banks 154, 158
Joint Ventures (JVs) 102–5, 109
Jones, R. 33, 35

Karakanian, M. 75
Karma 24
Karuna 18, 21, 31
Kassim, N.M. 7–8, 47–73
Keppel Corporation 98, 101–6
kiosks 75
Klausner, W. 24–5
Kmart 20

Knight, F. 154–5
Korea 27
Kreng Jai 17–18, 22, 26–7
Kudita 21
Kulviwat, S. 14–31

labour markets 3, 9–10, 114–33
laissez-faire 179
Lali, S. 96–7
land 158, 161–2
language 98, 145, 177–8
Laos 14
large corporations 77–80, 101, 126, 128
late developing countries (LDCs) 3
laws 2–3, 19–21, 24, 163
lay-offs 19–22, 116, 126–8
Le, N.T.B. 153–74
leadership 17, 25, 137, 143, 145, 149
Lee, G.O.M. 9–10, 114–33, 180
Lee, H.L. 130
lending 3–4, 11–12, 153–74, 178
Less Developed Countries (LDCs) 9, 34, 95, 97
Li, P.P. 105
liberalization 8, 23–4
licensing 105
Likert scale 7, 52, 81
Likierman, A. 35
line extensions 48
line quality 52–3, 60, 64–5, 67
Lion Group 101, 103, 105
Little, B.L. 79
local government 33, 50, 139–41, 146–9
logistics 105, 129, 159
long-term orientation 16–17, 19, 23, 27
Lüder, K.G. 33, 36–7, 41–2
Luo, Y. 105

MacLuhan, M. 123
macro level 107
macroeconomics 119, 158
Mahayana 25
maid levies 3
malaria 115
Malaysia 1–3, 6–9, 27, 120
   e-HRM 74–93
   future trends 175, 178–9
   internationalization 95–109, 180
   telecommunications 32–45, 47—73
Malthus, T. 122
managerialism 36–7, 42
managers 66–7, 75, 79–80, 85
   epidemics 128
   expatriation 137, 140
   lending 157, 159, 162, 165–6, 168–9, 171–2
Mandarin Chinese 178

manufacturing 2, 8, 21, 24, 104–5
   e-HRM 74–93
   epidemics 125–6, 133
manufacturing related services (MRS) 76
marital status 7–8, 54–6, 64–6
Market Development Scheme 92
market orientation 139, 154, 158
market segmentation 49
marketing 3, 8, 49–50, 54, 66–7, 79, 97
Martinez, Z.L. 138
masculinity 5, 16–17, 19, 21, 27
materialism 6, 17–19, 23, 25
Mathews, J.A. 105
Mayer, R.C. 155
media 1–2, 22–3, 75, 123
medical tourism 2
medium-term loans 164
Mercedes Benz 23
mergers and acquisitions (M&A) 97
Metta 18, 21,31
Mexico 104
Micro Accounting System (MAS) 36–7, 42–3
micro level 97, 107
micro-enterprises 76
microeconomics 119
Middle East 26, 121, 126
middle management 2
migrant workers 3
Miles, M.B. 100
military coups 25
Ministry of International Trade and Industry
   (MITI), Malaysia 75
Ministry of Manpower (MOM), Singapore 75,
   79, 125, 131
Ministry of Trade, Vietnam 161
Mintzberg, H. 137, 149
Mitsubishi Motors 2
modernization 175
Modernization and Automation Scheme 92
Modified Budgeting System (MBS) 36–7, 42
money 23
monitoring 37, 43, 120, 138, 140
   expatriation 148, 150
   lending 155, 159–60, 165
mortality 114–15, 121–2
motivation 79, 98, 102, 104
   expatriation 148, 150–1
   lending 163, 165–6
Mudita 18, 31
multiculturalism 47, 177
multinational corporations (MNCs) 26, 136–9,
   150–1
multinational enterprises (MNEs) 3, 9, 16,
   95–109, 123, 175, 179
multinational non-governmental organizations
   (NGOs) 135–51

multinational organizations (MOs) 135–6,
149, 151
multivariate covariance analysis (MANCOVA)
55, 59, 66
Murphy, J.L. 100
Myanmar/Burma 14, 102

Narula, R. 96
National Productivity Corporation, Malaysia 77
National Small and Medium Enterprise (SME)
Development Council 76
National Trades Union Congress, Singapore
131
National Wages Council, Singapore 130
Nestlé 20
networks 6, 9, 19, 99, 103–8
future trends 178
lending 156–7, 168, 171–2
New Economic Policy 2
new public financial management 42–4
New Zealand 6, 32
Newly Industrialized Countries (NICs) 3, 9,
95–101
Nguyen, T.V. 11–12, 153–74, 178
Nicaragua 104
Niffenegger, P. 3–6, 14–31, 177
nirvana 18, 25
non-governmental organizations (NGOs) 3,
11–12, 135–51
non-performing loans (NPL) 4, 15, 20–1, 164
non-profit organizations 50
North America 103, 108
North East Asia 1, 175

occupation 49, 54
O'Donnell, S.W. 138
Olson. O. 42
operationalization 52
Original Equipment Manufacture (OEM) 102,
105–6
Outline Perspective Plans (OPP) 92
outsourcing 22, 75, 78, 80, 83, 92
overwork 79
Ownership Location Internationalization (OLI)
96

P&G 20
pandemics 179
paternalism 21, 156
pay-slips 85
Pearson correlation 55
Pendlebury, M.W. 6–7, 32–45
pensions 83, 85
People's Republic of China (PRC) *see* China
performance appraisal 8, 47–67, 74, 84–6
personnel departments 79

Petti grew, A.M. 137
Pfeffer, J. 138
Philippines 27, 104, 116
pink books 164
plagues 121–2
planning 37, 139
polarization 147
politicians 33
politics 1–2, 25, 34, 105, 107
expatriation 137, 139–40, 142, 144,
148–50
future trends 178–80
lending 156, 166
population 3, 15, 179
portals 75, 79
postal services 67
poverty 25, 27, 139, 144–5
power 4, 16–17, 20–1, 27, 143, 180
pregnancy 3
private sector 6, 12, 33, 41–3
e-HRM 92
lending 153–4, 158, 161, 166, 170
privatization 126, 178
Product Life Cycle model 96, 98
professional associations 80
professionalism 41
profit 2, 8, 33, 66–7, 136–7
profit and loss accounts 33
Programme Performance Budgeting System
(PPBS) 36
programming 17
property rights 11, 153–4, 164, 170, 178
Proton 2
PSA Corporation 126, 128
psychic distance 98
psychology 120, 123, 133, 155
psychometrics 55–6
public sector 32–3, 36–7, 40, 42–3
Purnell, D. 11, 135–51, 180

qualifications 41, 43
quality circles 43
Quality Enhancement Scheme 92
quarantine 116, 124
questionnaires 7, 40–1, 52, 54–5, 81–3
quotas 2, 102

race 80
Raffles Group 132
Rama IX King 23
Rama V King 23–4, 26
raw materials 76–7
real estate 161–2
recession 125
recommendations 168
recruitment 8, 10, 34, 43, 74

e-HRM 83–4, 86
epidemics 128
redundancies 116, 127
referrals 156
regionalization 98–9, 103–4
registration fees 53
registration information 161, 163
regulation 6, 12, 19, 23–4, 138–9, 147, 158
Rehabilitation Fund for Small- and Medium-
scale Industries 92
relationships 53, 99, 136, 157
    business 19, 22, 26–7, 78, 105–8,
    167–8
    expatriation 138–41, 145–6, 148–9,
    151
    interfirm 155–8
    lending 167–9, 171
relative convergence 177
reliability estimates 55
religion 17–18, 50, 140, 144–5, 148, 177
repeat purchases 48
reporting practices 6, 19, 34–5, 40, 44, 143, 146
repurchases 48–9
reputation 103, 167, 170
research and development (R&D) 103–4
response rates 40, 54, 81
responsiveness 135–9, 143–5, 147, 150
restaurants 10, 125, 127, 133
restructuring 20–2, 24, 26
retail 10, 22, 50, 102, 124–5, 127
retention 8, 47–67
Ricks, D.A. 138
risk 3, 11–12, 17, 153–5, 157
    future trends 180
    lending 164, 170–2
Robinson, M. 35
role theory 28
Roman Catholics 123
Romm, C.T. 137
root mean square residual (RMR) 55–6
Rowley, C. 1–13, 175–81
Rutherford, B.A. 33

Salancik, G. 138
salaries 85, 90
Saleh, Z. 6–7, 32–45
sample size 54–5, 67, 101–2, 109
SARS Relief Tourism Training Assistance 130
scandals 33
scene-setting 1–13
scholarships 43
schools 123, 131
scrutiny 35
security 89–90, 100, 126, 164
self-reliance 22–3, 25
September 11 2001 126, 179

service quality 47, 50, 52–3
service sector 10, 114–33
Severe Acute Respiratory Syndrome (SARS)
    10, 12, 114–33, 179–80
Shin Corp 2
shocks 10, 120, 122–4, 133, 179–80
short-term loans 164–5
Siam 23
Siam Cement Group 20
SilkAir 126
Sim, A.B. 8–9, 95–109, 178
Singapore 1, 3, 8–10, 75, 79
    future trends 175
    internationalization 95–109, 178–80
    language 178
    SARS 114–33
    shocks 179
Singapore Airlines (SIA) 116, 126–7, 130, 132
Singapore Human Resource Institute and
    Remuneration Data Specialists 129
Singapore Tourism Board 131
Skills Redevelopment Programme 128
Small and Medium Industries Development
    Corporation (SMIDEC) 75
small and medium sized enterprises (SMEs)
    bank lending 153–74
    definitions 75–6, 82
    e-HRM 74–93
    role 3, 8, 11–12
social pressure 138, 150
socialization 144, 148
software 55, 80, 91
Sound Blaster 103
South Korea 97, 116, 120, 124, 180
Southern Africa 115
Spanish Flu 122
Spearman coefficient 55
Spirit of Chinese Capitalism 99
spiritualism 5, 17–19, 25
Sri Lanka 101–2
start-up firms 172
state 2, 9, 12, 40, 98–9, 107–8, 178
State Bank of Vietnam 164
state-owned banks 154, 158–9, 161, 165–6,
    168–70, 178
stock markets 3, 100, 132, 178, 180
strategy formulation 3, 137–40, 142, 148–50
structural adjustment 24
structure 3, 34, 148, 150–1
subcontracting 2, 78, 105
subsidiaries 11, 20, 79, 98, 100
    epidemics 126
    internationalization 104, 109, 126
    NGOs 135–40, 142–51
suffering 24–5, 27
suicide 3

superannuation 35
supply 10, 22, 105, 120–1, 128, 179
support offices (SOs) 140–1, 143–4, 146,
    148–50
surveys 7, 40, 54–5, 81, 83–4, 151, 154
sustainability 23, 26–7
Suutari, V. 136
Sweeney, J.C. 53
Switzerland 16
synergy 104, 106

Taiwan 27, 97, 103, 117, 120, 180
takeovers 2
Tan Tock Seng Hospital 117, 119
tariffs 2
taxation 2, 24, 99, 161
teamwork 145, 147, 149
technology 3–4, 8–9, 14–15, 21–5
    accounting 42
    acquisition 101–6
    e-HRM 74–5, 78–82, 87–8, 90–1
    epidemics 122
    internationalization 97, 101, 105–7
    level 83–4, 89
    niche 108
    proprietary 96
    SARS 123
Technology Acquisition Fund 92
Technology Development Scheme 92
telecommunications 2, 7, 47–73, 103
Temasek Holdings 2
tendering 35
Thai language 178
Thailand 1–3, 5–6, 116, 175
    cultural imperatives 14–31
    history 177–80
    SARS 117
Theravada 25
third parties 156, 168
Third World 96–7
Third World Multinational Enterprises
    (TWMNEs) 95, 97–8
TOA Paint Manufacturers 21
Tolentino, P.E. 96
total quality management 43
tourism 2, 10, 24, 116, 123–4
    epidemics 126–7, 130–2
    future trends 179–80
trade 14, 23, 98, 164
training 7, 21, 35, 41, 44, 74
    e-HRM 78, 82–4, 86, 89, 91–2
    epidemics 128, 130–1
    expatriation 144
    internationalization 99
    NGOs 146

transitional economies 153–5, 157, 170,
    172, 178
transparency 19, 41, 163–4
travel 114–16, 122, 124, 129, 132
trust 11–12, 19, 22, 26, 53
    definition 155
    expatriation 148
    interfirm 165
    internationalization 106
    lending 153–74
    mechanisms 167–71
trustees 155
trustors 155
tsunamis 179–80
turnover 75–6

Ubekkha 18, 31
umbrella approach 137, 149
uncertainty 10–12, 115, 120, 123
    avoidance 5, 16–17, 22, 27, 164–5,
        170–1
    epidemics 126
    future trends 180
    lending 153–74
underwriting 157
unemployment 10, 21, 114–33
    benefit 19–20
United Kingdom (UK) 6, 16, 32, 34–5, 42–4
United Nations Programme on HIV/AIDS
    (UNAIDS) 115
United States (US) 4, 14–16, 20
    accounting 32, 36
    culture 27
    e-HRM 79
    future trends 177, 179
    internationalization 101–4
    SARS 117, 123, 126
unskilled workers 20–1
Uppsala model 96, 98, 101
urbanization 115

valuation 33
values 3–4, 14–15, 17–19, 23–4
    culture 26–7
    expatriation 137–8, 140, 144–5,
        148, 150
    history 177
    internationalization 99, 103, 107
van Hoesel, R. 95, 99, 105
varimax rotation 55
Vernon, R. 96
Vietcombank 178
Vietnam 1–3, 11–12, 102, 175
    banks 153–74
    ethnicity 178–9
    NGOs 135–51

SARS 115, 117
shocks 179
Vietnamese language 178
Vinamilk 3
visas 139
Volkswagen (VW) 2
voters 25

Walsh, D. 100
Walters, J.A. 137, 149
Warner, M. 1–13, 114–33, 175–81
warning systems 120
Watson Wyatt Consulting 75
websites 81, 83–5, 100
western world 3–4, 6, 9, 14–16
    culture 18–21, 23–7
    expatriation 145
    history 177–8
    internationalization 95–101, 104,
      106–8

lending 155, 171
    telecommunications 50, 66
white-collar employees 126, 128
Wholly Owned Subsidiaries (WOS) 104
wireless technology 83
witchcraft 122
word-of-mouth advertising 48, 54
Workforce Development Agency (WDA) 128
World Bank 24, 119
World Health Organization (WHO) 114, 126–7
World Tourism Organization 124
World Trade Organization 2

Y2K Grant 92
Yale 24
Yeung, H.W.C. 98, 105

Zhu, Y. 11, 135–51, 180

For Product Safety Concerns and Information please contact our EU
representative GPSR@taylorandfrancis.com Taylor & Francis Verlag GmbH,
Kaufingerstraße 24, 80331 München, Germany

Printed and bound by CPI Group (UK) Ltd, Croydon, CR0 4YY
01/05/2025
01858362-0003